POSTCARD HISTORY SERIES

Ohio's Lake Erie Vacationland

IN VINTAGE POSTCARDS

POSTCARD HISTORY SERIES

Ohio's Lake Erie Vacationland

IN VINTAGE POSTCARDS

R. Wayne Ayers

ARCADIA PUBLISHING

ISBN 978-0-7385-0738-5

Published by Arcadia Publishing
Charleston, South Carolina

Printed in the United States of America

Library of Congress Catalog Card Number: 00-105232

For all general information contact Arcadia Publishing at:
Telephone 843-853-2070
Fax 843-853-0044
E-mail sales@arcadiapublishing.com
For customer service and orders:
Toll-Free 1-888-313-2665

Visit us on the Internet at www.arcadiapublishing.com

Contents

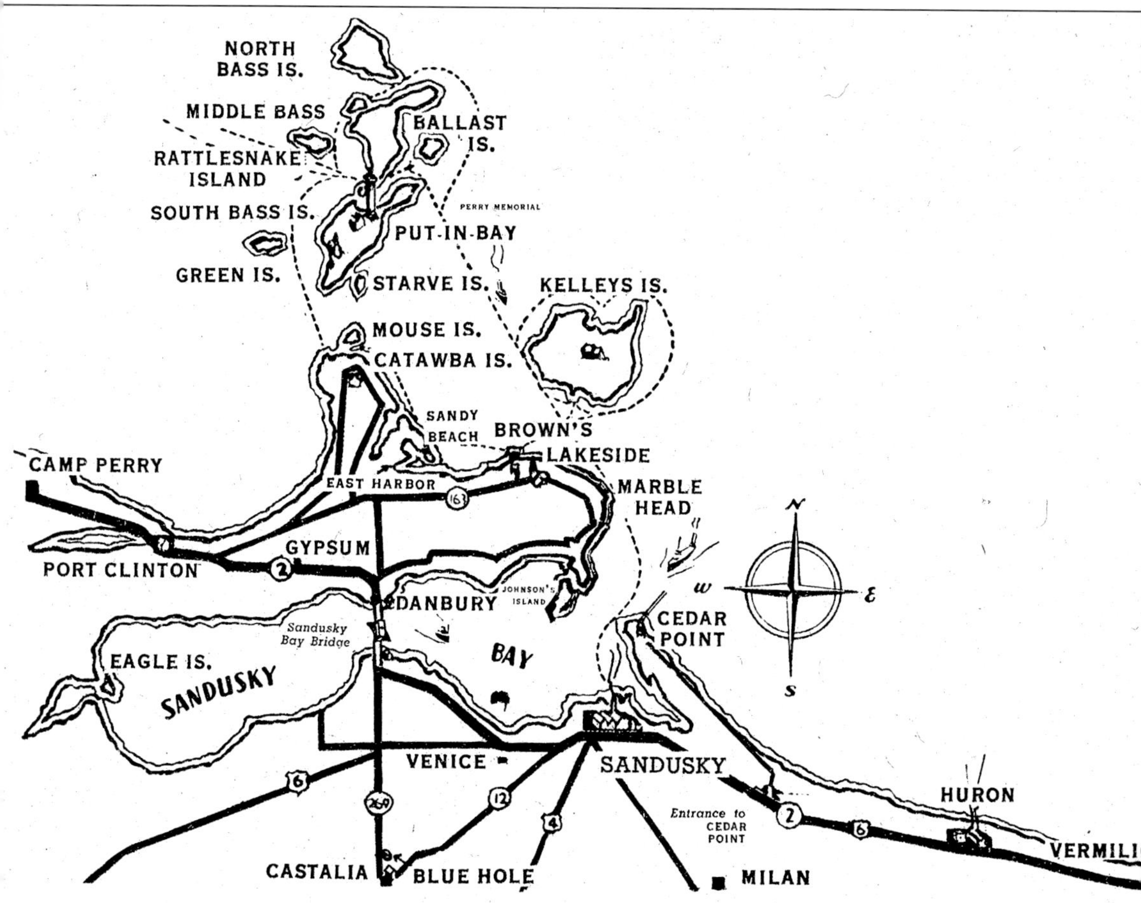
NORTH BASS IS.
MIDDLE BASS
BALLAST IS.
RATTLESNAKE ISLAND
SOUTH BASS IS.
PERRY MEMORIAL
PUT-IN-BAY
GREEN IS.
STARVE IS.
KELLEYS IS.
MOUSE IS.
CATAWBA IS.
SANDY BEACH
BROWN'S
LAKESIDE
CAMP PERRY
EAST HARBOR
163
MARBLE HEAD
GYPSUM
PORT CLINTON
2
DANBURY
JOHNSON'S ISLAND
CEDAR POINT
Sandusky Bay Bridge
EAGLE IS.
SANDUSKY
BAY
N
W
E
S
VENICE
SANDUSKY
6
269
12
4
HURON
Entrance to CEDAR POINT
CASTALIA
BLUE HOLE
MILAN
VERMILI

DEDICATION

This book is dedicated to my wife, Nancy, whose creative ideas, organizational skills, and support of this project made it all possible.

INTRODUCTION

Western Lake Erie began to blossom as a resort area in the mid-1800s. It came into full bloom around the turn of the century when a boom in steamboat navigation brought thousands of tourists on excursions to Put-in-Bay, Cedar Point, and spiritual retreats at Lakeside on Marblehead.

Large Victorian hotels, some still thriving today, were constructed to accommodate the throngs of visitors. Steamboats—some so large and luxurious they were literally floating hotels—were built in boatyards that dotted the lake shore, and then pressed into service ferrying tourists between the resorts and population centers of Buffalo, Cleveland, Detroit, and other smaller ports.

Each tourist center developed its own special character, and each has retained its own particular identity to this day.

Put-in-Bay, in its heyday, was one of the top tourist destinations in the U.S. It was a social Mecca, and was considered the place to be seen. The Victory Hotel, the largest wooden structure in the country before it burned to the ground in 1919, featured gardens, an indoor pool, and a dining room capable of seating two thousand people. Numerous smaller hotels such as the Beebe, Put-in-Bay House, Crescent, and Park (of which two are still standing), sprung up to meet the demands of the throngs of visitors drawn to social activities such as boating and wine-making. The area also featured many natural attractions like caves, rock cliffs, and lake breezes. The town of Put-In-Bay featured game parlors, souvenir shops, bowling, restaurants, and dance halls.

Today, Put-in-Bay retains much of its quaint (though raucous) character with unique shops, restaurants, and indoor/outdoor bars. The world's longest bar is here, and live entertainment abounds. Large jet-powered boats, such as the *Jet Express I* and *II*, ferry visitors from docks in Port Clinton and Catawba to the pleasures of "the Bay". The Heineman winery and Crystal and Victory caves still attract crowds of visitors, as they have for over a century.

Kelleys, the largest of the Lake Erie Islands, is more sedate than Put-in-Bay, though just as picturesque. Tourism is increasing, and visitors are drawn to the Victorian homes that dot the shore, along with an increasing number of shops and eateries. Natural attractions include the Glacial Grooves (a remnant of the Ice Age), and Inscription Rock, thought to be carved by an ancient civilization.

Cedar Point was, and remains today, an amusement park. The Victorian version touted promenades, beach frolics, arcade games, and beer gardens in place of the roller coasters, waterslides, giant Ferris wheels, and other thrill rides of today. The Victorian Cedar Point was every bit as popular in its time as the mammoth park is today. Accommodating a large segment of the visitors was the Breakers Hotel, built in 1904 and still the queen of Cedar Point hotels today. Other notable hotels, long gone, included the White House, Cedars, and Bay Shore.

At **Lakeside**, the Chautauqua of Lake Erie, a more contemplative atmosphere prevailed. A few hotels, such as the stately wooden Lakeside Hotel, served and still serve the faithful seeking peace, relaxation, and spiritual renewal. "Lakeside cottages" were built and have been, in many cases, passed from generation to generation. Notable speakers filled the days with spiritual messages as part of the on-going Chautauqua experience, born in Chautauqua, New York.

Marblehead Peninsula is home to upscale condos, and the summer and retirement homes of Cleveland, Detroit, and Columbus natives. The picturesque town of Marblehead, home of renowned artist Ben Richmond, features galleries and shops, motels and condos, bed-and-breakfasts, a picturesque shoreline on both Lake Erie and Sandusky Bay, and the famed Marblehead Lighthouse.

The Lighthouse, the oldest still in operation on the Great Lakes, dates to 1821. Its beacon has guided many a sailor past the rocky cliffs of Marblehead for nearly two centuries. Its picturesque appearance and noted history make it a prime attraction throughout all the islands. Hundreds of items, from towels to yard ornaments, bear its likeness. The original keeper's house, about a mile from the lighthouse, is being restored and is now open for tours, as is the lighthouse, on designated weekends during the season.

Port Clinton, noted for its fishing industry, is today the "walleye capital of the world" and home to a sizable fleet of sport fishing boats that prowl the lake from spring to fall, and return with sizable catches of walleye, perch, and bass. Neighboring Catawba Island boasts a sizable peach-growing industry, thanks to the temperature-moderating influence of Lake Erie.

Sandusky, the metropolis of the area, was (and remains) a popular embarkation point for excursions to Cedar Point and the islands. Cleveland and Detroit boats often made a stop here. The city was once seen as a possible terminus for the Ohio-Erie Canal, and grandiose plans were made for its development. When that failed to materialize, Sandusky settled back to small city status. Its beautiful downtown park system and harbor on Lake Erie today give the city a graceful charm that delights visitors and residents alike.

Vermilion, billed as "Harbour Town 1847," boasts a quaint downtown, picturesque lagoons bordered by New England style clapboard homes, a grassy park in the center of town, and the respected Great Lakes Nautical Museum on the waterfront. Once a fishing village (the last commercial fishery closed in the 1980s), the area features numerous sea captains' homes dating to the 1800s.

Ohio's Lake Erie Vacationland was, and remains, a fascinating part of the country. It is full of history, scenery, and recreational opportunities. It's an area with much to see and do, and, as this book attests, it is an area that has changed only gently, preserving and enhancing the best of the old while augmenting its attractions with the new and exciting.

One

Port Clinton and the Catawba Shore

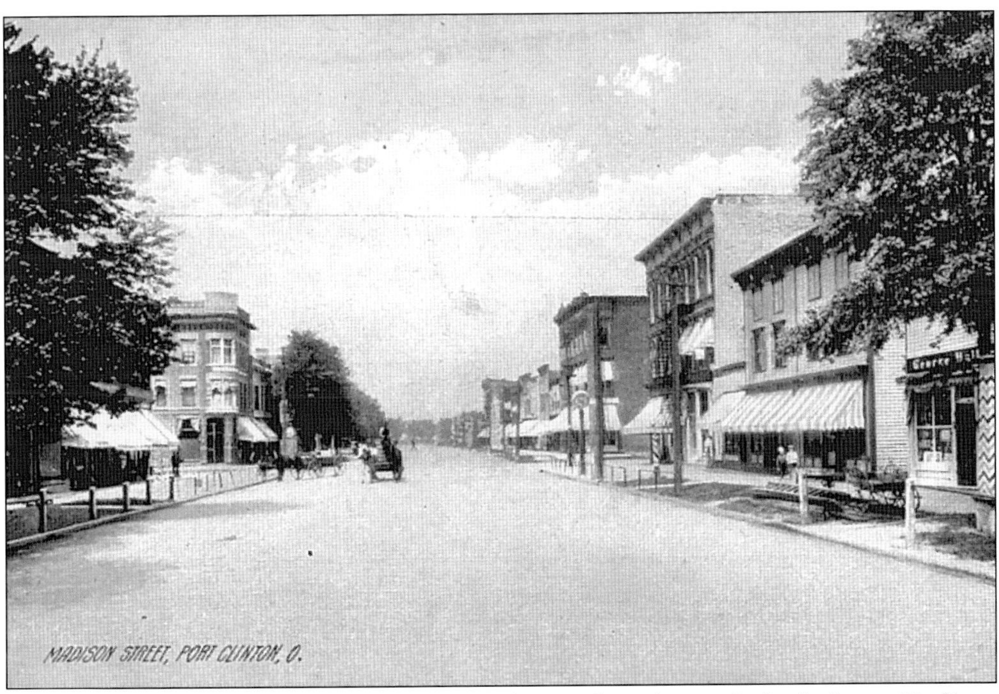

Horse-drawn carts and hitching posts are featured in this early look down Madison Street in Port Clinton. Note the predominance of awnings that helped keep the stores cool and sheltered shoppers from the summer sun.

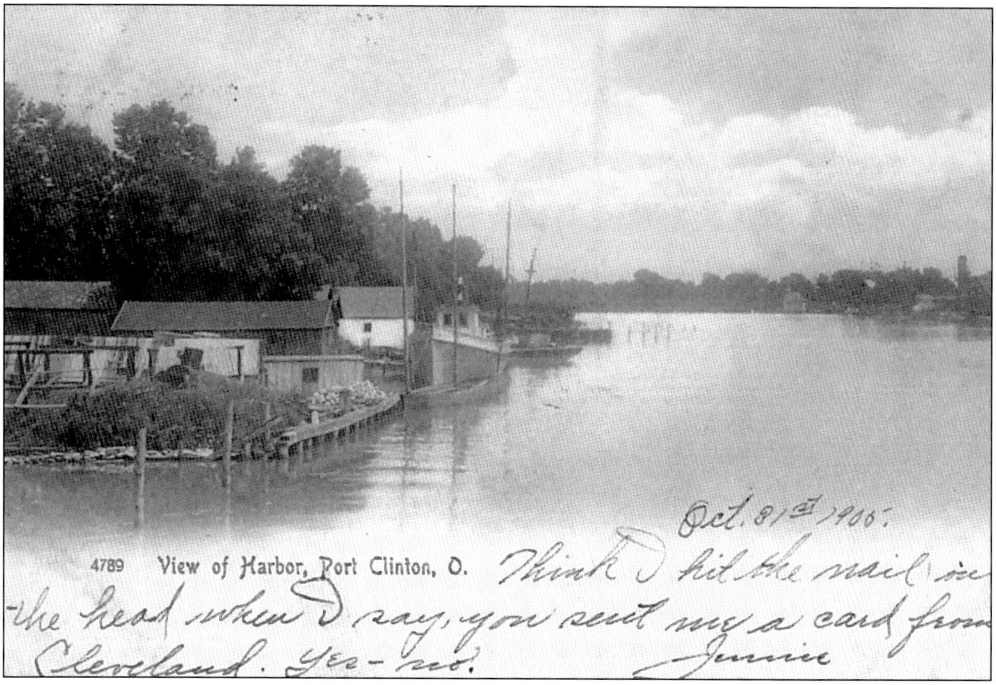

The Harbor at Port Clinton, somewhat sleepy in this 1905 scene, was headquarters for the huge fishing industry in the area.

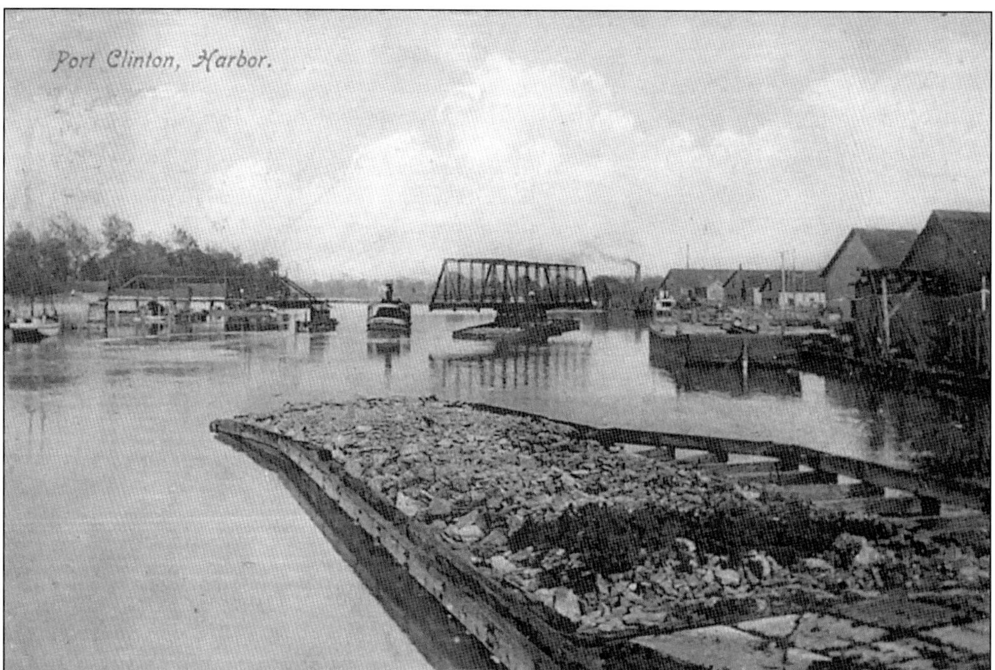

In a busier scene, the famous "swinging bridge" turns to allow a tug to pass, while numerous boats can be seen at the docks.

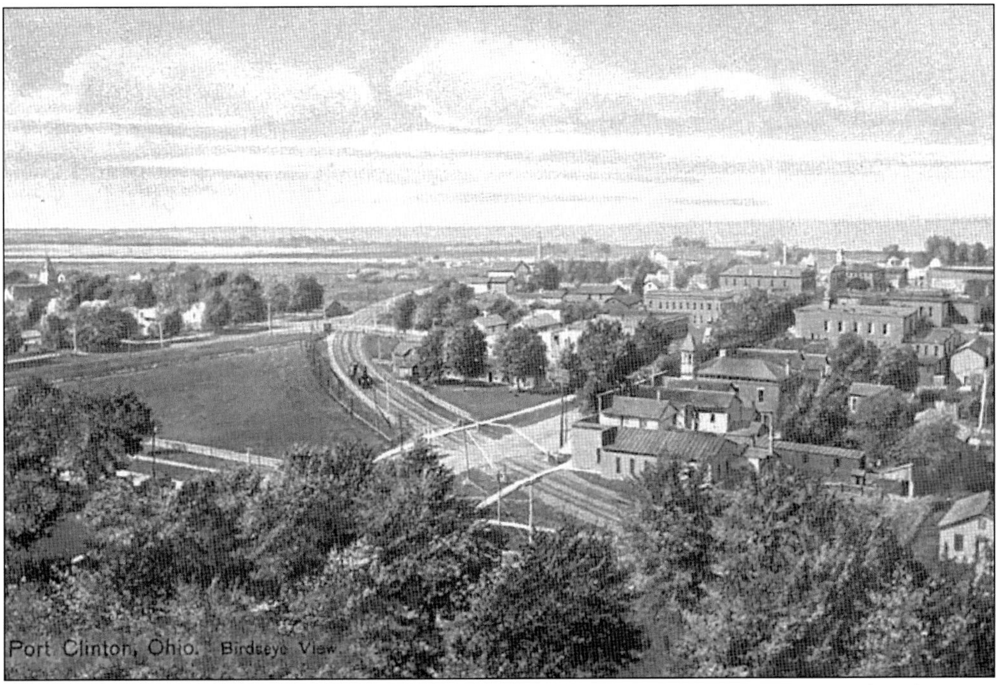

This bird's-eye view of Port Clinton, looking north toward Lake Erie, is dated 1908. Most of the buildings still exist today.

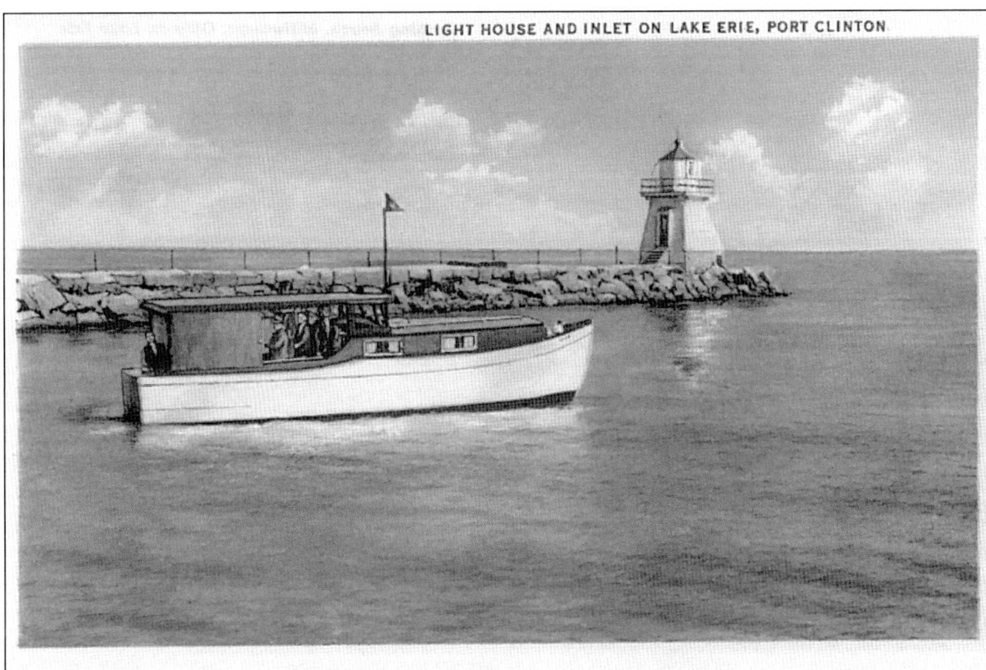

A new west pier light was erected at the inlet to Port Clinton, replacing the old brick lighthouse that was demolished in 1899.

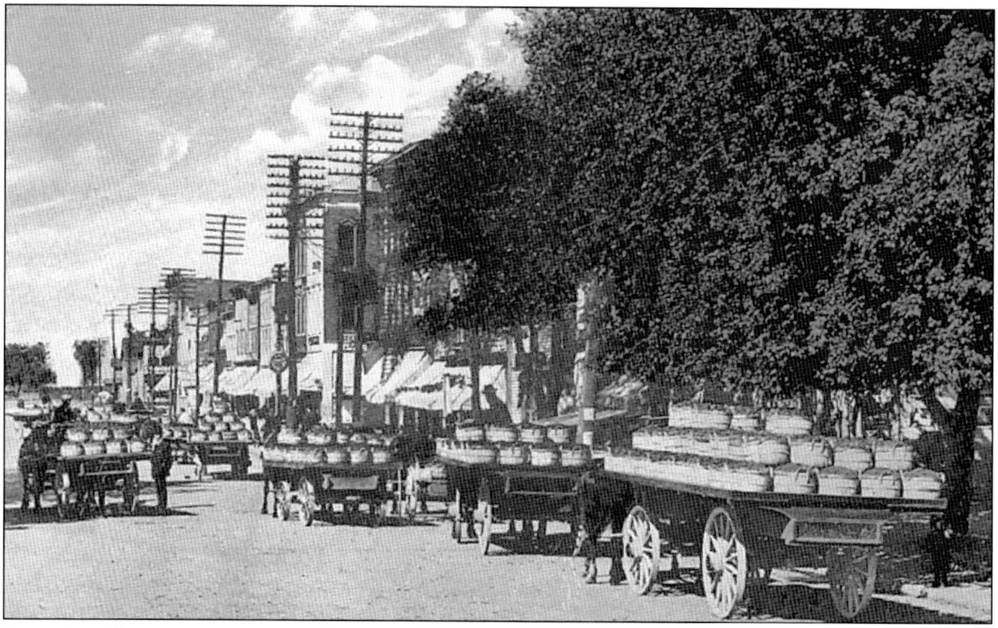

In a bustling scene, Port Clinton prepares for the Peach Auction, as growers from nearby orchards bring their produce to town. The moderating influence of Lake Erie on year-round temperatures makes the area ideal for growing warm-weather fruits such as peaches and grapes. Today, numerous peach varieties are harvested along the lakeshore from Toledo to Buffalo.

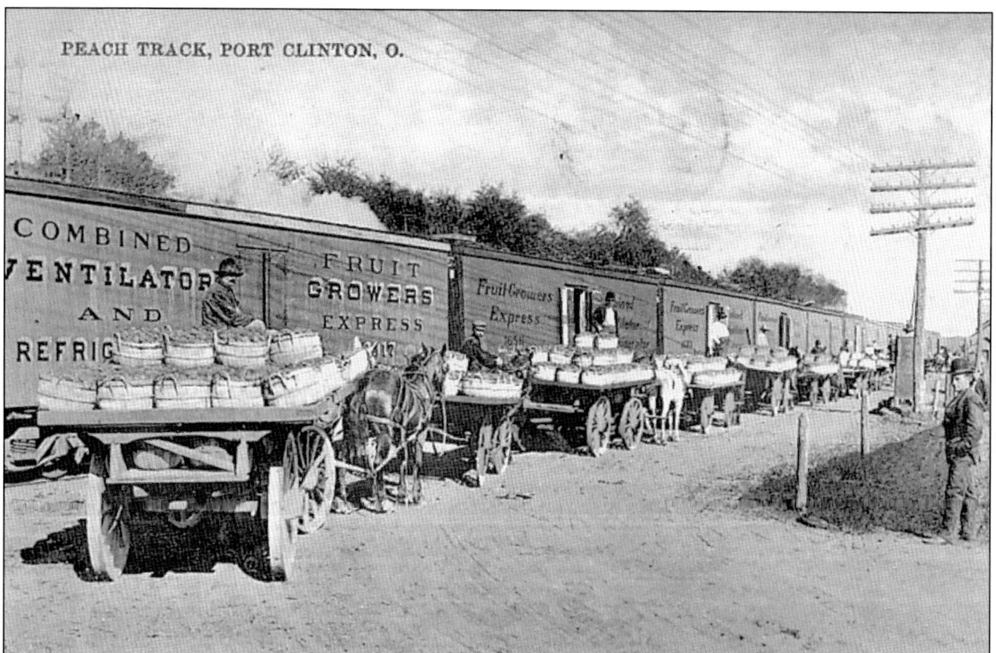

Here, peach growers line up to load their crop into refrigerated cars for shipment around the country.

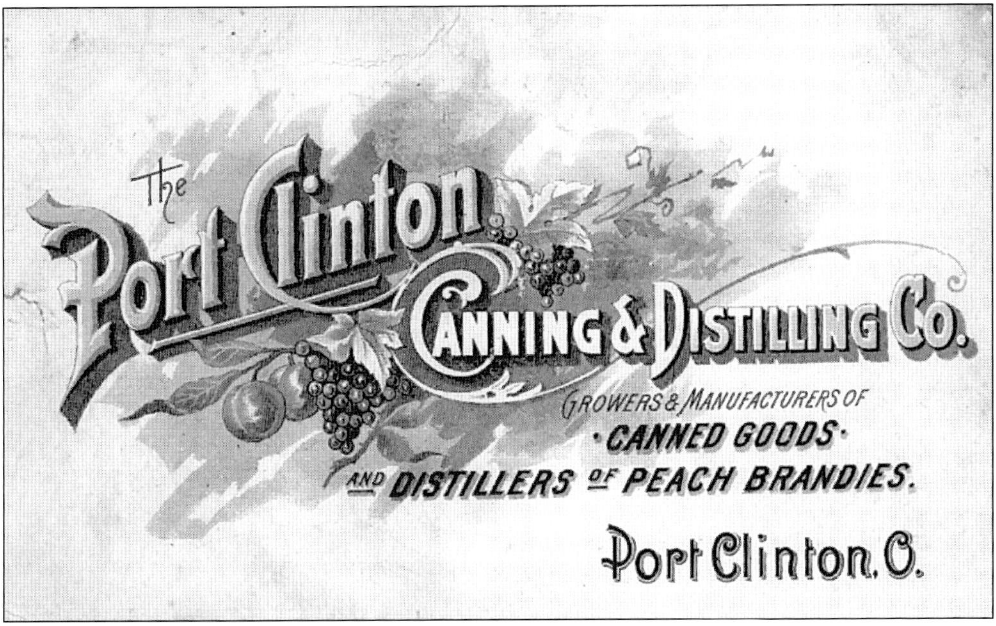

Peaches were canned and distilled into brandy at the Port Clinton Canning and Distilling Company. Port Clinton has long been famed for its peach crop, and the growth and processing of peaches was a major industry in Ottawa County at the turn of the century.

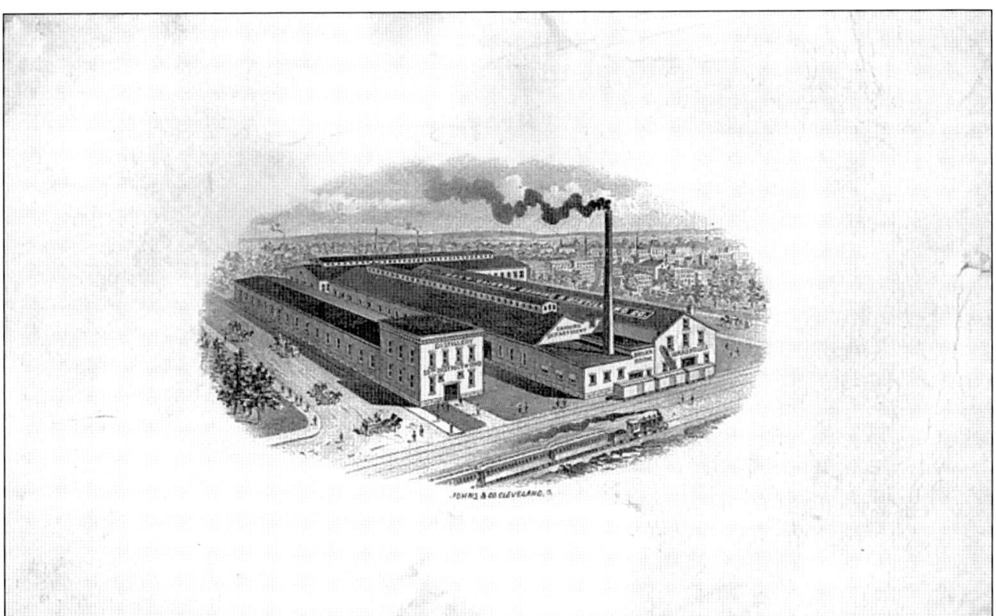

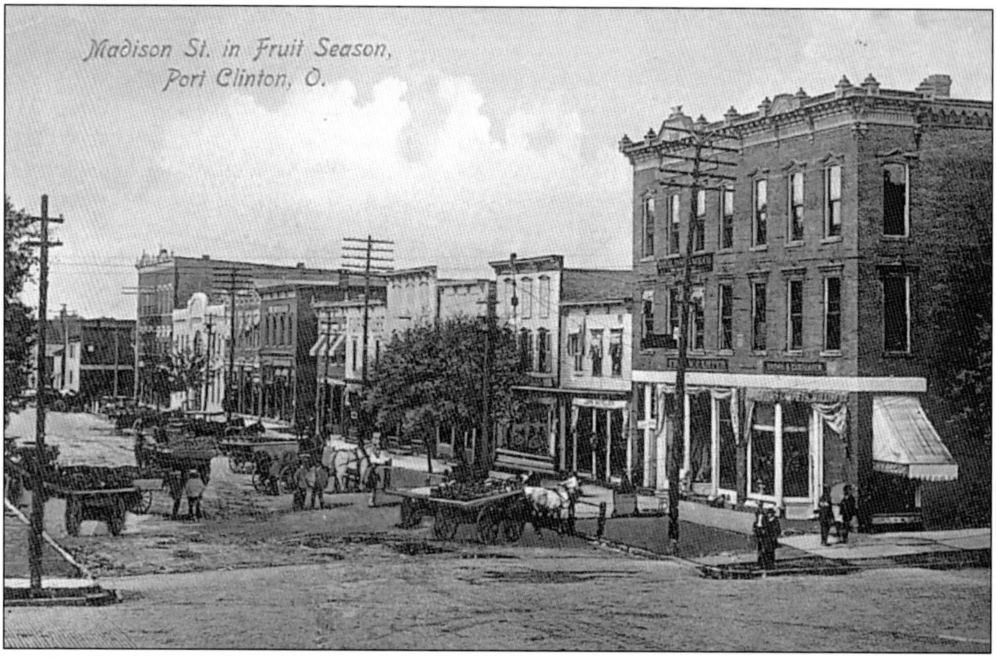

Looking north on Madison Street, again in fruit season, this view shows some of the early downtown businesses which included a furniture store, a milliner, dry goods, a carpet store, and an insurance office.

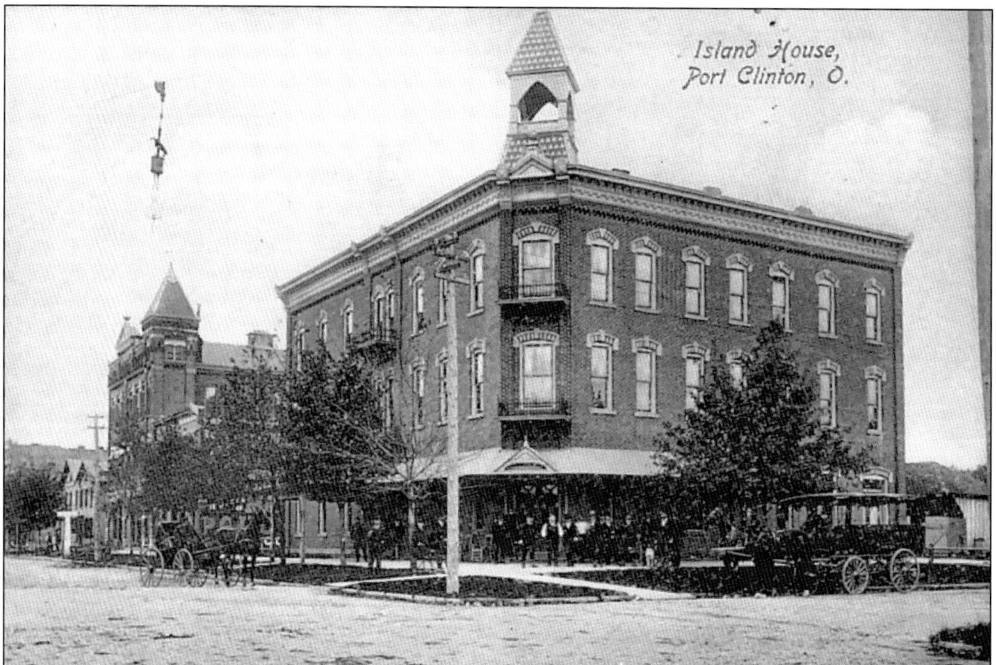

Carriages and hotel guests are on view at the famous Island House in Port Clinton. The hotel, still popular today, opened its doors in 1888, replacing the old Island House that was built in 1840 and burned in 1882.

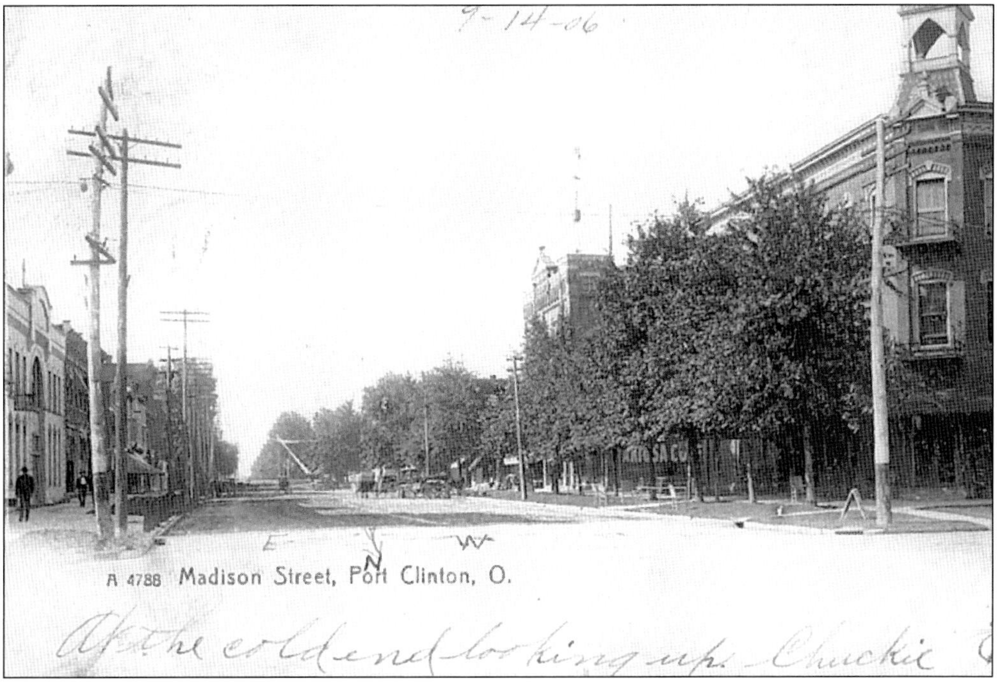

In this postcard dated "9-14-06," the Island House, on the corner at the right, looks much the same as it did in the earlier view, bottom opposite, except for the taller, fuller shade trees lining Madison Street.

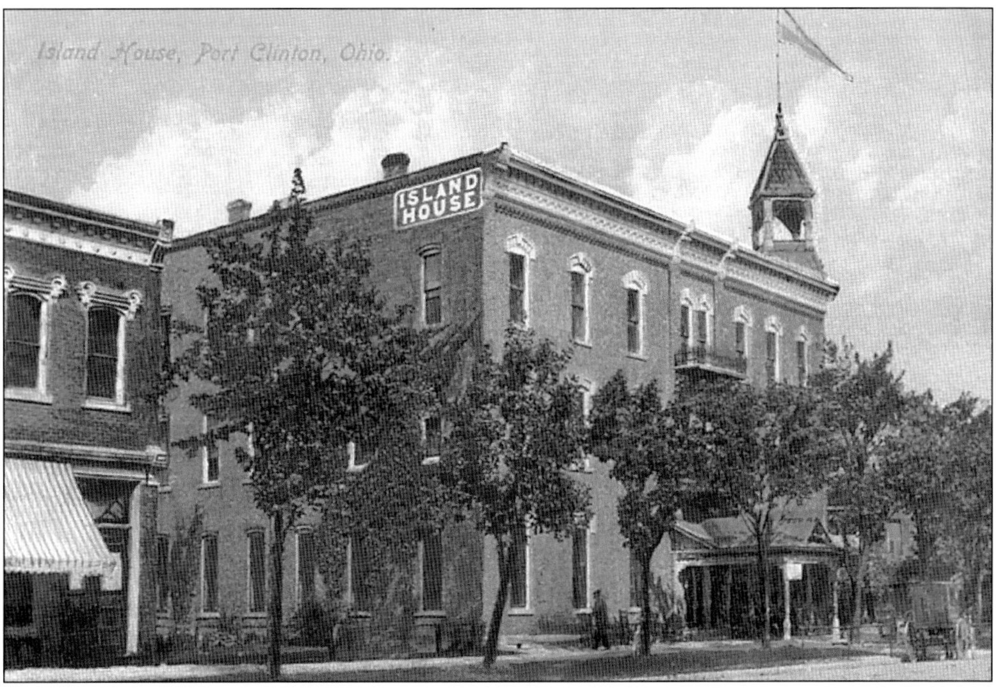

This is another early view of the Island House. Note the carriage at the front door.

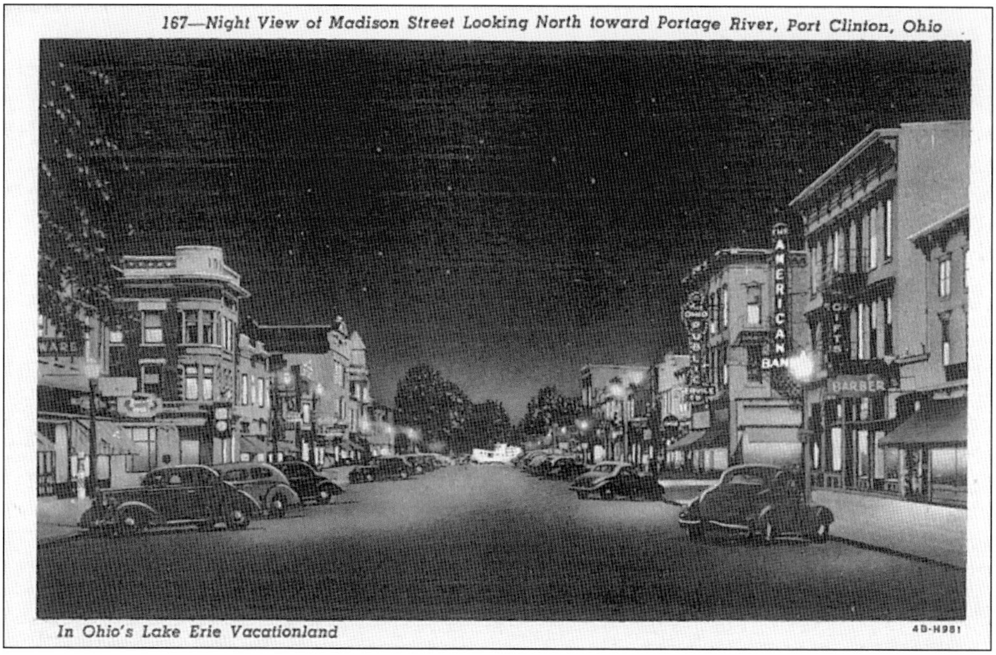

Downtown Port Clinton was bustling at night, according to this 1940s view. However, this is probably a daytime view that has been retouched to give it a nocturnal look.

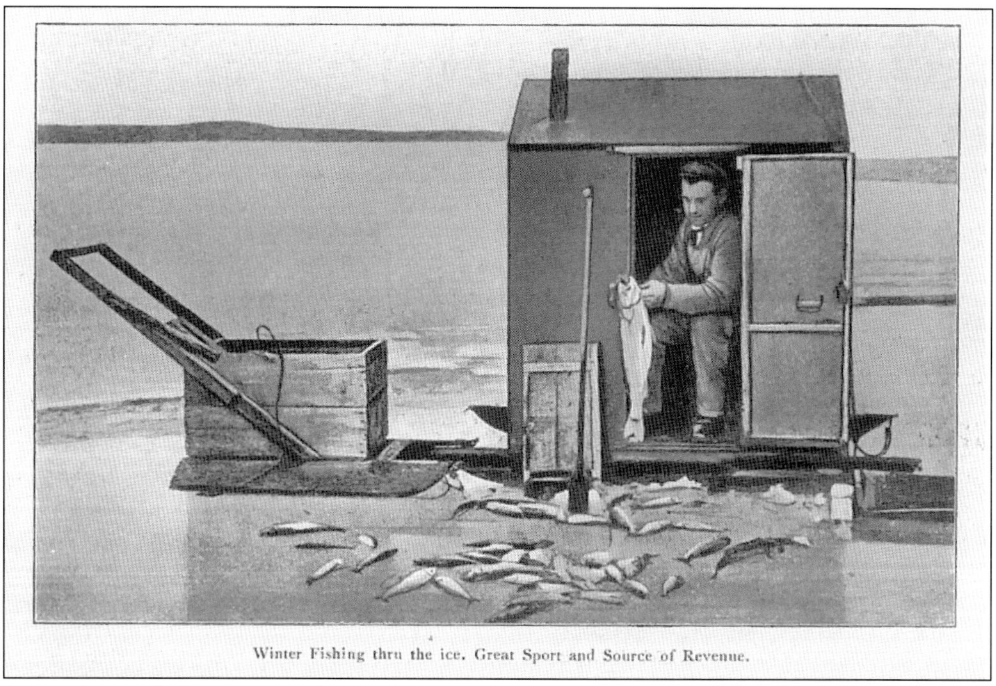

An early ice fisherman is shown here with a plentiful catch. The shallow waters of western Lake Erie freeze solid most winters, enabling participation in this sport that is still popular today. Fishermen bring their ice shanties complete with heaters, cut a hole in the ice, and drop a line.

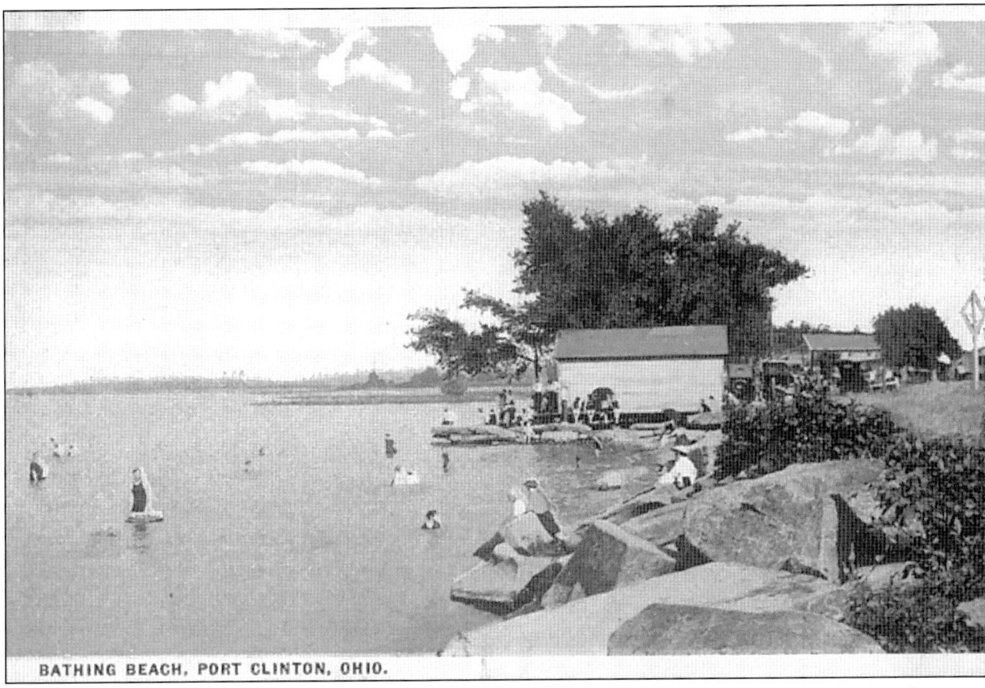

The Lake Erie shore at Port Clinton provides a shallow bathing beach. In the distance is the Catawba shoreline.

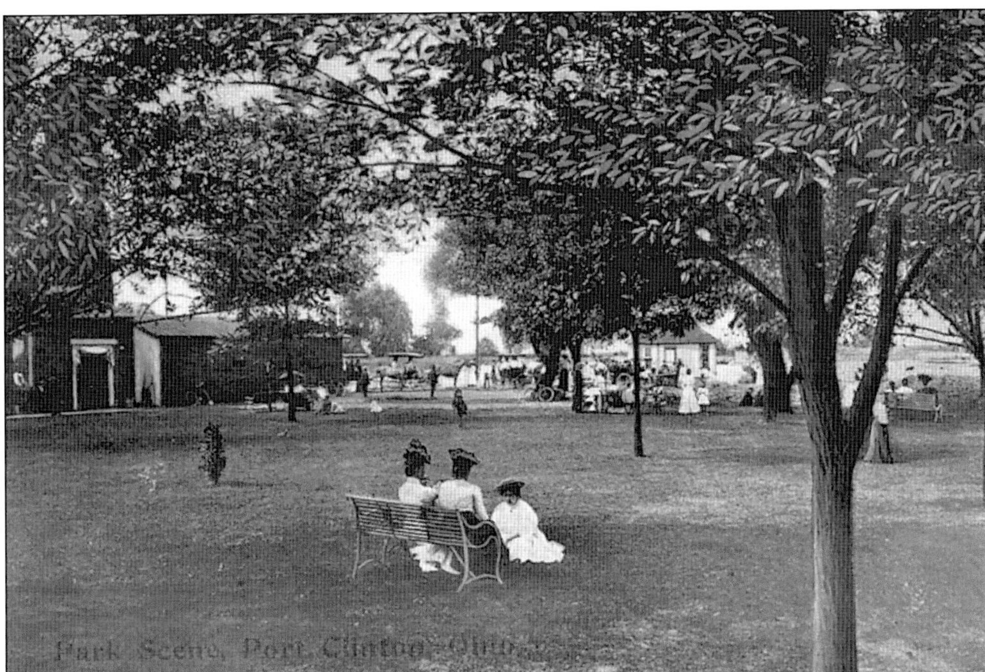

Bicycles and carriages transported visitors to the park on the lakeshore in the early 1900s. Ladies in Victorian hoop skirts and hats enjoy the cool shade.

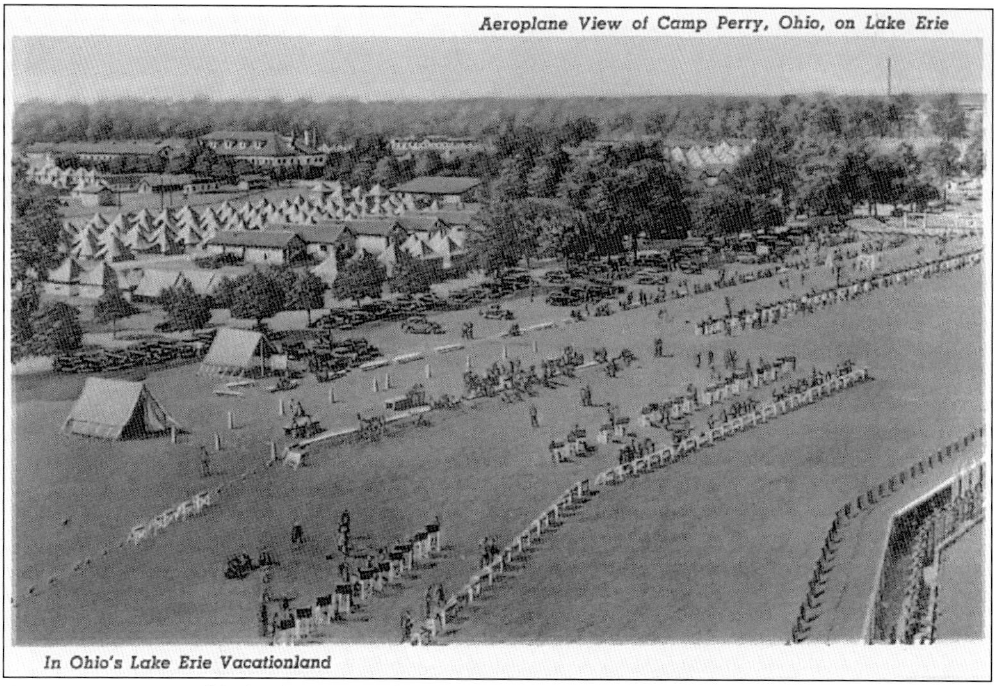

Camp Perry, established in 1906, is famous for the National Rifle matches held here each summer.

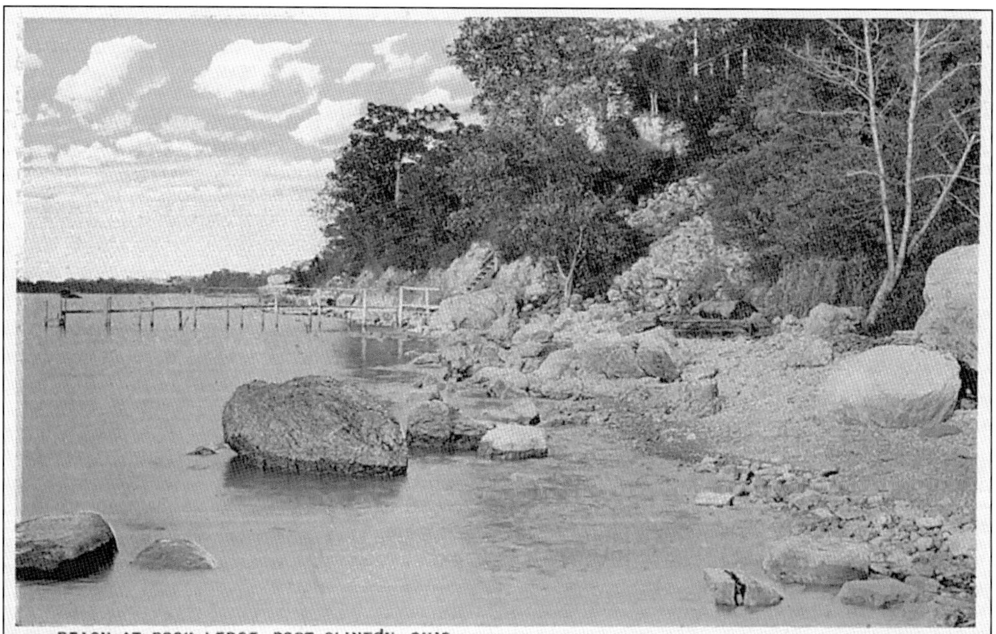

Rock Ledge, near Port Clinton, is a picturesque area with stunning rock cliffs jutting into the lake. Today the spot boasts two bed and breakfast inns dating to the early 1900s, one of which, the Rock Ledge, is visible at top right.

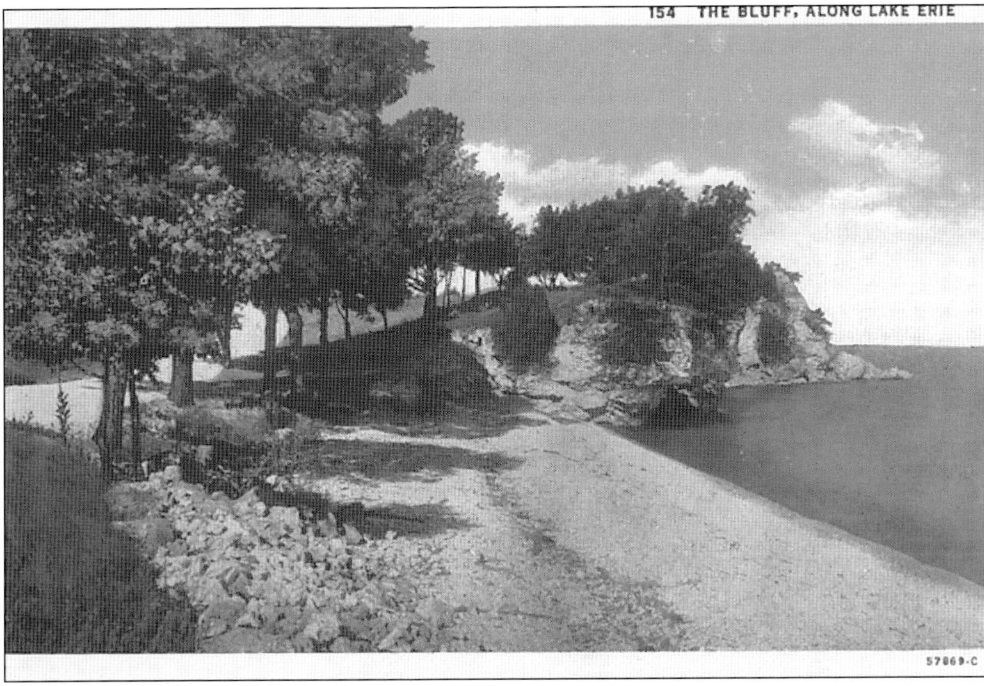

This shale outcropping on Catawba Island along Sand Road is today famous for its expansive views of Lake Erie. Catawba Island, actually a peninsula, used to be an island before a storm created the spit of sand now known as Sand Road, which connects it to the mainland.

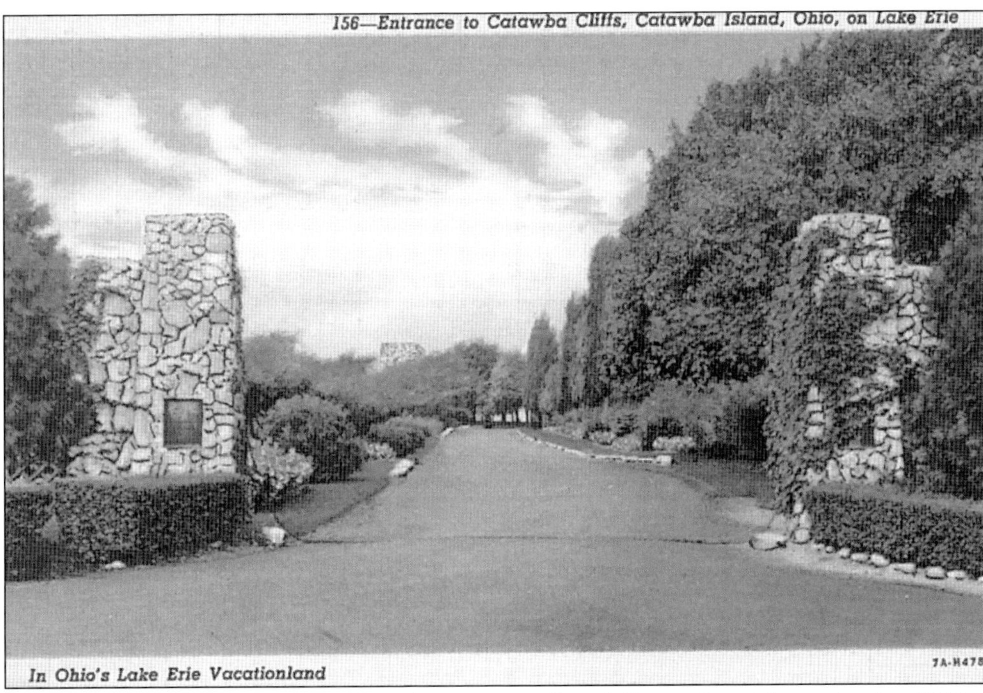

This formal entryway led to the exclusive Catawba Cliffs residential area in the 1940s.

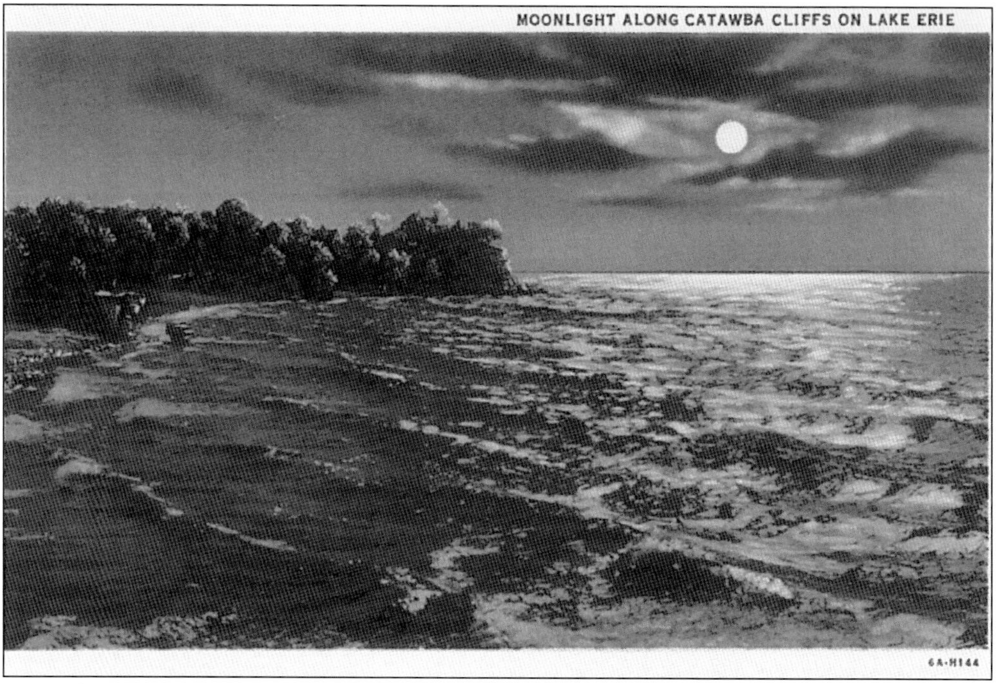

Several unique rock homes grace the beautiful cliffs of Catawba.

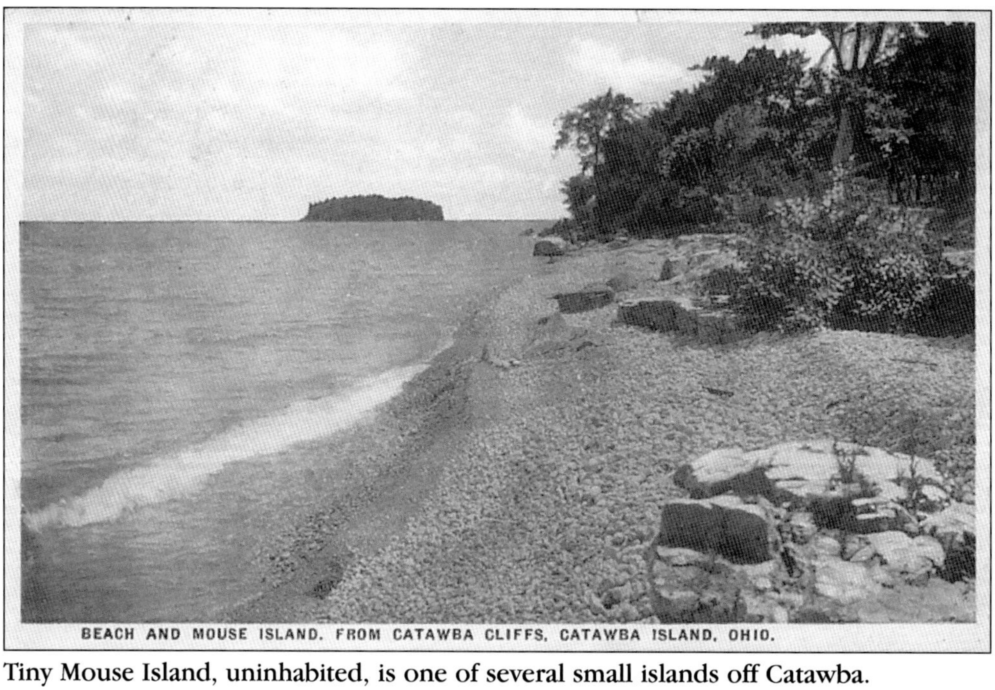

Tiny Mouse Island, uninhabited, is one of several small islands off Catawba.

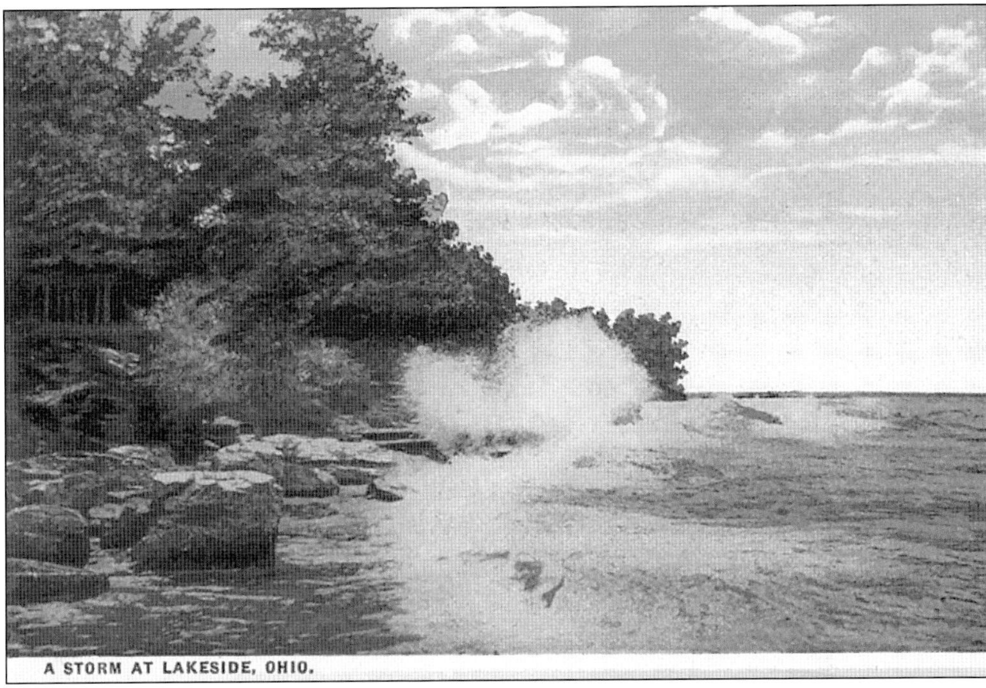

Lake Erie, known as "The Cat" by the Erie Indians, can whip up fierce storms with little notice because of its shallowness.

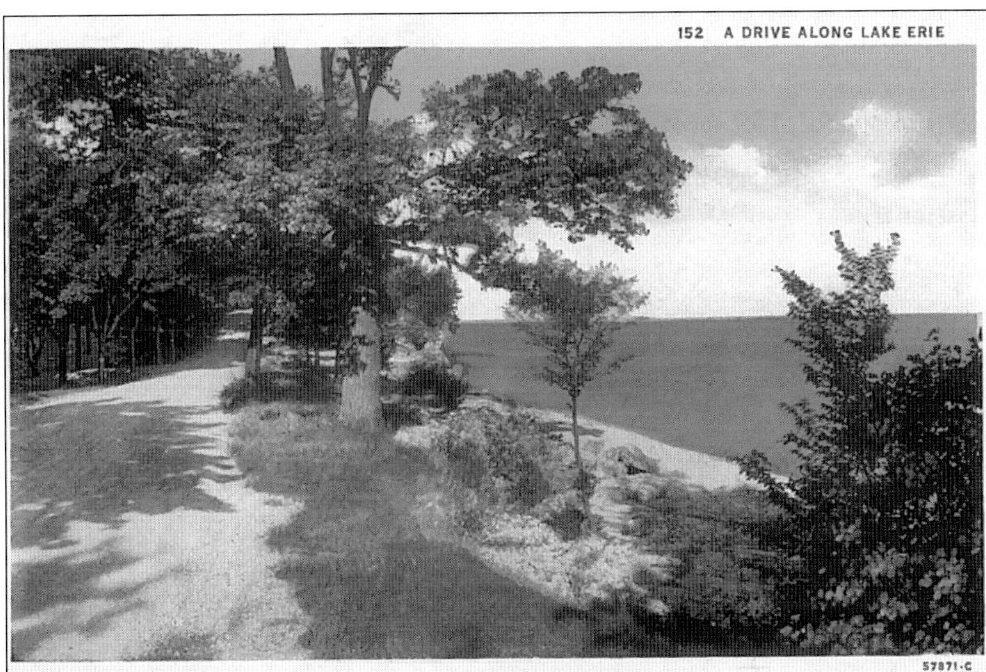

A more peaceful setting is Catawba's Sand Road, when it was truly a *sand* road.

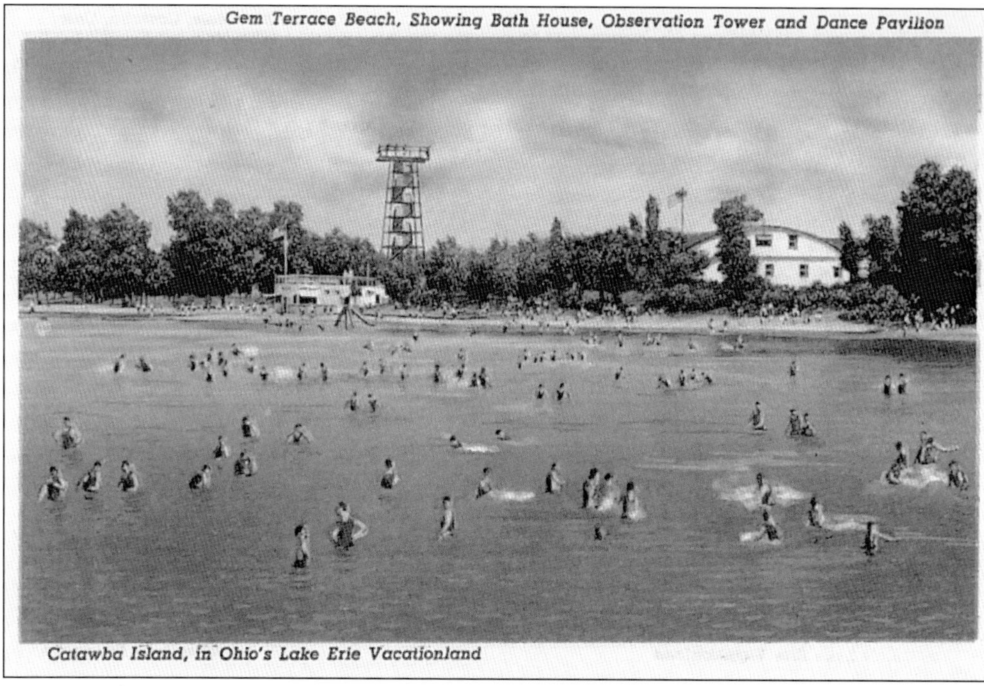

Gem Beach was a popular recreation destination on Catawba for years. Seen here are the bathhouse, observation tower, and dance pavilion.

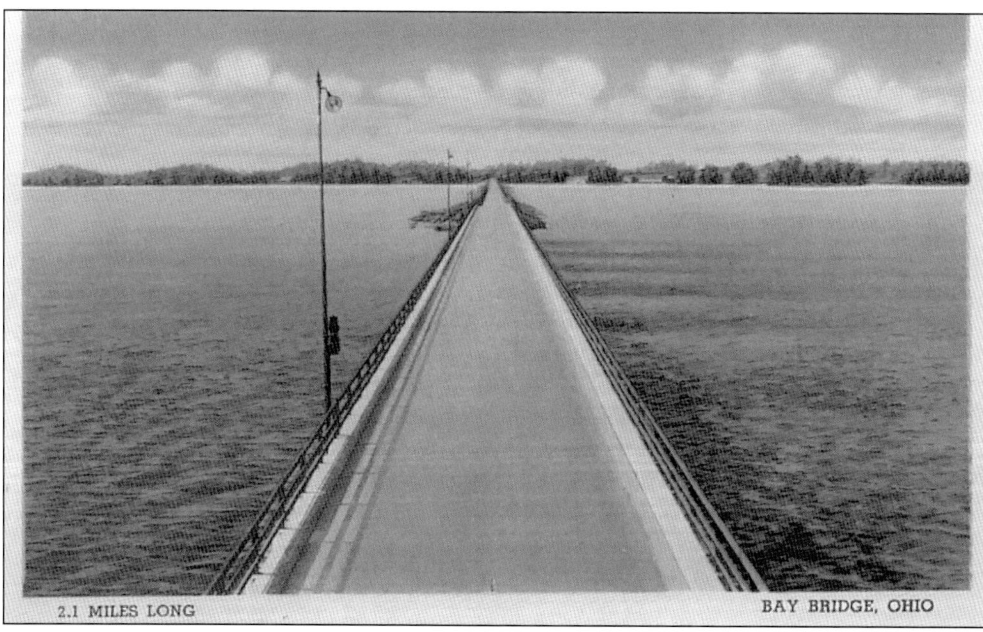

The auto bridge across Sandusky Bay carried motorists to Marblehead, Catawba, and Port Clinton before its replacement by the high-span Thomas A. Edison Memorial Bridge.

Two

Cedar Point

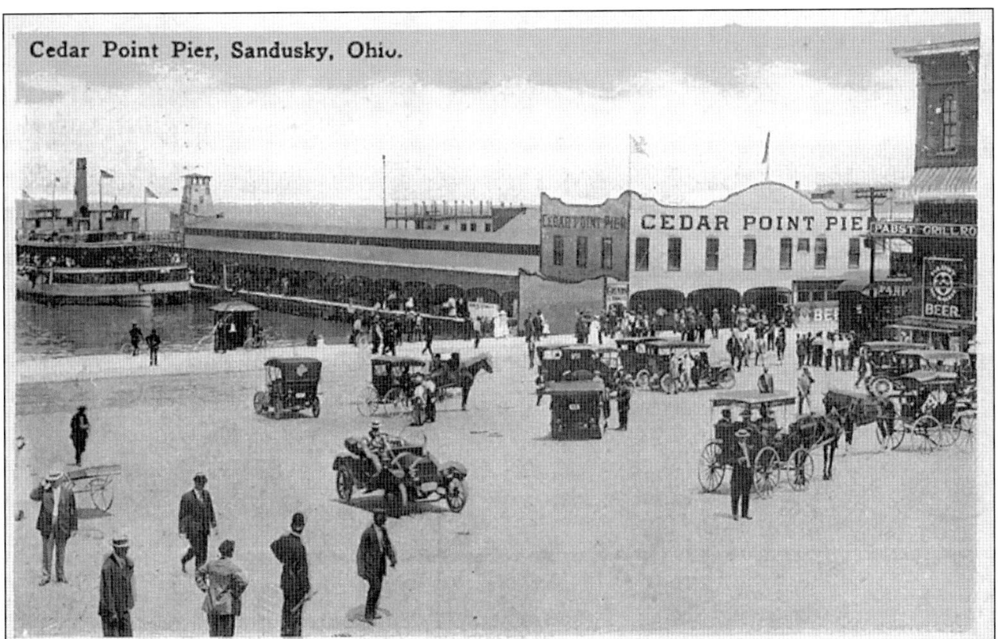

A view of the Cedar Point Pier in Sandusky shows horseless and horse-drawn carriages discharging passengers, while a steamboat awaits departure. Excursionists could enjoy a cold brew at the Pabst Grill Room or a smoke at the cigar and tobacco stand (at center).

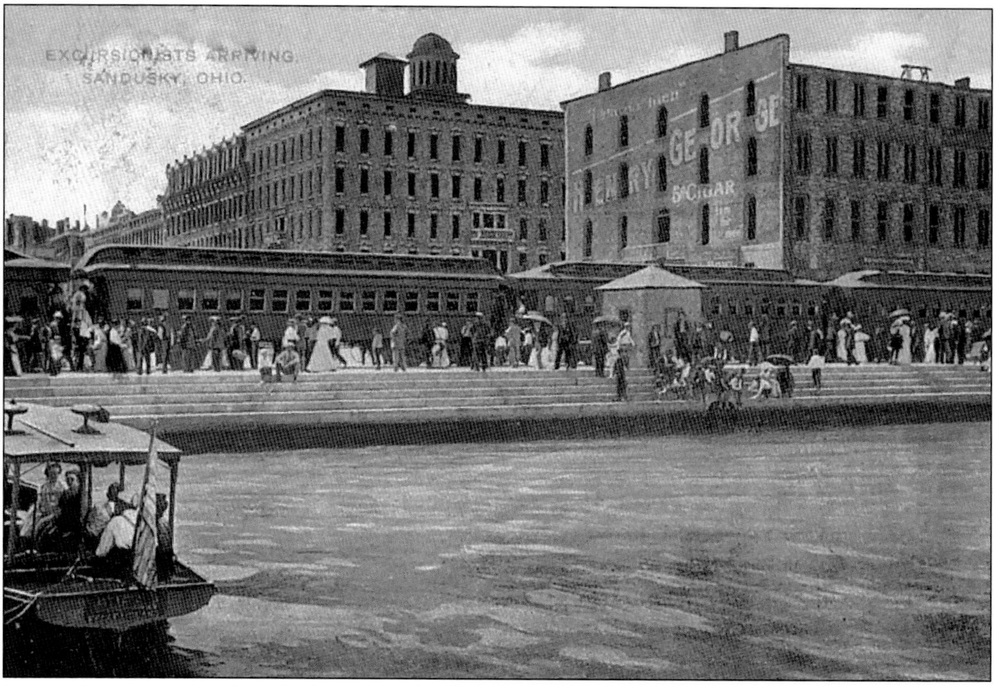

Excursionists arrived at Cedar Point by boat, train, and carriage. Here, train passengers disembark at the pier in Sandusky to await steamboat passage to Cedar Point.

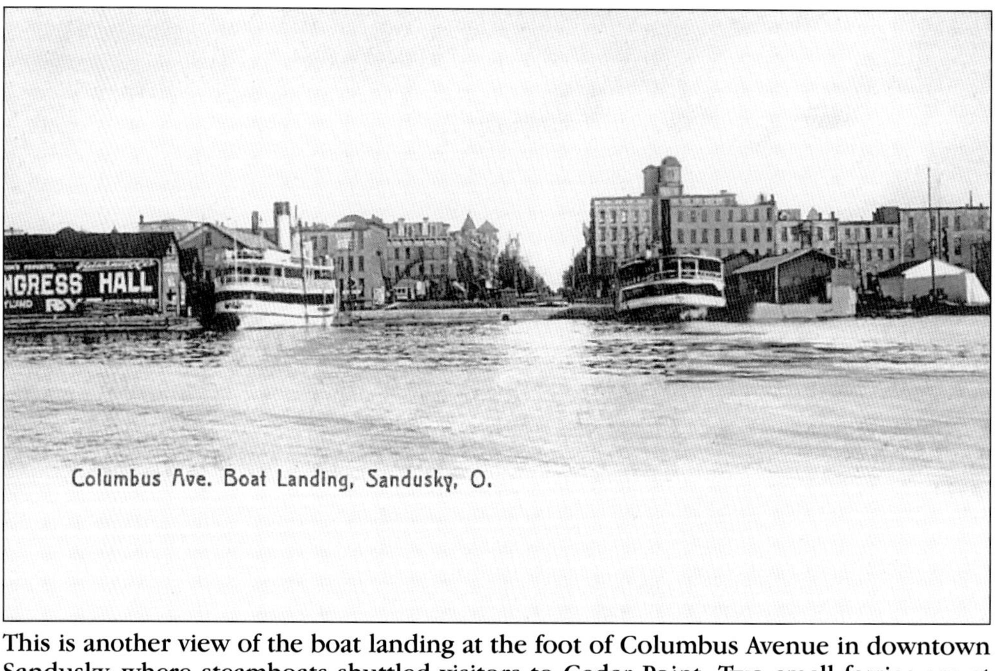

This is another view of the boat landing at the foot of Columbus Avenue in downtown Sandusky, where steamboats shuttled visitors to Cedar Point. Two small ferries are at the dock awaiting passengers.

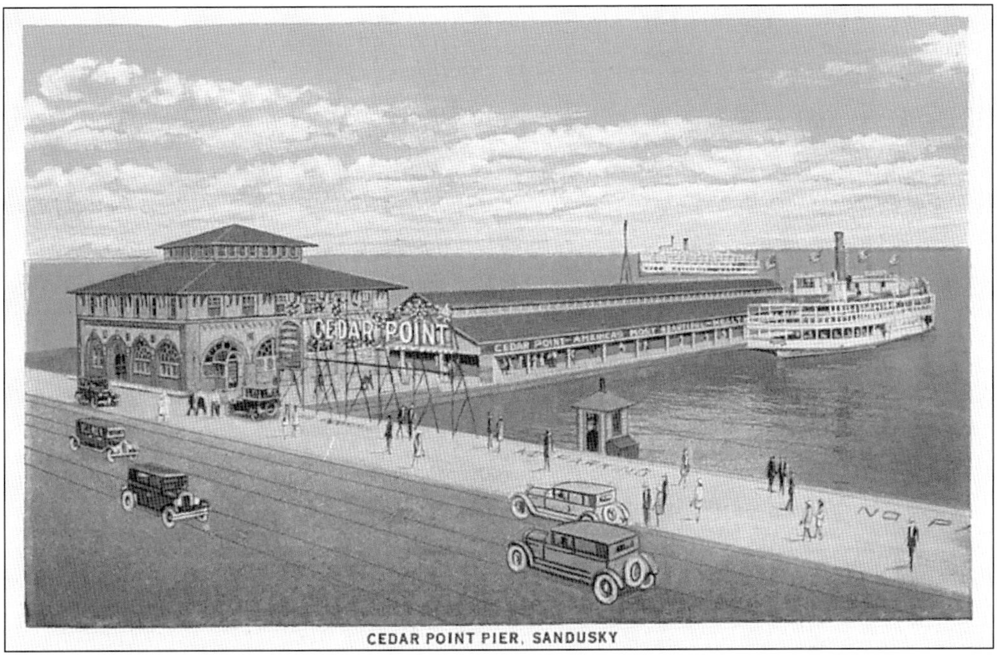

Automobiles are prominent in this view of Sandusky's Cedar Point Pier in the 1920s. The rise in automobile travel led to the demise of the large passenger steamship lines by the 1930s.

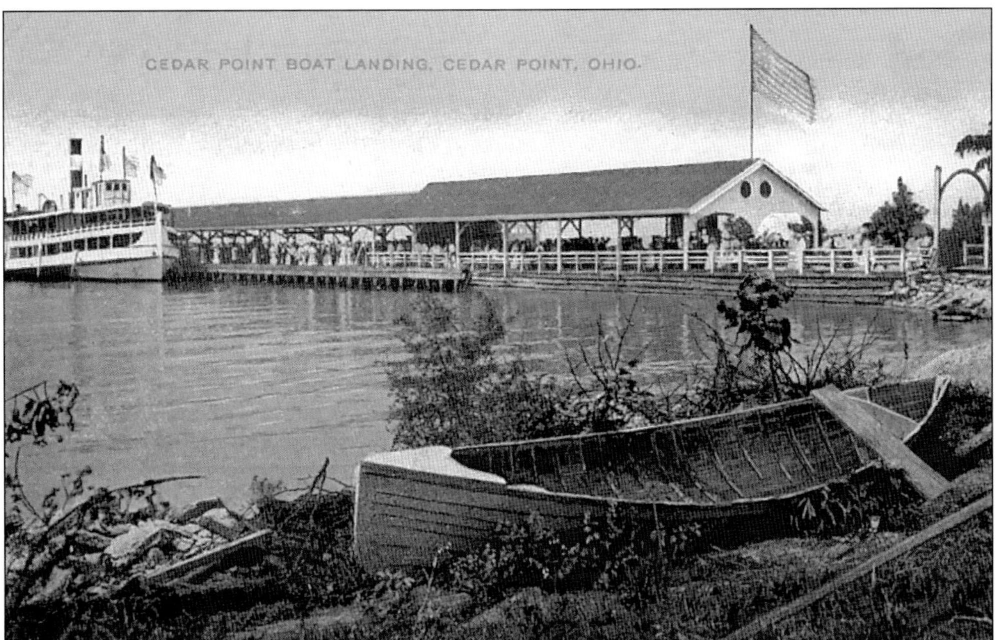

This is an early view of the boat landing at Cedar Point.

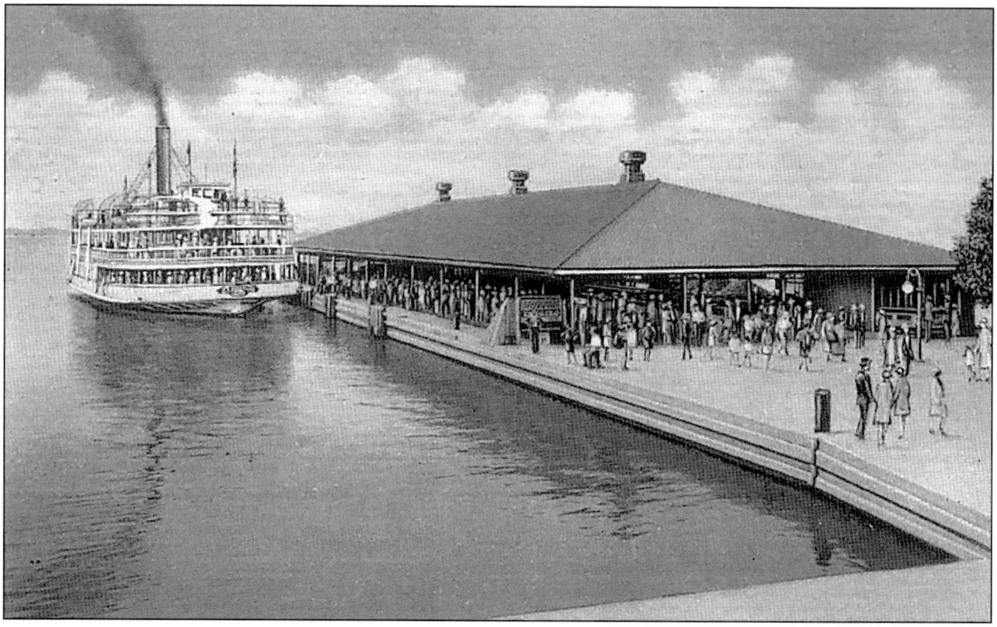

Passengers are shown arriving at Cedar Point on the *G. A. Boeckling*. The boat was named in honor of the longtime Cedar Point manager. The "G. A. Boeckling Co., Sandusky, Ohio" published this postcard.

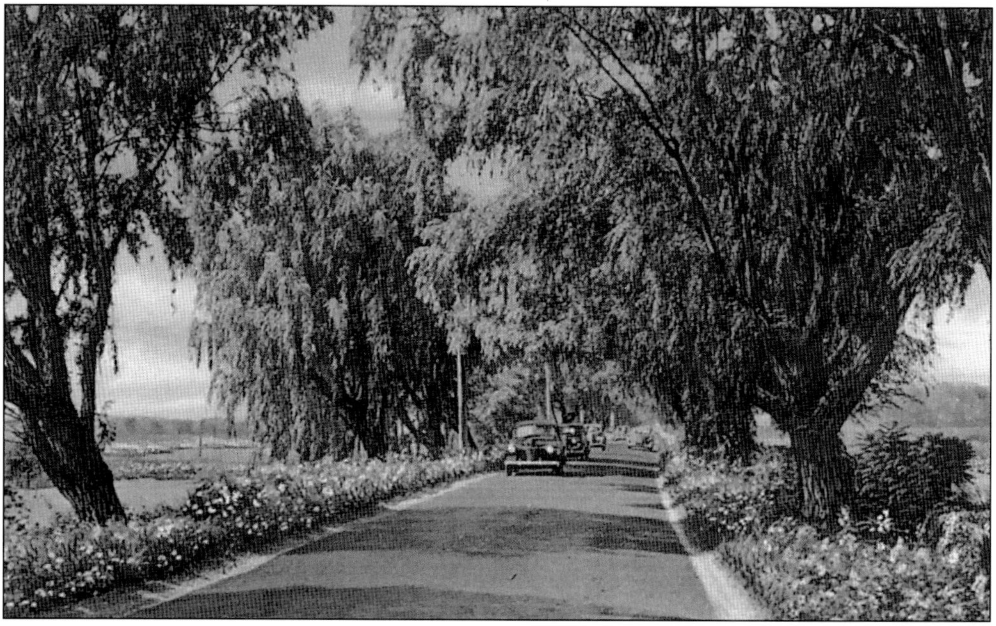

The automobile age ushered in the opening of the Cedar Point Auto Road. Now a scenic back road, this was the only land access to Cedar Point prior to the opening of the Cedar Point Causeway in 1957.

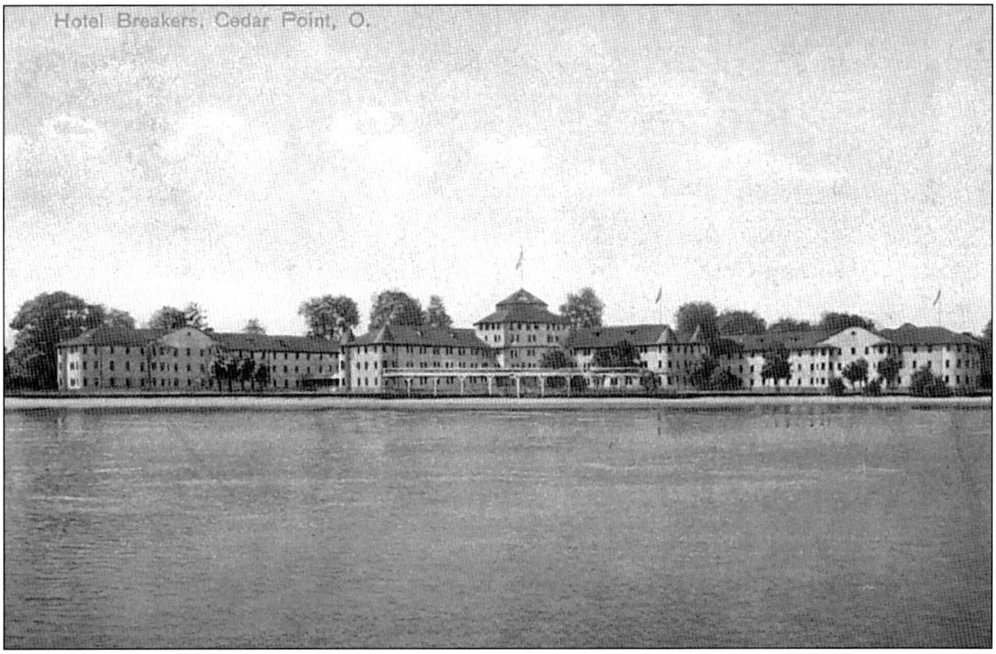

The massive Breakers Hotel has been welcoming guests to Cedar Point since its opening in 1905. This 1906 card shows the hotel's appearance, little changed from today, shortly after its completion.

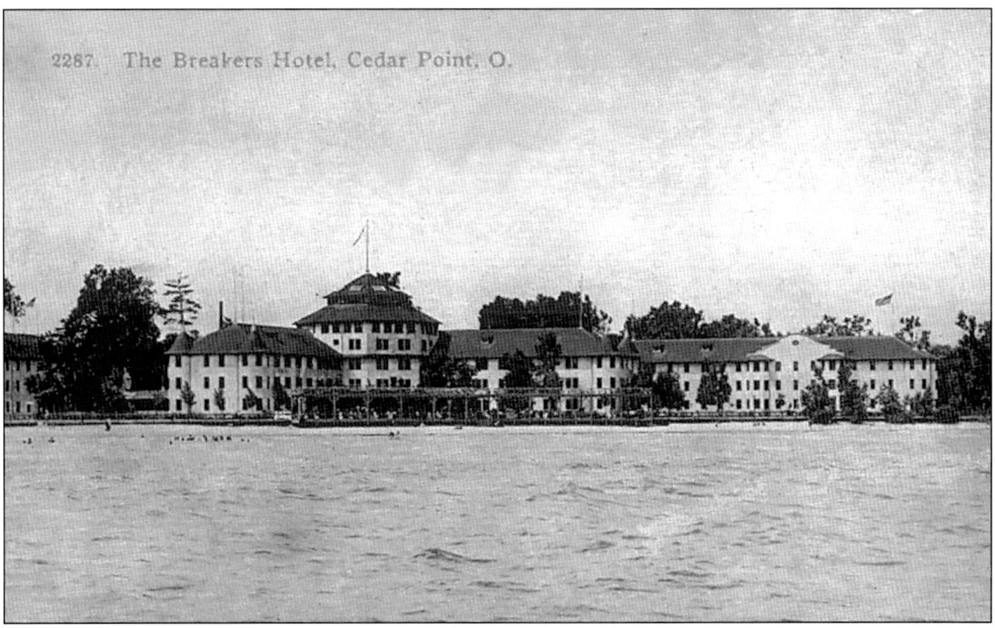

The Hotel Breakers is shown several years after its opening in this view. Note the young trees, which now tower over the hotel.

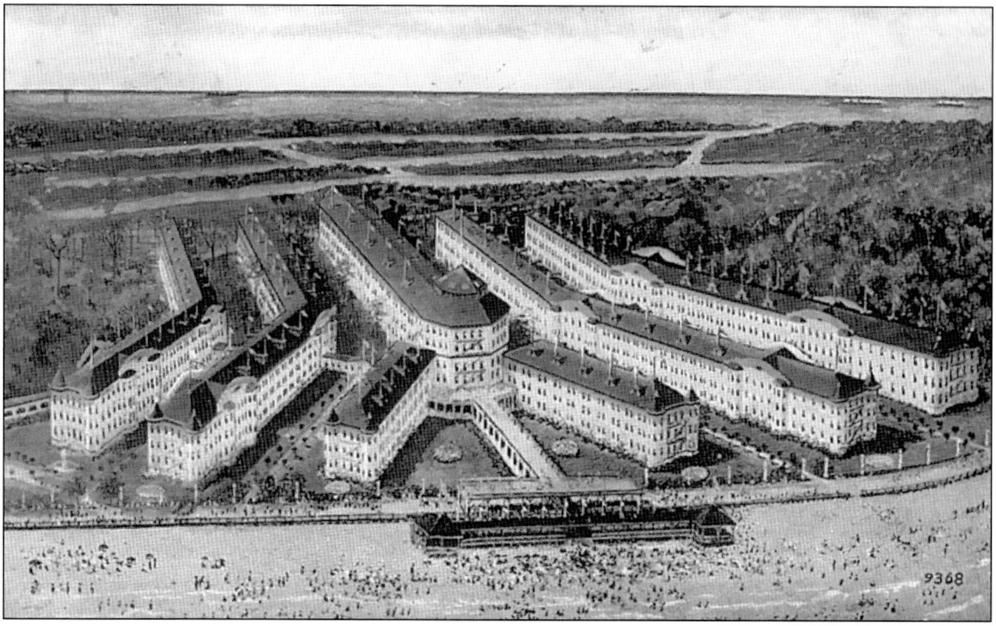

The Breakers is described in an early promotional brochure as "one of the largest and best equipped hotels in America...It covers over eight acres of ground and contains more than a thousand rooms, every one of which affords an unobstructed view of the bathing beach and Lake Erie's broad expanse."

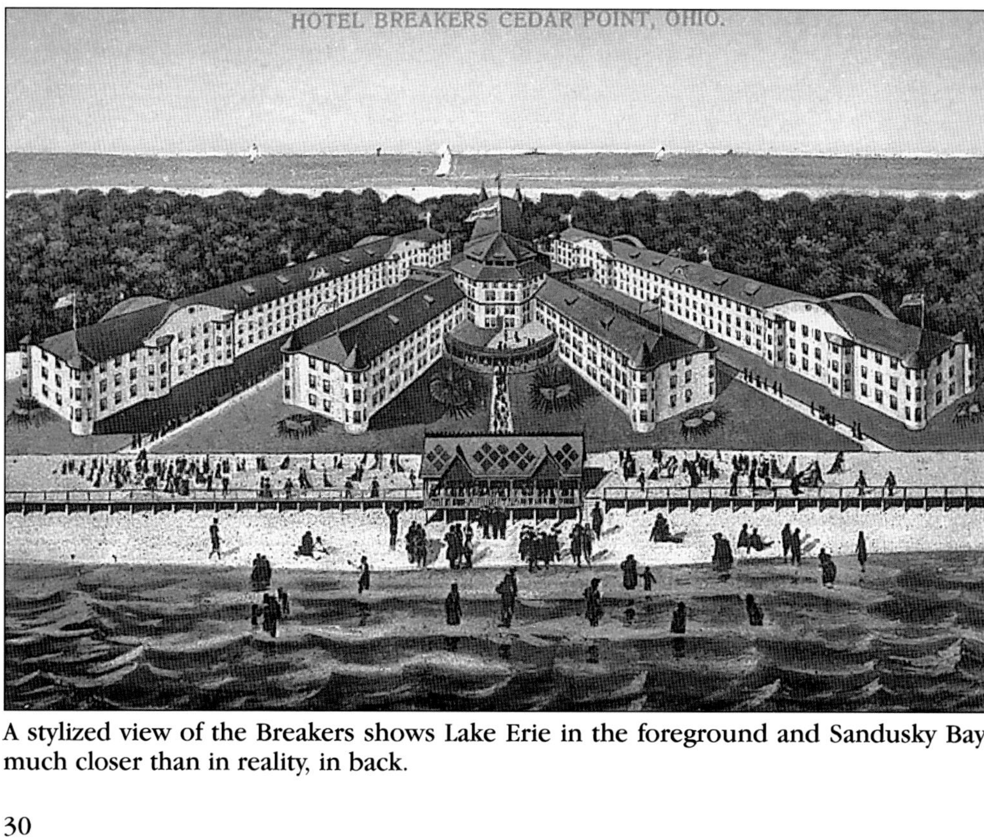

A stylized view of the Breakers shows Lake Erie in the foreground and Sandusky Bay, much closer than in reality, in back.

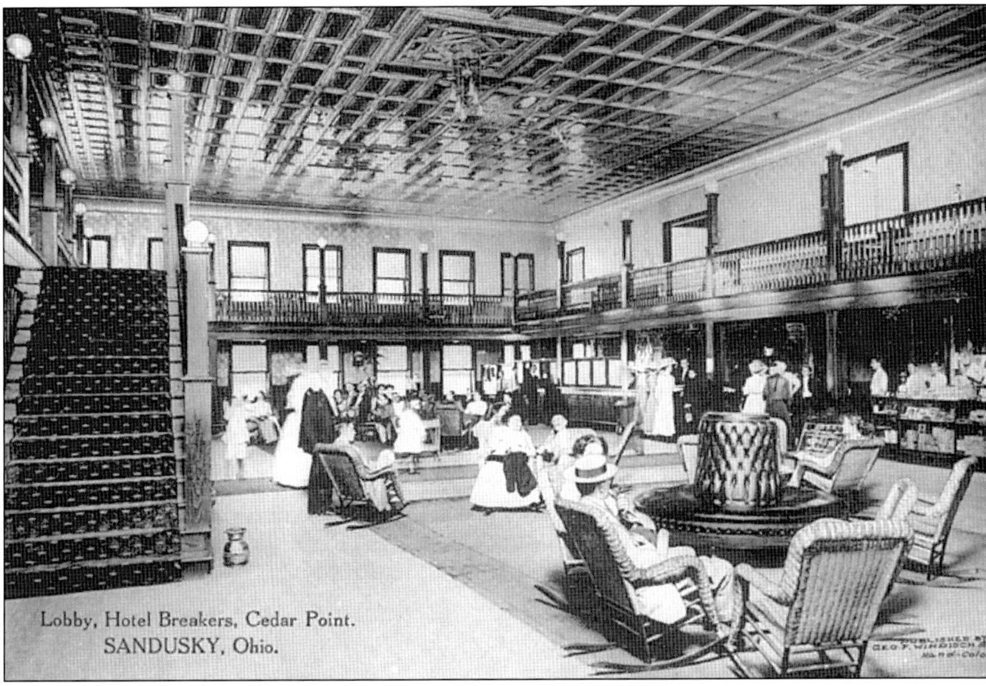

The lobby of the Breakers, replete with wicker furnishings and ornate balconies, has welcomed Presidents Taft, Wilson, Harding, Coolidge, Roosevelt, and Eisenhower. Other notable guests included Annie Oakley, John Philip Sousa, John D. Rockefeller, and Tyrone Power. Note the spittoon at the foot of the stairs.

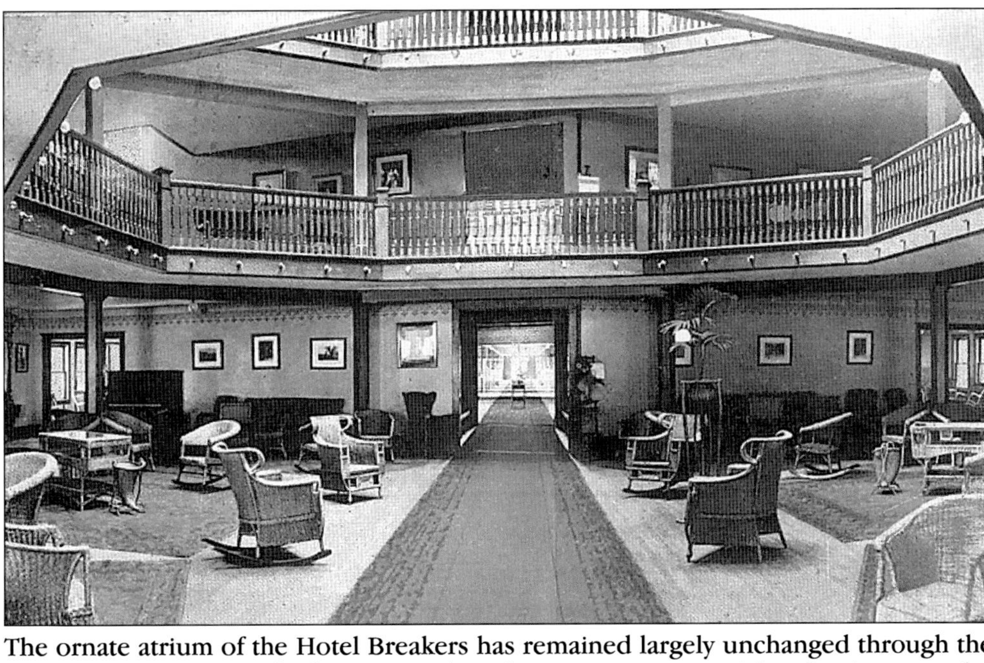

The ornate atrium of the Hotel Breakers has remained largely unchanged through the years. The electric light bulbs surrounding the atrium were considered quite a wonder in 1916, when this card was postmarked.

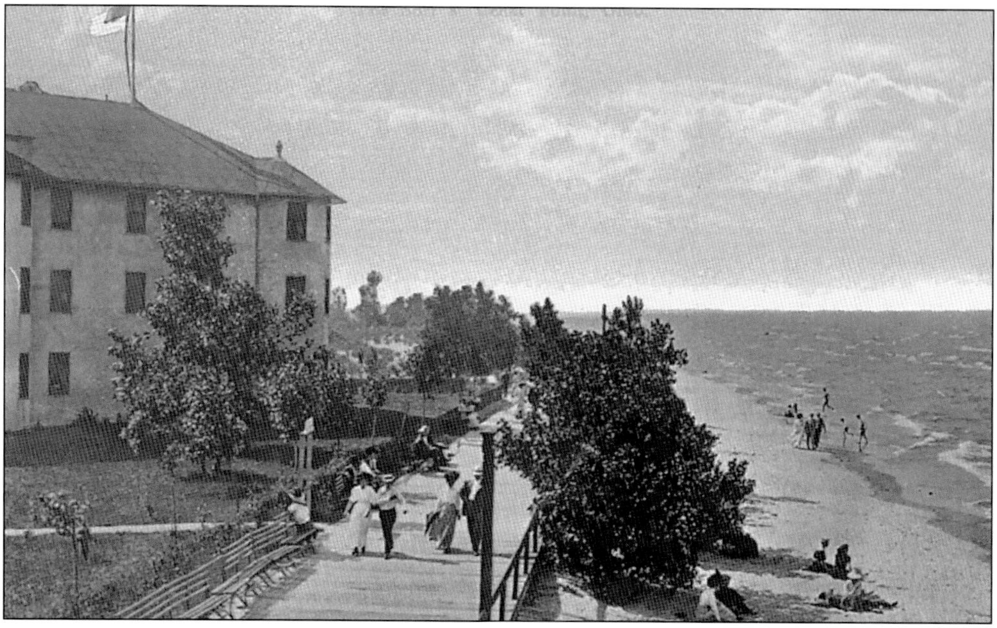

Couples stroll past the Hotel Breakers in this scene featuring the famous Cedar Point boardwalk. The boardwalk still attracts promenaders, although concrete has replaced the wooden walkway.

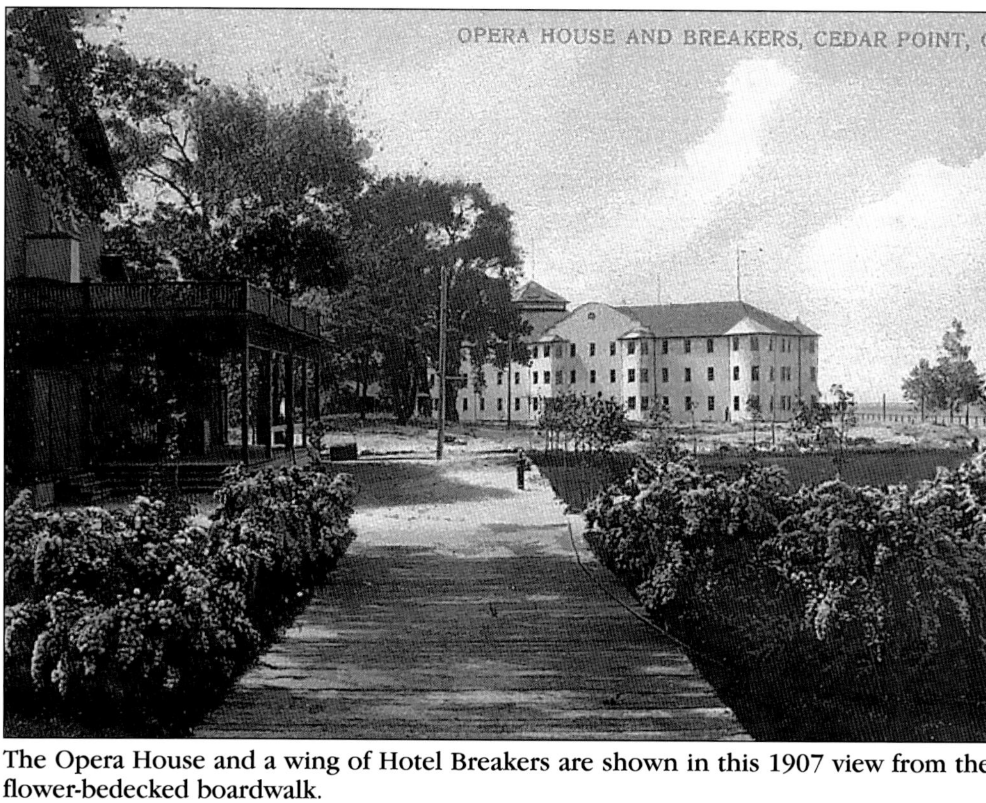

The Opera House and a wing of Hotel Breakers are shown in this 1907 view from the flower-bedecked boardwalk.

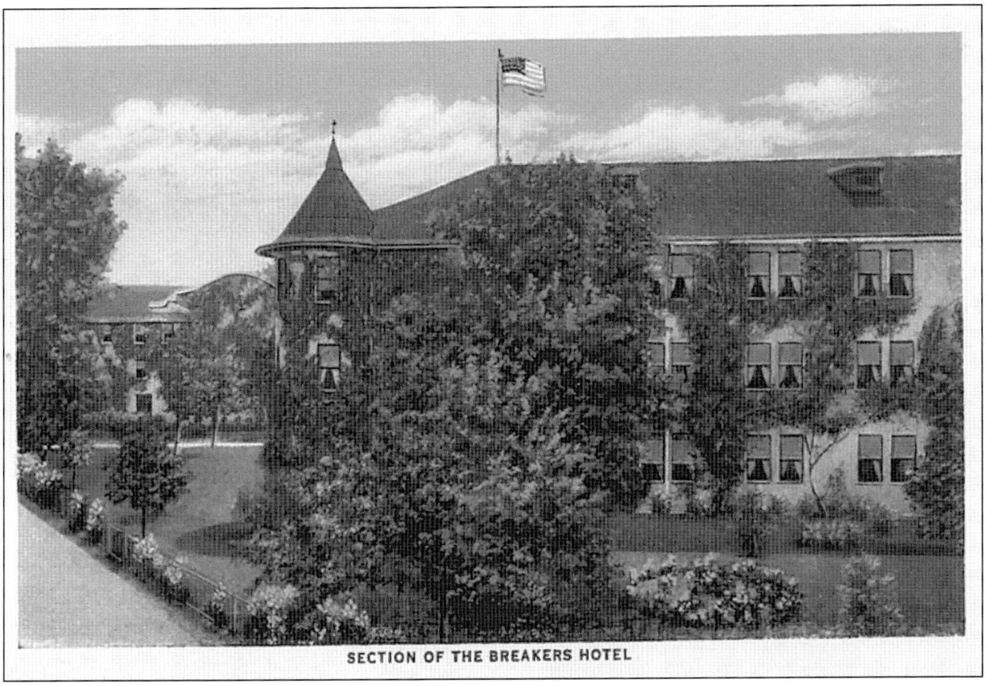

Greenery and plantings enhanced the beauty (and coolness) of the Breakers.

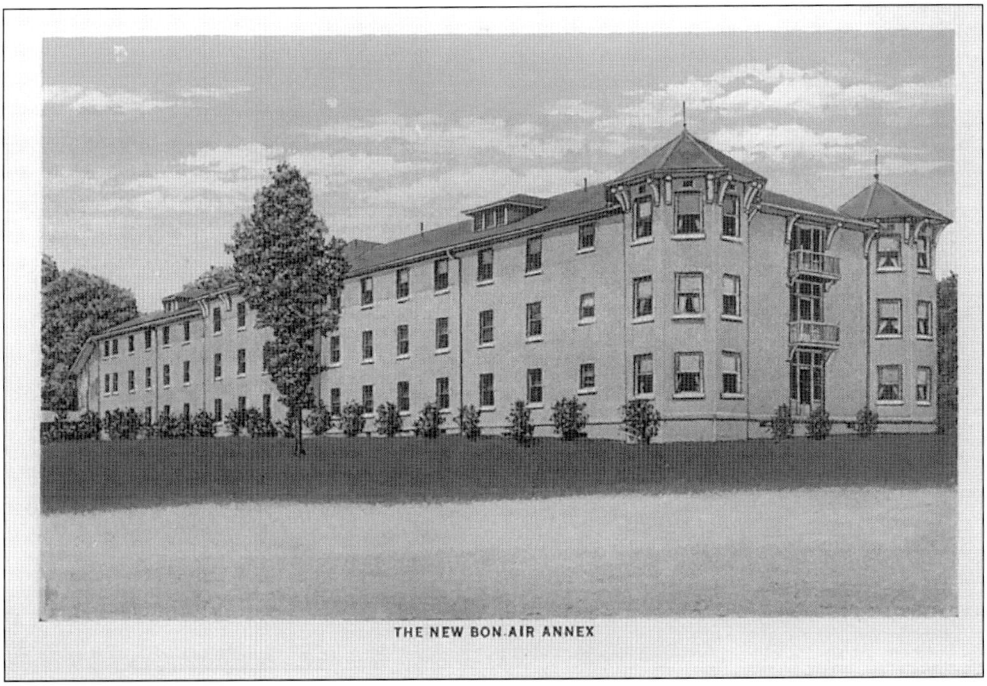

The Bon-Air wing expanded the Breakers in the 1920s.

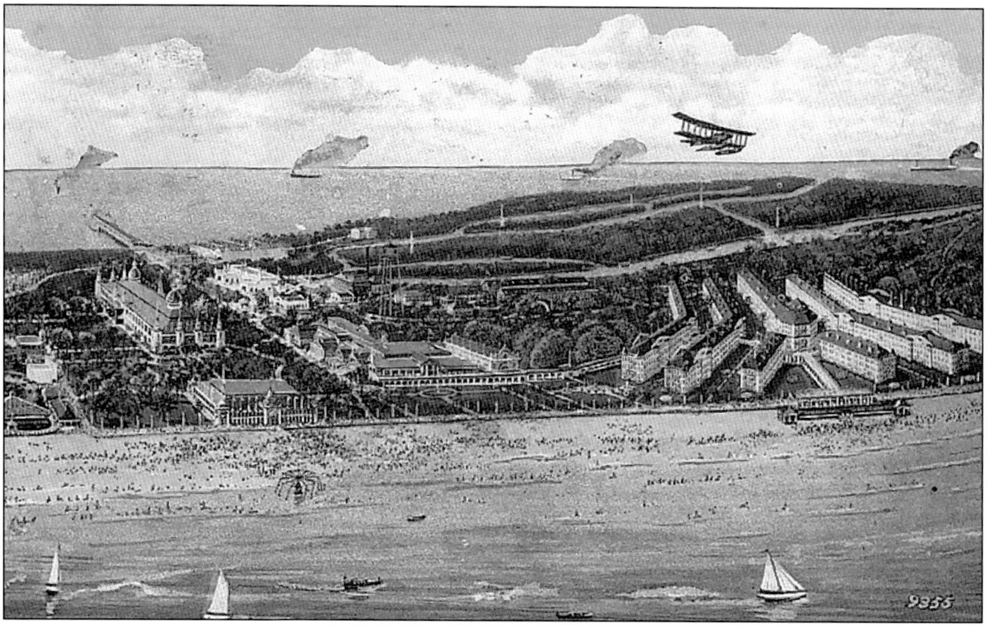

A main attraction of Cedar Point was, as it is today, the beach, touted as the widest and finest in Lake Erie. Many visitors flocked to the wide, sandy expanse and cool waters of Lake Erie every summer.

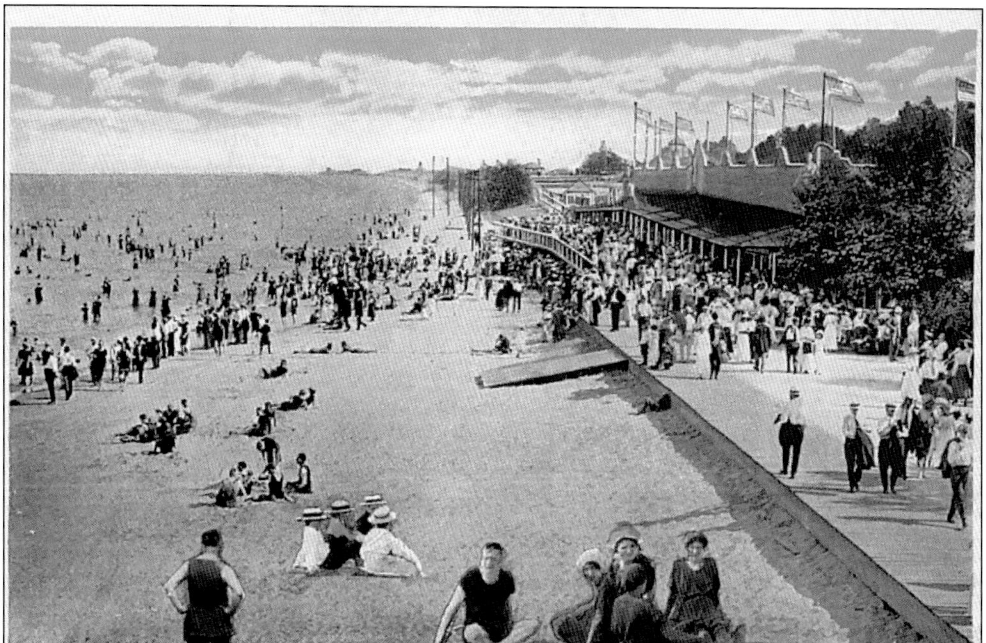

117. BATH HOUSE, BOARDWALK AND BEACH, CEDAR POINT, OHIO.

The boardwalk and bathhouse can be seen in this view.

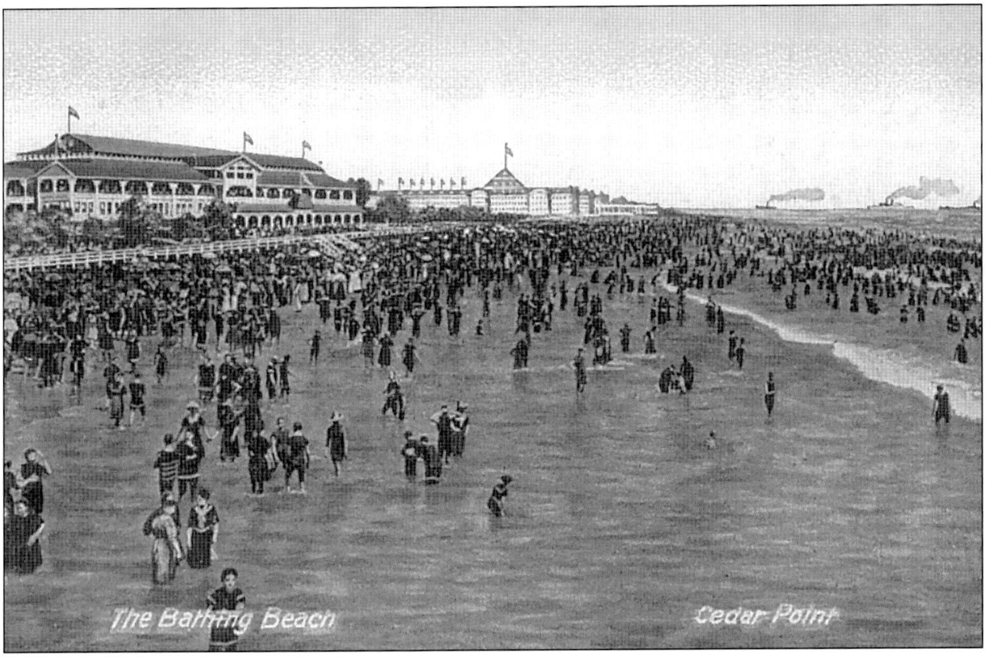

The famous bathing beach at Cedar Point hosted thousands of beachcombers in their bloomers. Shown in the background is the world's largest bathing pavilion and Hotel Breakers.

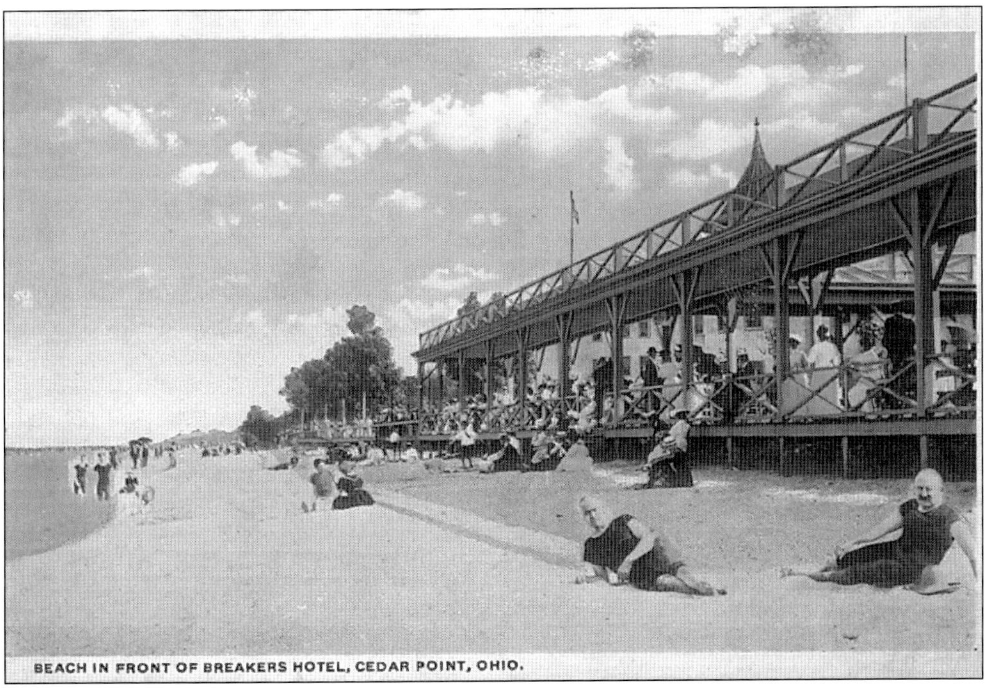

This is the beach in front of the Hotel Breakers.

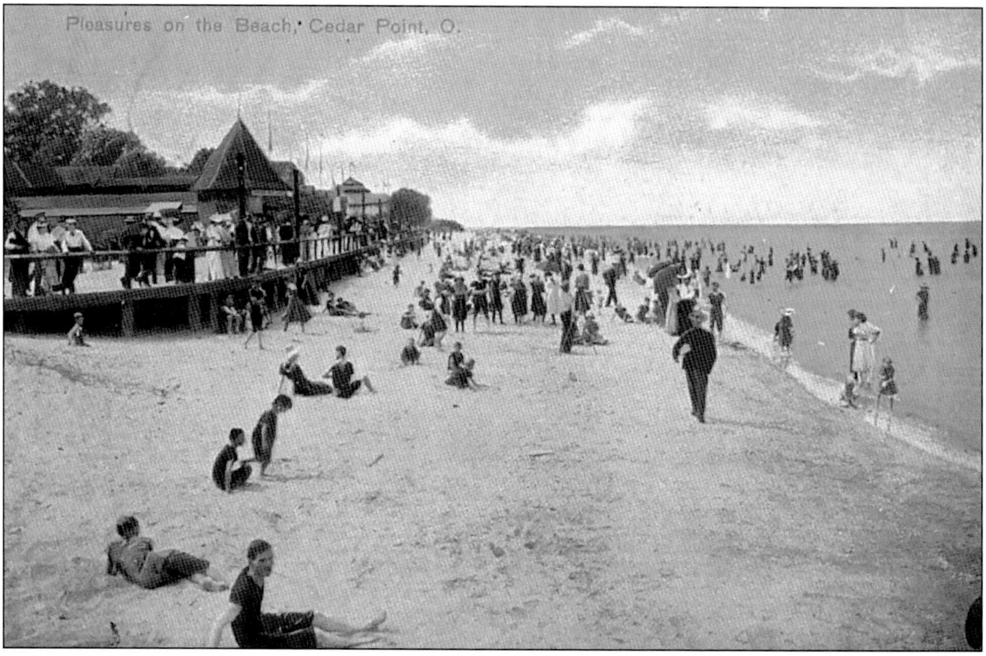

Then, as now, crowds flocked to the beach at Cedar Point on a hot summer's day. The building shown on the left offered "Souvenir Post Cards."

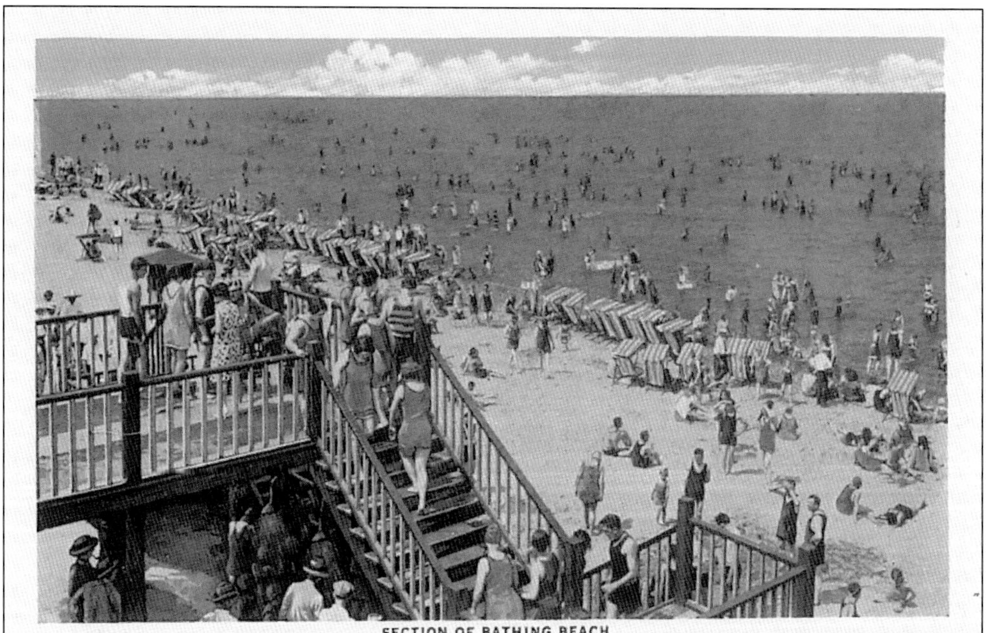

Beachgoers climb the steps to the Pavilion. Covered chairs were popular in the early days as they are now.

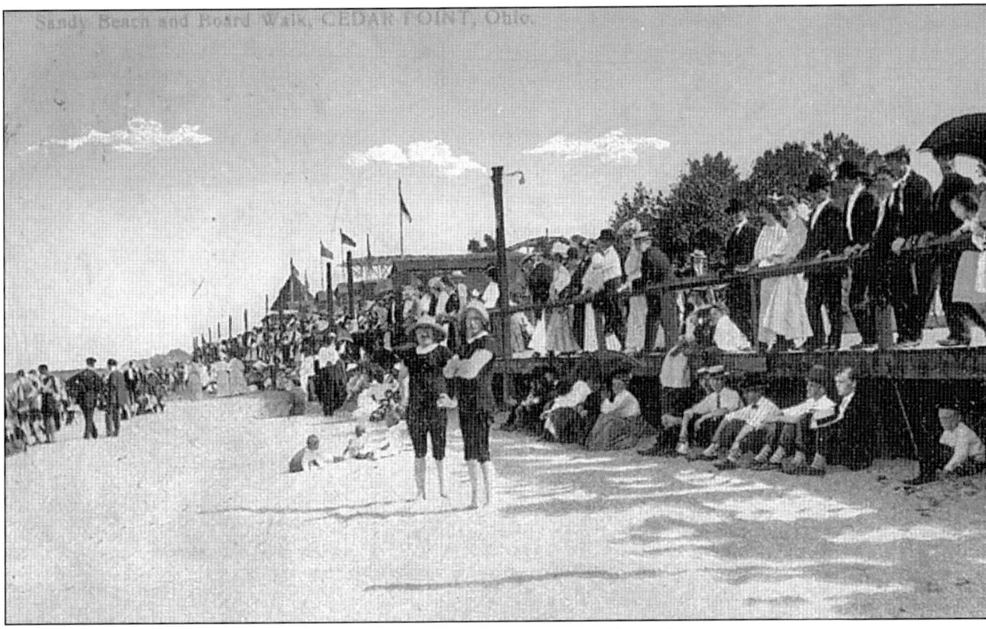

Formally attired visitors enjoy a summer's day at the beach.

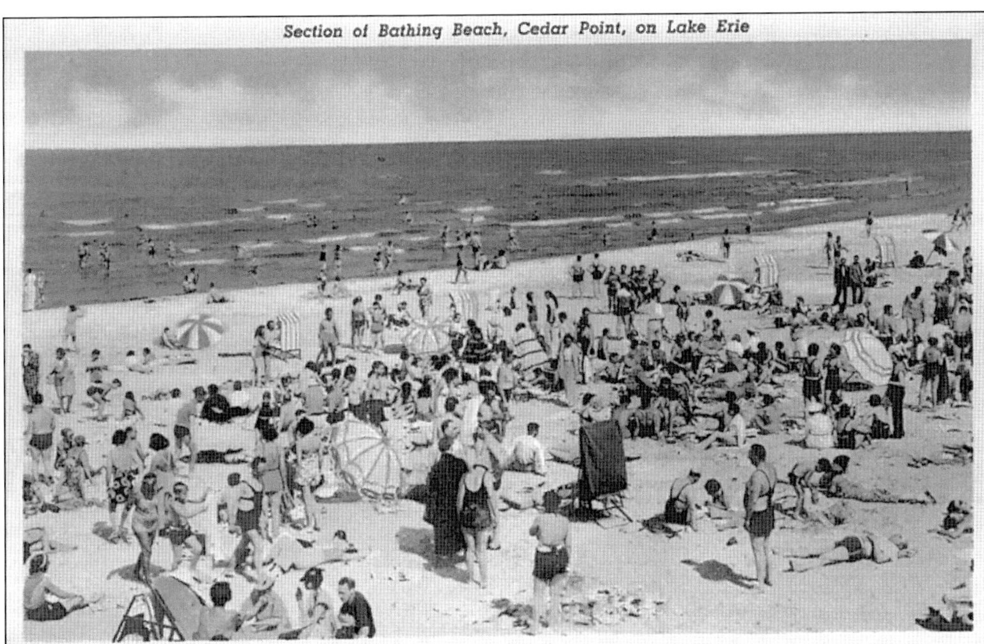

The beach at Cedar Point, shown here in the 1940s, has remained one of the finest on Lake Erie. Note the change in bathing attire from earlier views.

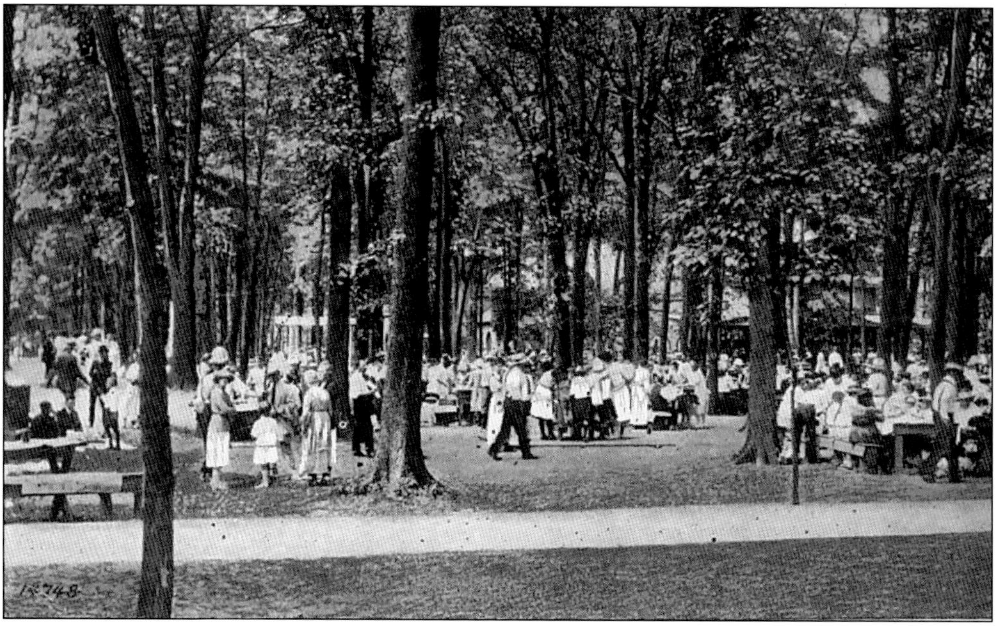

Picnicking was a popular pastime at early Cedar Point. Excursioners decked out in their finest attire—straw hats, starched collars, ties, and suspenders for the gentlemen and dresses with high heels for the ladies—enjoy a day's outing among the tall cedars, that "reaching skyward raise their fringes of green against the blaze of sky," according to the promotional text on the postcard folder.

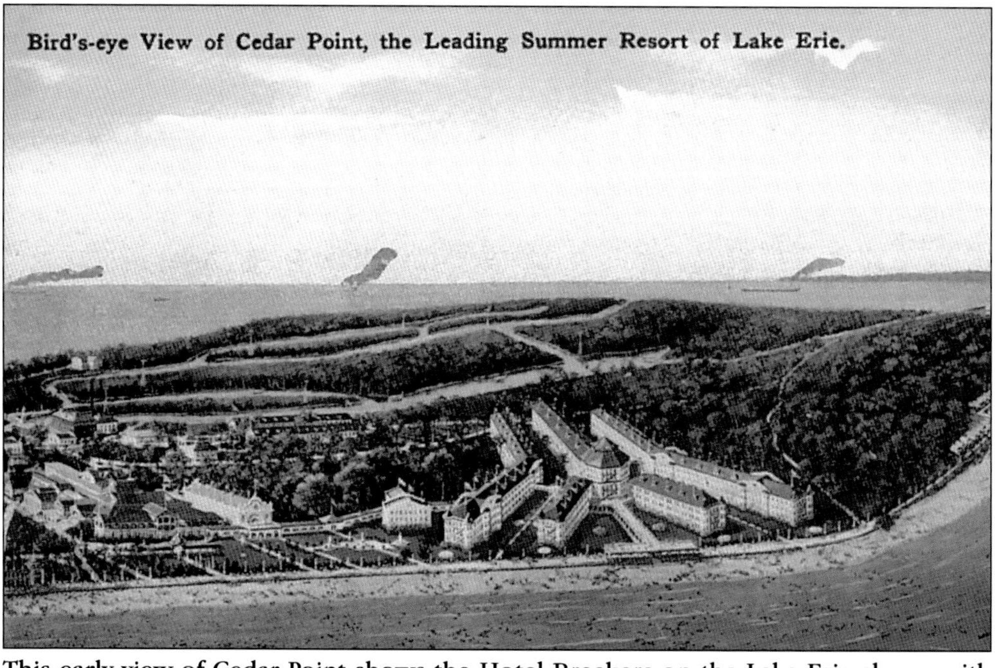

This early view of Cedar Point shows the Hotel Breakers on the Lake Erie shore, with the lagoons in the background and Amusement Circle on the left.

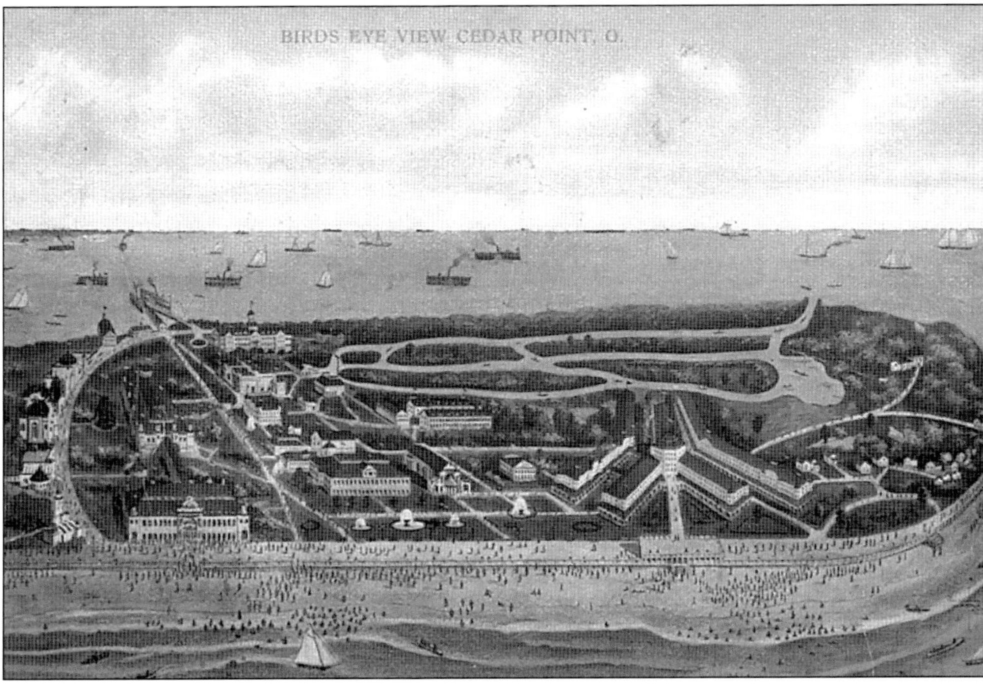

This bird's-eye view has more detail, and shows the lagoons, which still exist today, and the Hotel Breakers, along with the early amusement arcade, Grand Pavilion (lower left, next to the beach), the Bay Shore Hotel (upper left), and White House Hotel (on the beach with fountains).

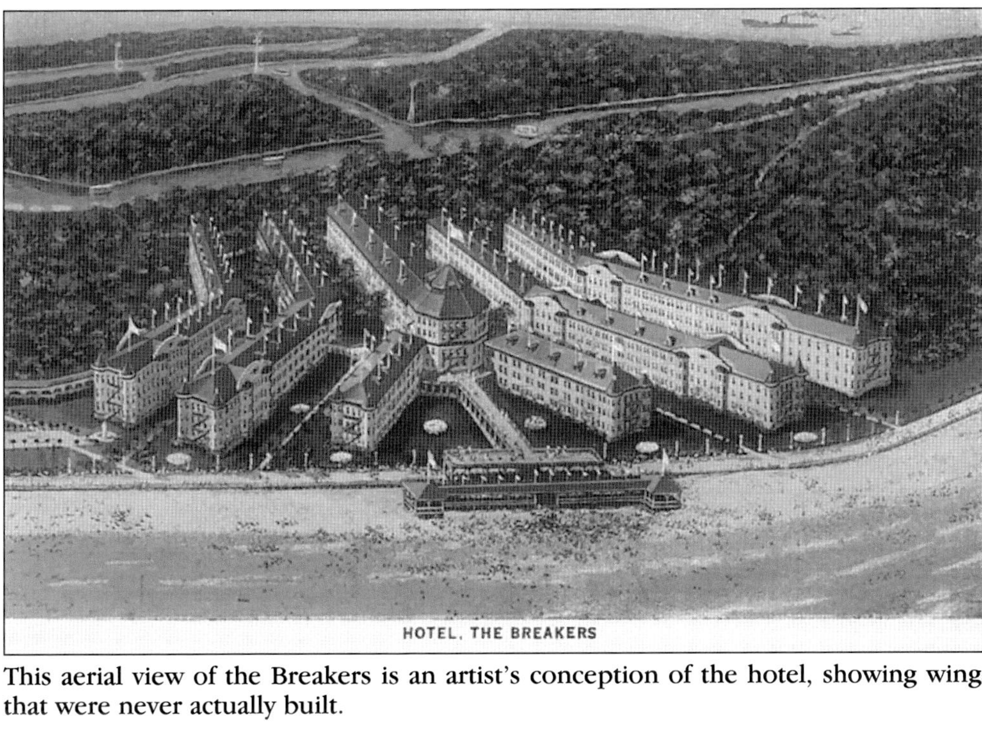
HOTEL, THE BREAKERS

This aerial view of the Breakers is an artist's conception of the hotel, showing wings that were never actually built.

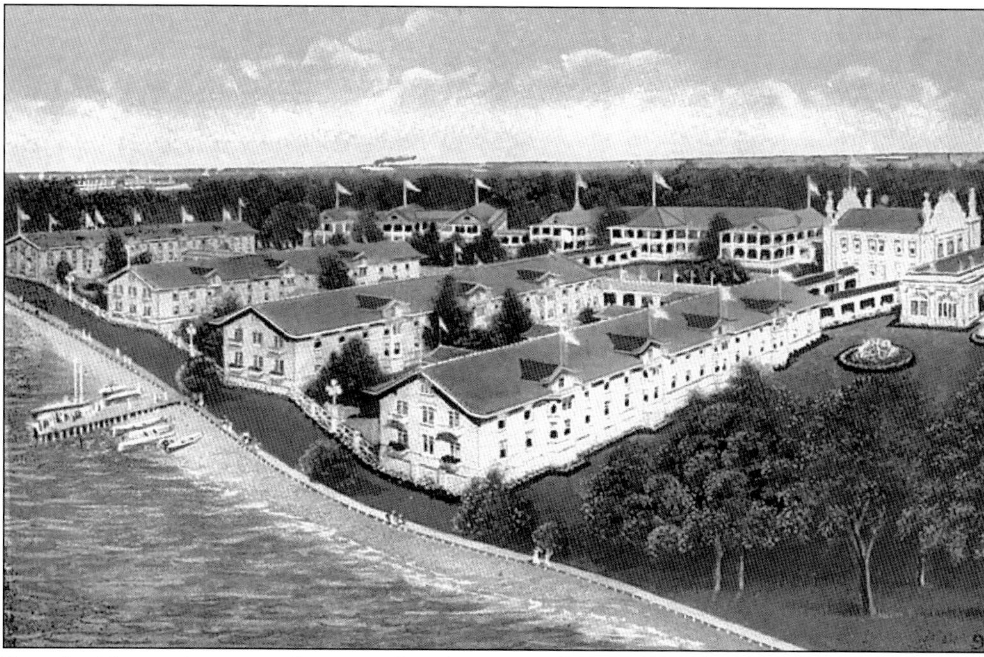

Faced with surging attendance and a shortage of overnight accommodations at Cedar Point, the Cedars hotel was constructed for the 1915 season, incorporating several buildings of the original White House Hotel. The Cedars welcomed guests until its closure in the 1930s and is today used as an employee dormitory.

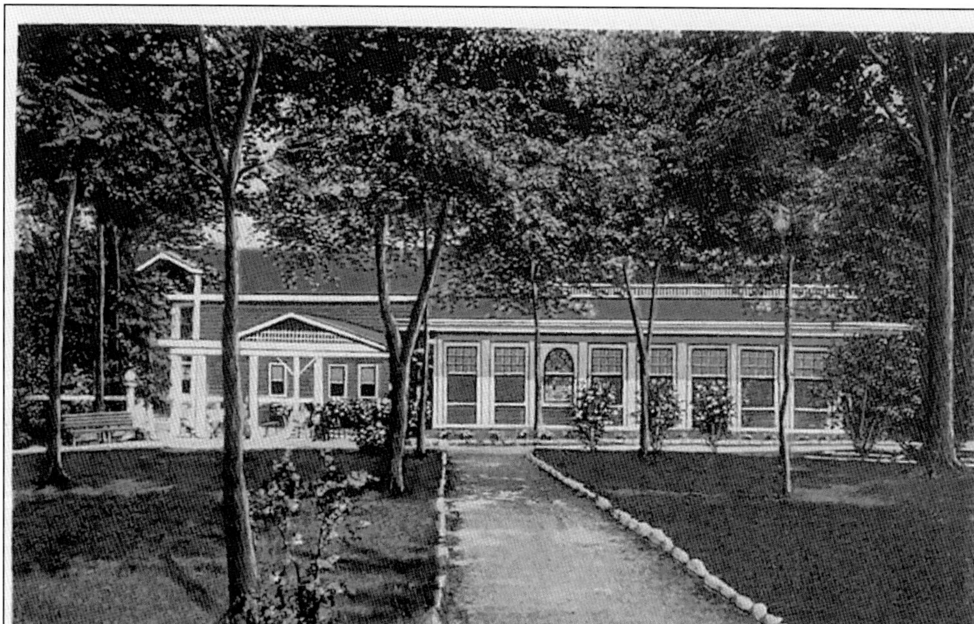

THE HOTEL CEDARS ENTRANCE

The Hotel Cedars featured 270 guestrooms, its own cafeteria, and a gift shop.

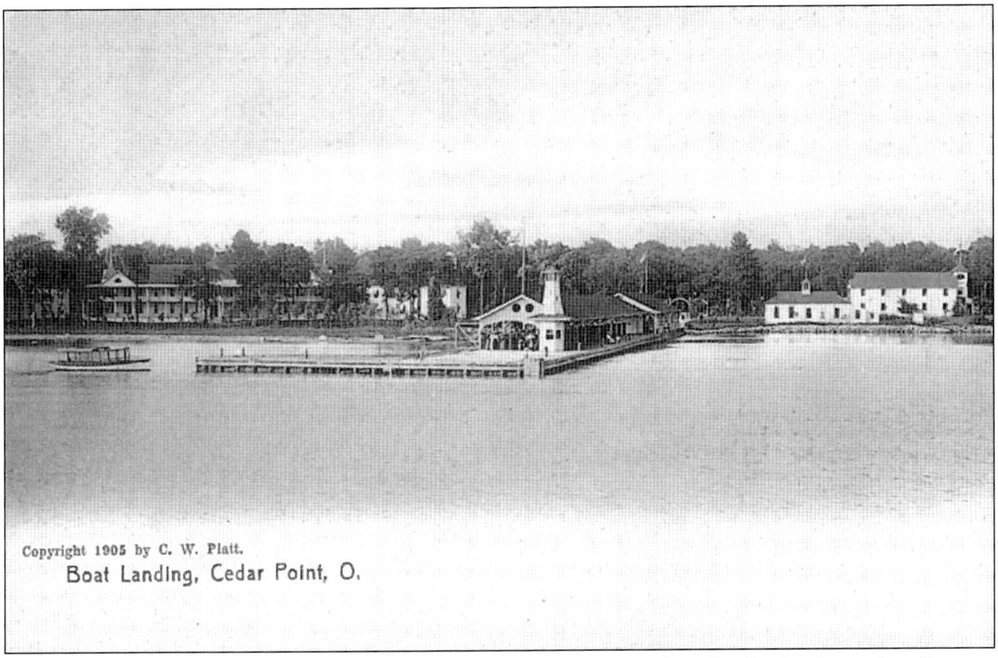

The White House Hotel (left) and Bay Shore Hotel (right) flank the boat landing at Cedar Point in this 1905 view.

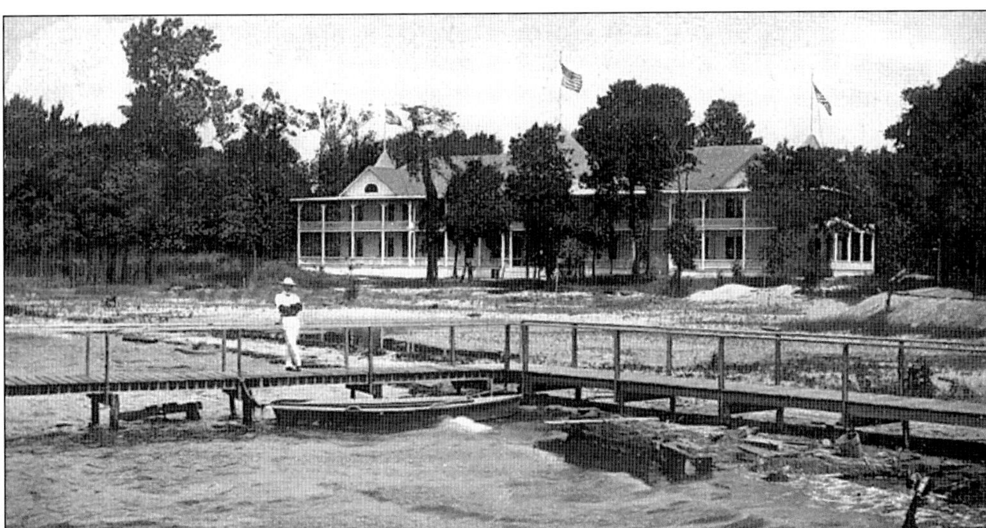

An early promotional booklet provides this description of the White House at Cedar Point: "Located on the Bayshore, the White House affords its guests a delightful view of the ever-moving panorama of shipping, together with pleasure craft of every variety. This, it will be seen, is ample accommodation provided for those who would forget the heat and dust of crowded cities."

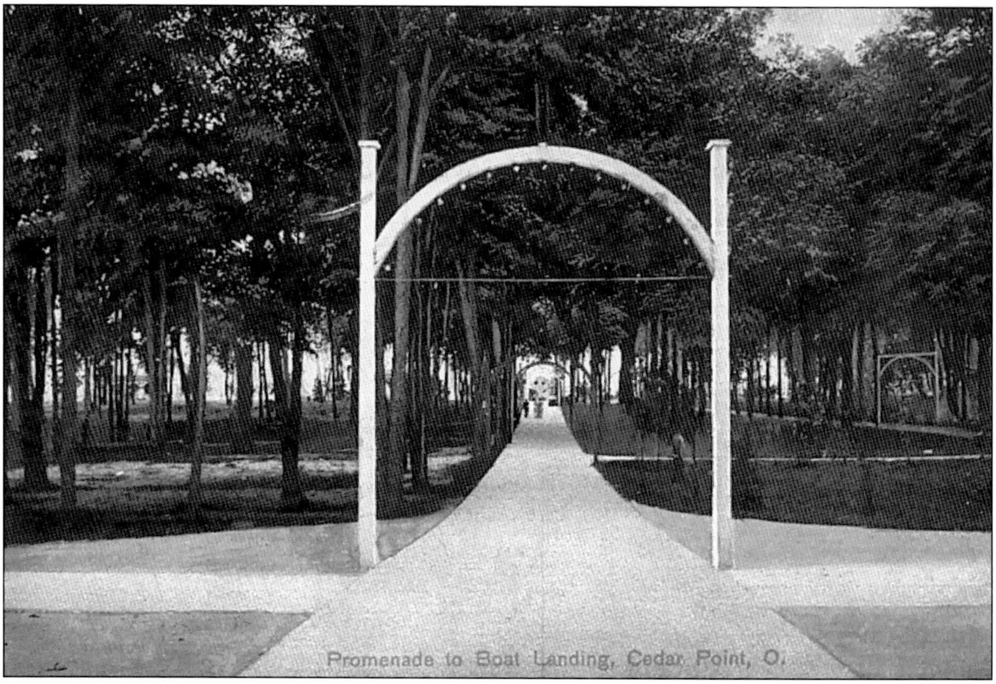

An entrance arch topped with multi-colored electric lights and a tree-lined promenade provided a grand walkway to the boat landing.

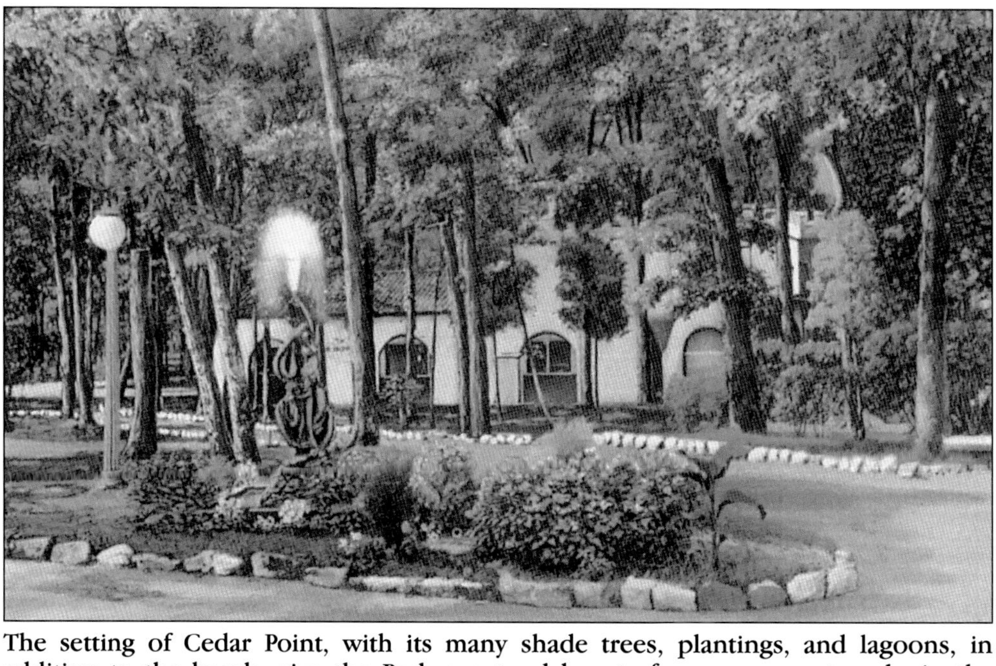

The setting of Cedar Point, with its many shade trees, plantings, and lagoons, in addition to the beach, give the Park a natural beauty few amusement parks in the country can match.

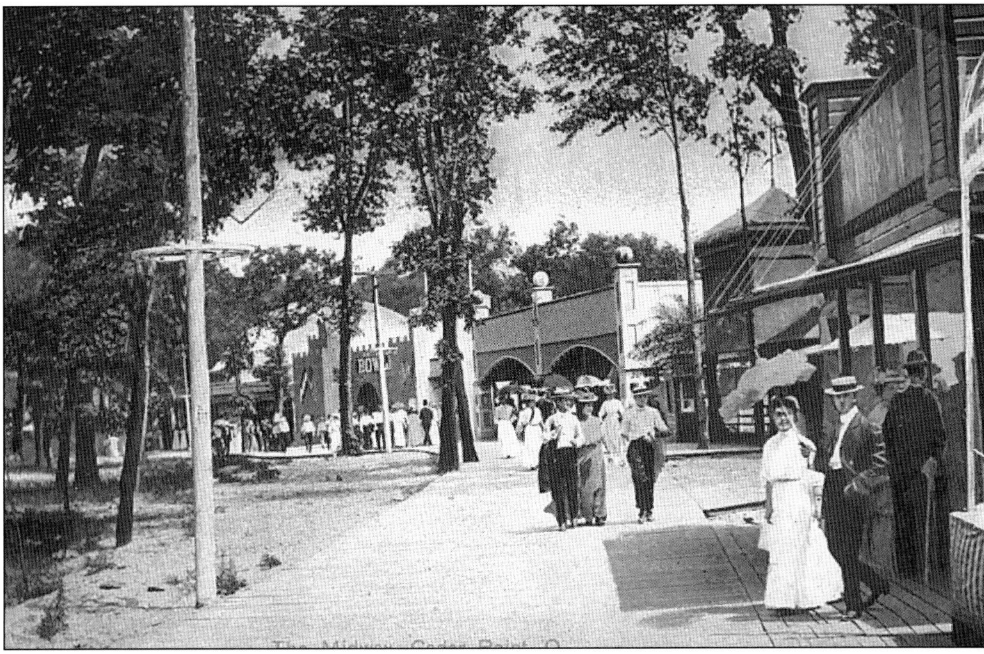

Early guests in Victorian finery stroll in the Amusement Circle, the entertainment center of Cedar Point.

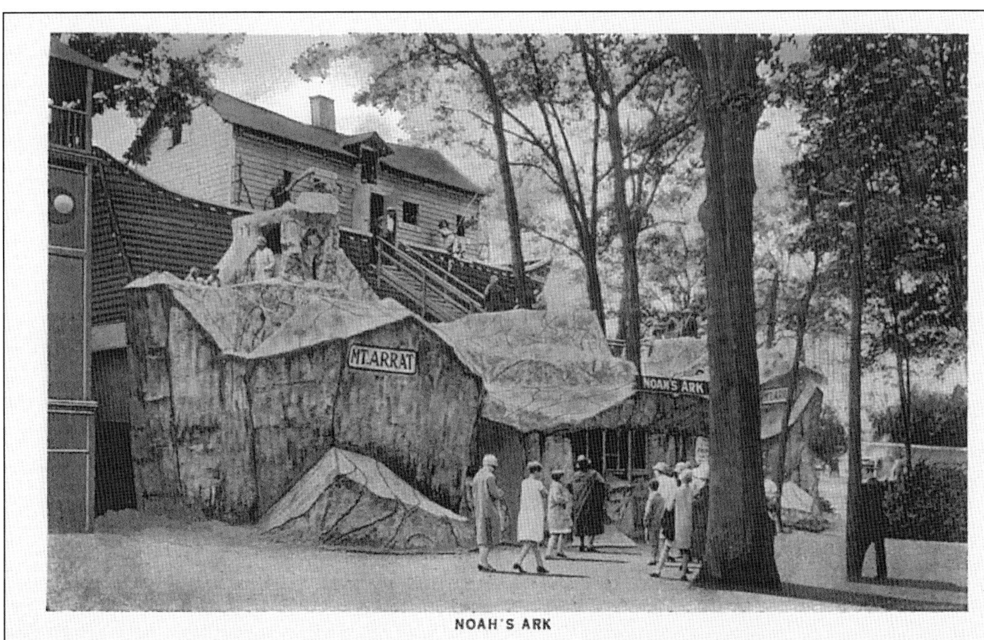

Noah's Ark funhouse, built in 1925, featured a boat replica resting along Mt. Arrat.

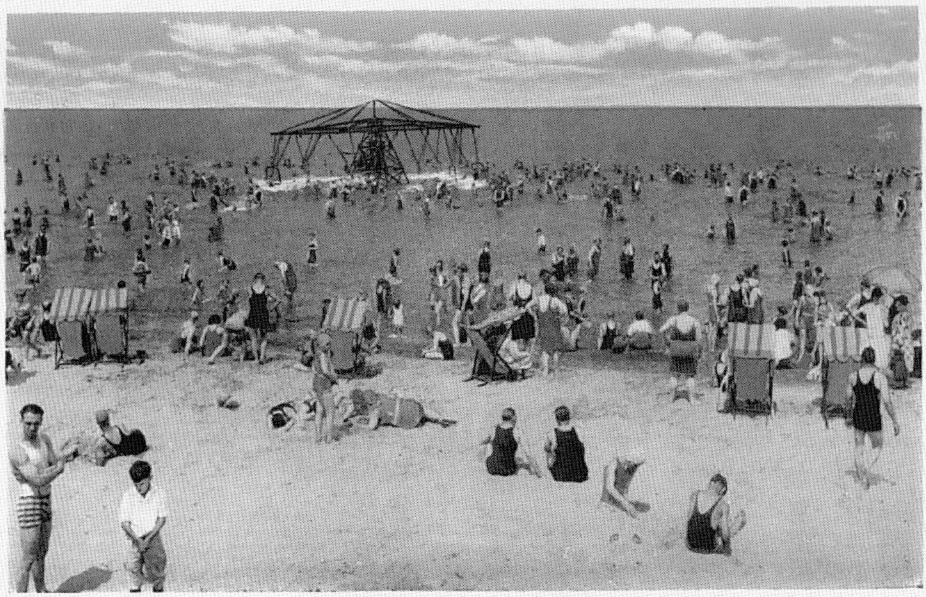

SECTION OF BATHING BEACH

The Wheel was an early waterfront thrill ride.

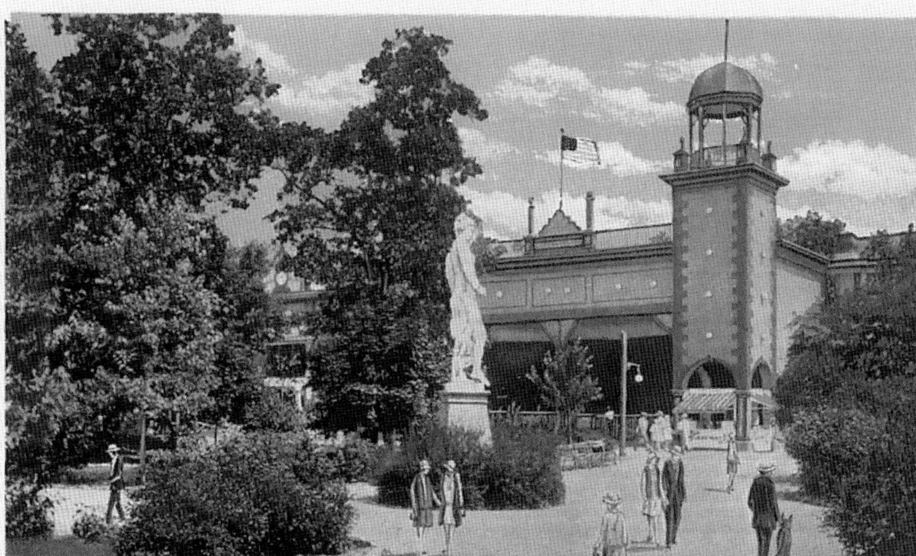

ONE OF MANY BEAUTIFUL WALKS

A scenic walk past oversized statuary and the Tumble Inn is shown in this view of the Amusement Circle.

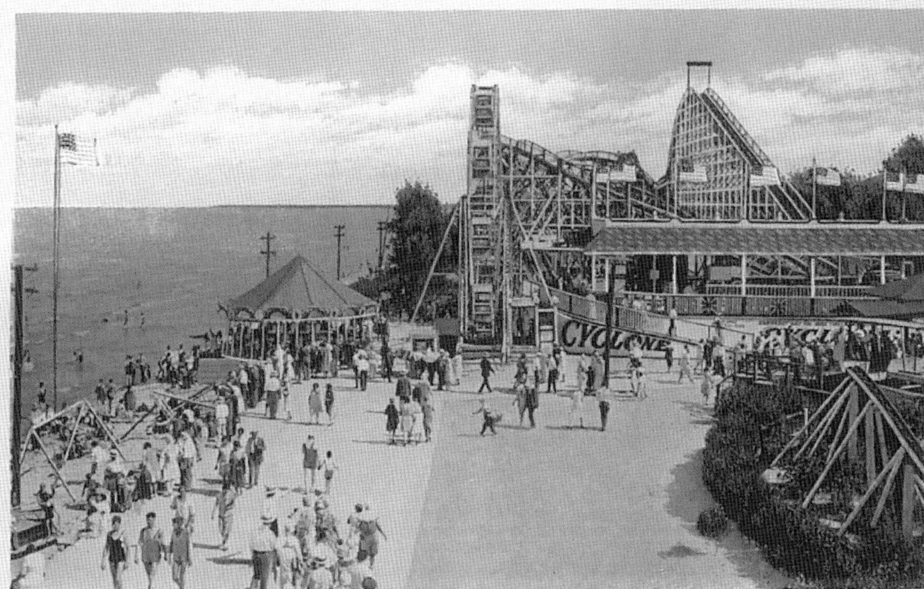

CYCLONE RACER, FERRIS WHEEL AND MINIATURE MERRY-GO-ROUND

The massive Cyclone Racer was Cedar Point's major attraction when it premiered in the late 1920s, initiating a tradition of bigger and more thrilling roller coasters that has made Cedar Point the Roller Coaster Capital of the nation. The merry-go-round and Ferris Wheel continue as popular rides in the current park. The Cyclone survived into the early 1950s.

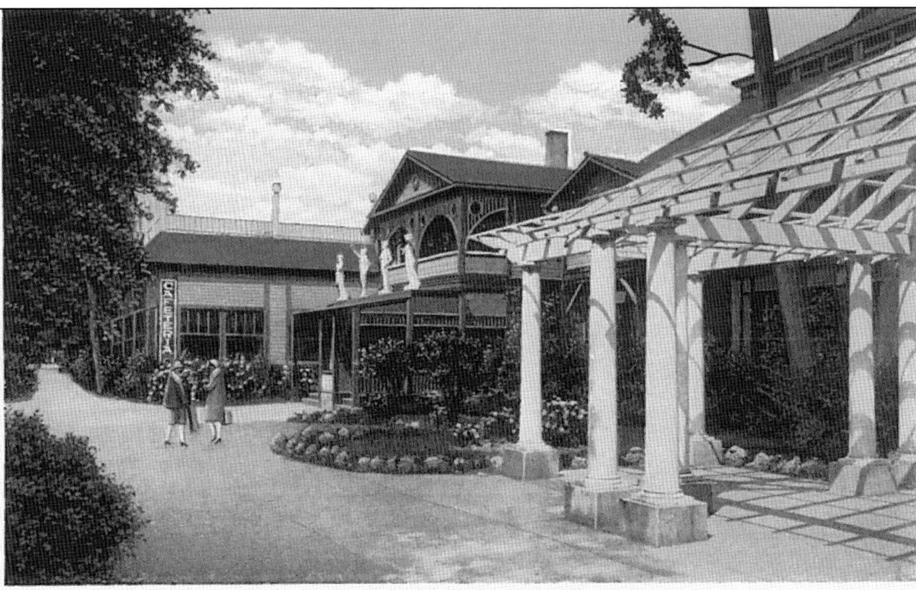

LARGE GRILL AND CAFETERIA

"Flapper" ladies contemplate a visit to the Cafeteria Moderne (left) or the Green and Silver Grill (right). This early postcard folder promised "Mammoth Dining Rooms—Luncheonettes and Cafeteria—where popular prices prevail."

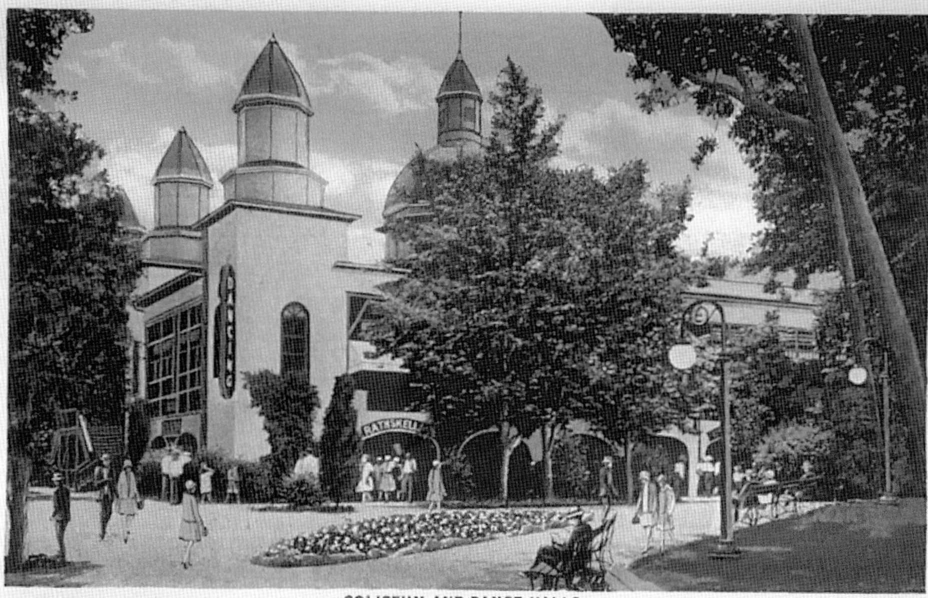

COLISEUM AND DANCE HALLS

A popular Cedar Point attraction was dancing and imbibing at the Rathskeller and Beer Hall.

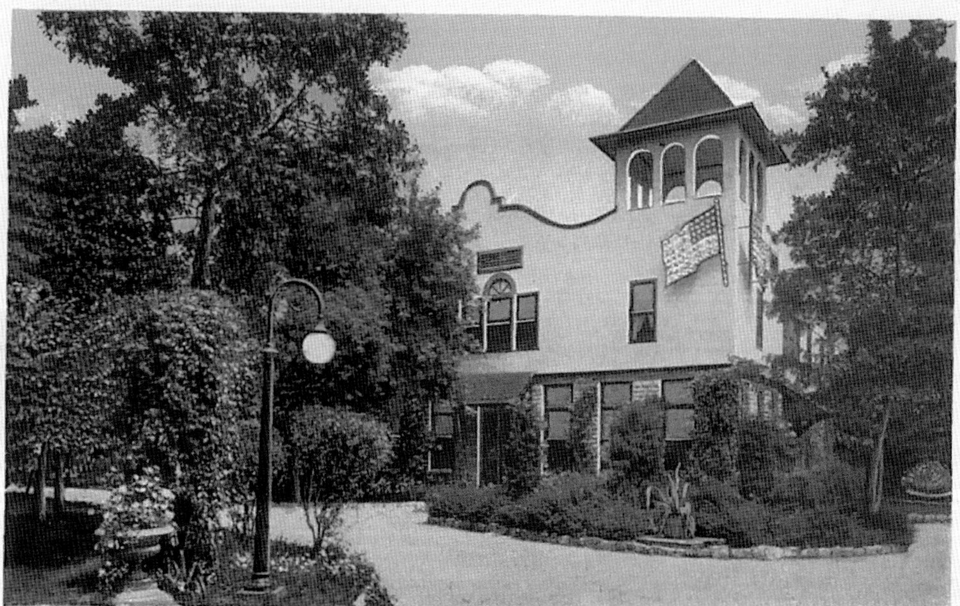

ADMINISTRATION BUILDING

The new Administration Building, constructed in the 1920s, was the hub of resort management.

Three

Put-in-Bay and the Islands

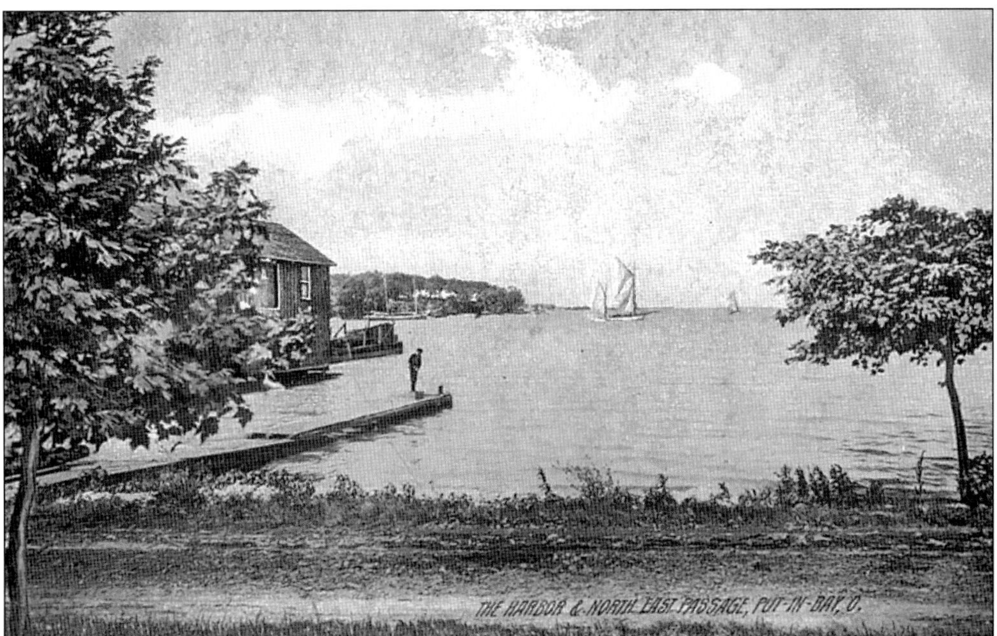

This early Put-in-Bay harbor scene looks out toward the Northeast Passage. Schooners appear to be the primary transport.

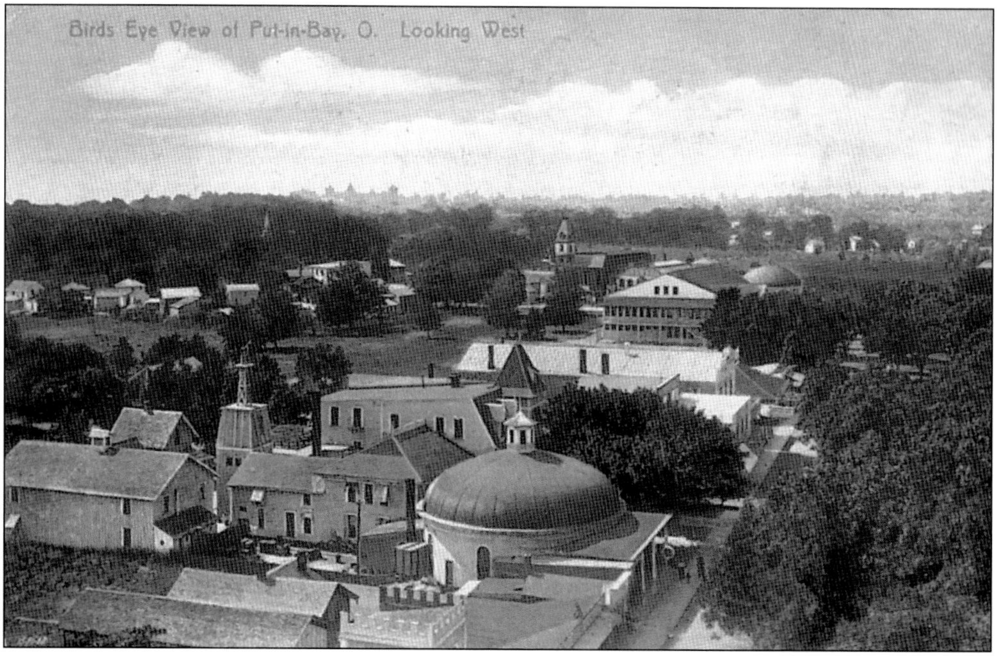

This 1911 bird's-eye view of Put-in-Bay looks west from the Round House Bar, past the Colonial to Catawba Avenue. The Town Hall on Catawba, still standing, can be seen in the middle (building with tower). The Round House Bar was constructed in Toledo, dismantled, and reconstructed in Put-in-Bay in 1873. Now painted bright red, it remains a popular tourist attraction.

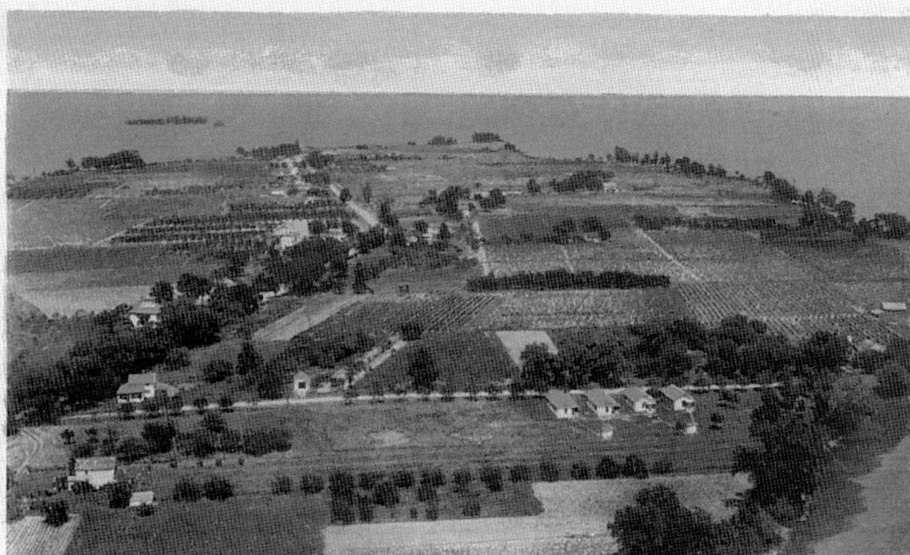

VIEW OF ISLAND FROM PERRY MONUMENT

This view of vineyards dotted with cottages and homes, looking westward from Perry's Monument, is virtually unchanged today.

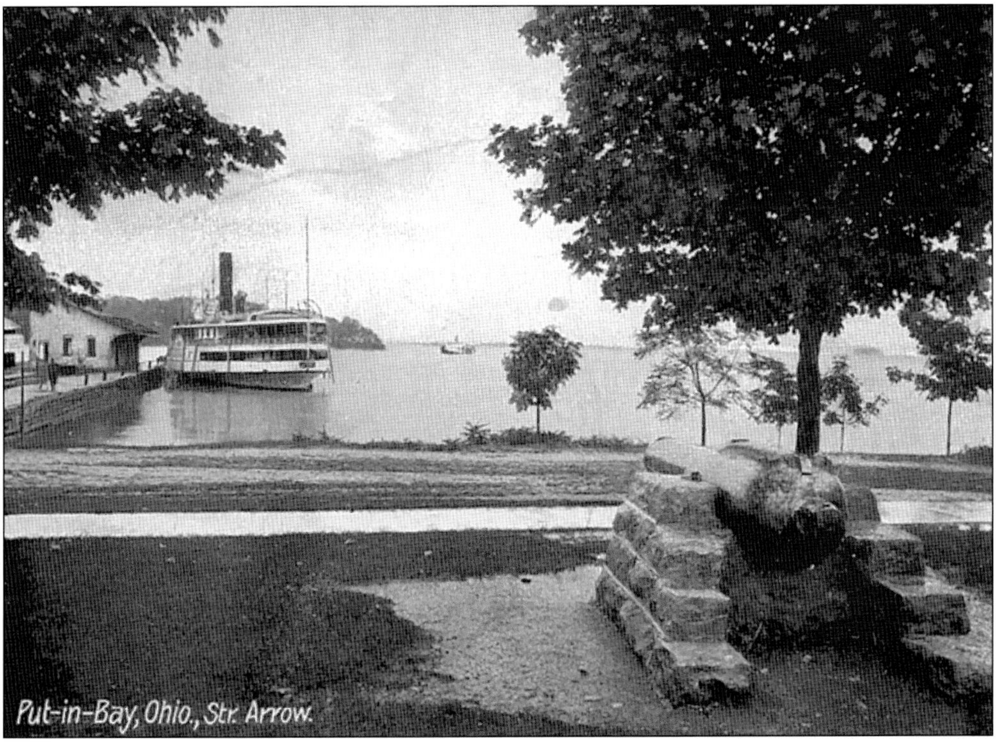

The steamer *Arrow*, which ran between Sandusky and Put-in-Bay from 1895 to 1922, is shown at the dock. The cannon in the foreground is still a fixture at DeRivera Park.

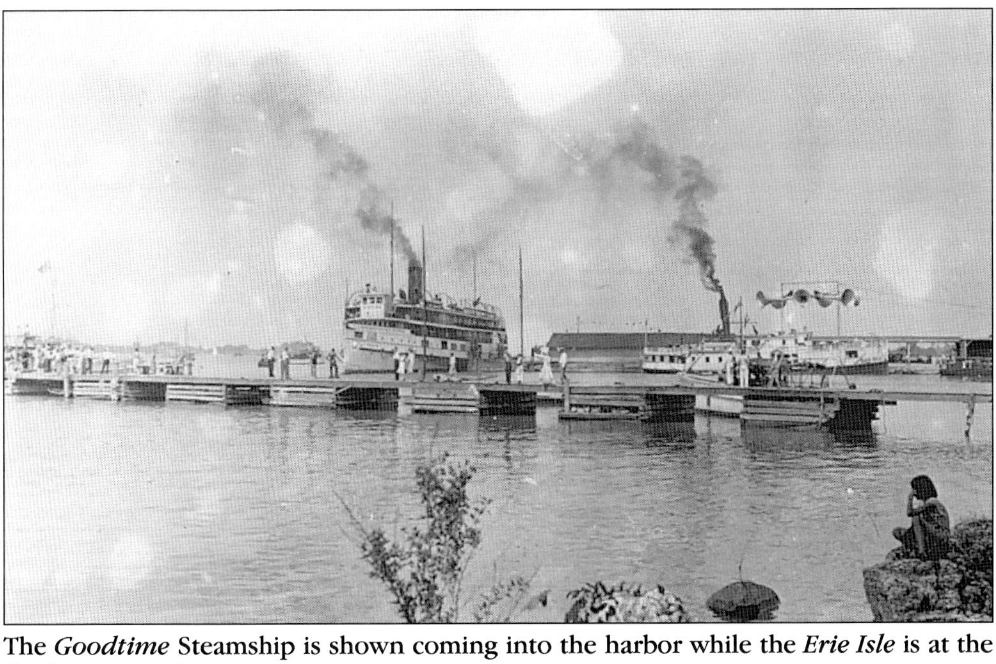

The *Goodtime* Steamship is shown coming into the harbor while the *Erie Isle* is at the dock in Put-in-Bay.

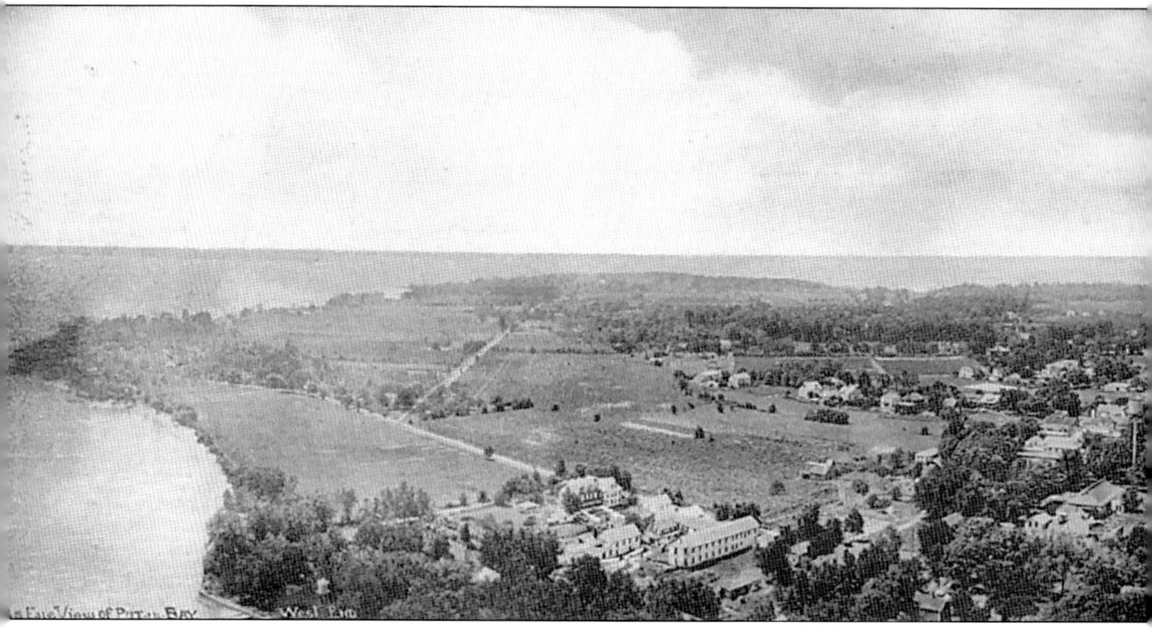

This early panorama shows the harbor with steamboats, the downtown area, and large areas

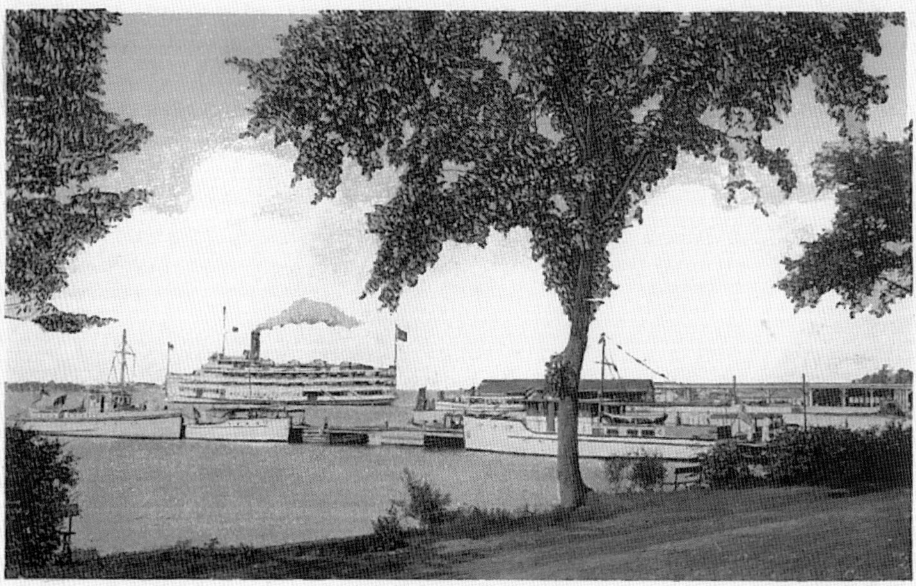

VIEW OF HARBOR AND FOX PIER

The dock at Put-in-Bay is shown with the steamer *Put-in-Bay* coming in. The harbor, in its heyday, was a stopping point for all manner of watercraft, from huge steamboats to schooners and rowboats. Today, private pleasure crafts and ferries dominate the dock space.

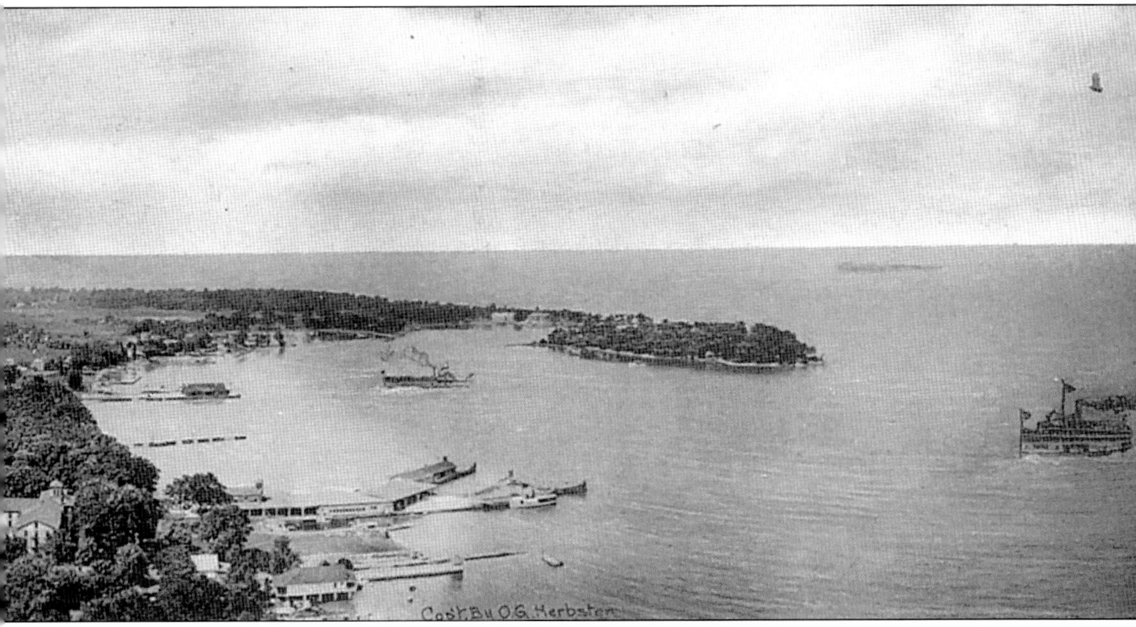

of grape vineyards that supplied the wine industry that dominated the early economy.

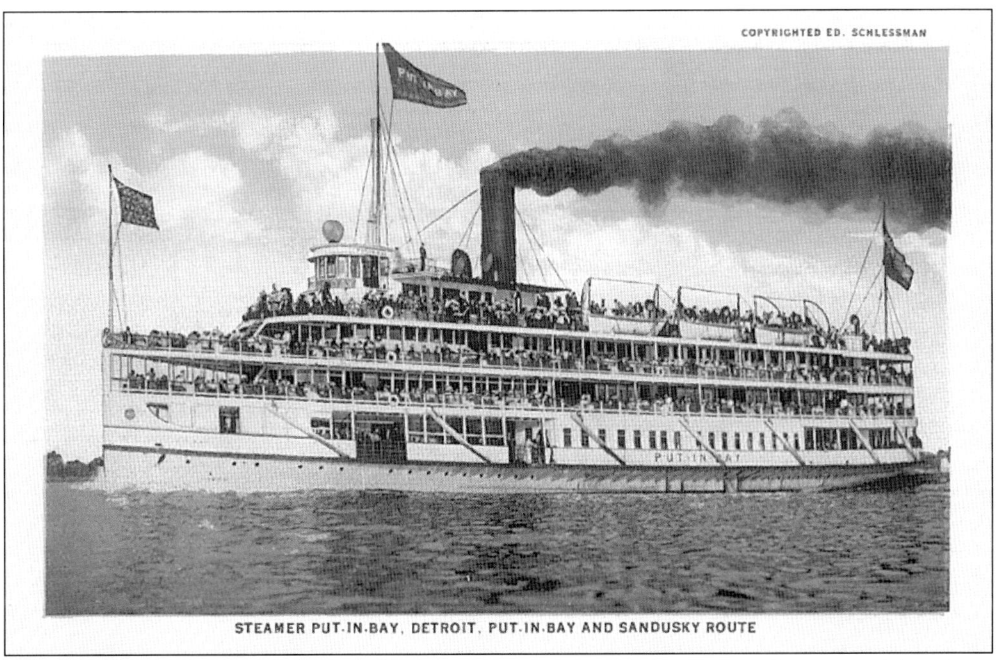

The steamer *Put-in-Bay*, capable of carrying 3,500 passengers and powered by three thousand horsepower, pulls into Put-in-Bay harbor.

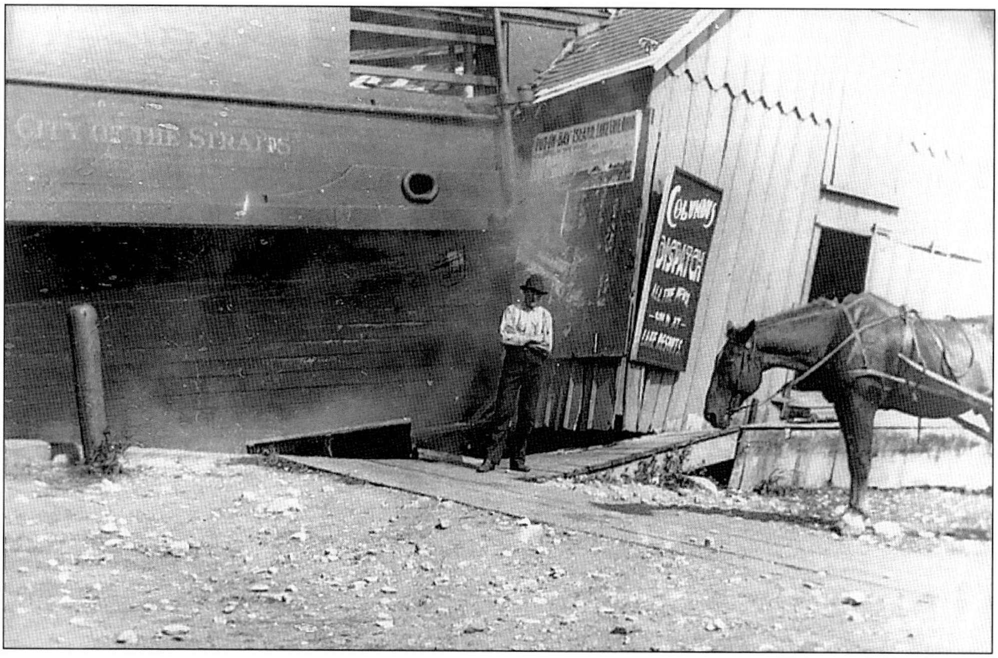

The *City of the Straits* steamer apparently smashed into a shack at Put-in-Bay's downtown dock. The gentleman and the horse appear nonplussed by the action.

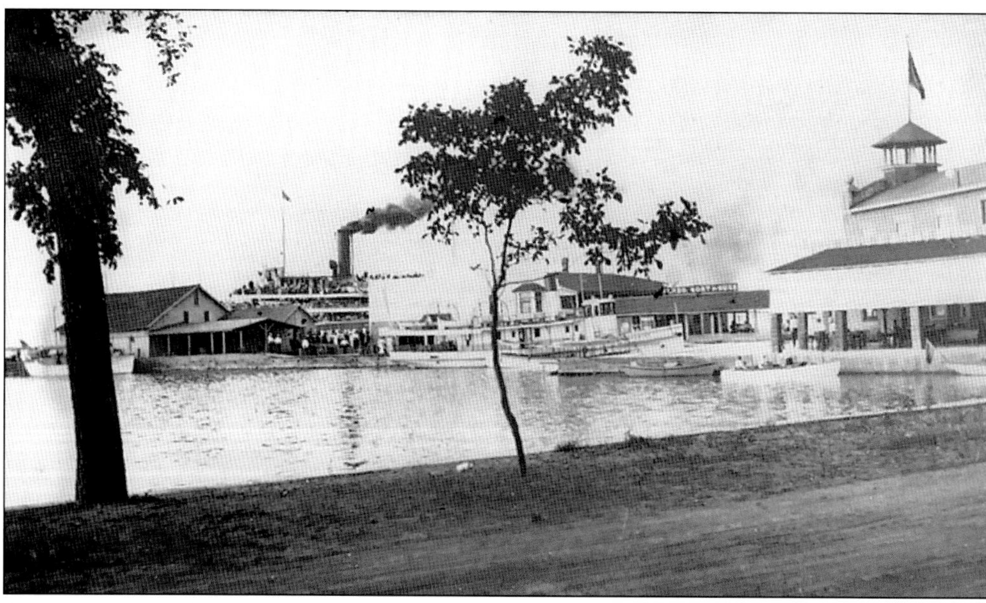

A passenger-loaded steamer is shown arriving on a busy day at the dock. Ladd Boat House, forerunner of today's Ladd's Marina, can be seen in the foreground.

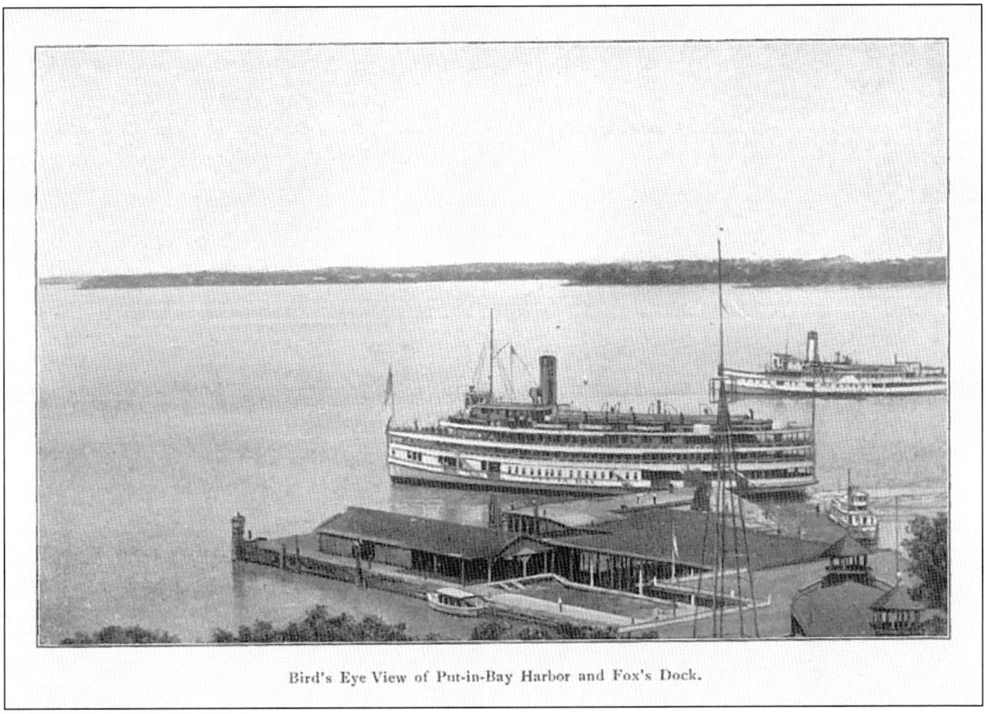

This bird's-eye view looks across the harbor toward Kelleys Island from Fox's Dock. The ever-present steamer *Put-in-Bay* is pulling out, likely headed to Detroit. It was the custom of the islanders to assemble on Labor Day, the last day of tourist season, to bid farewell to the *Put-in-Bay*.

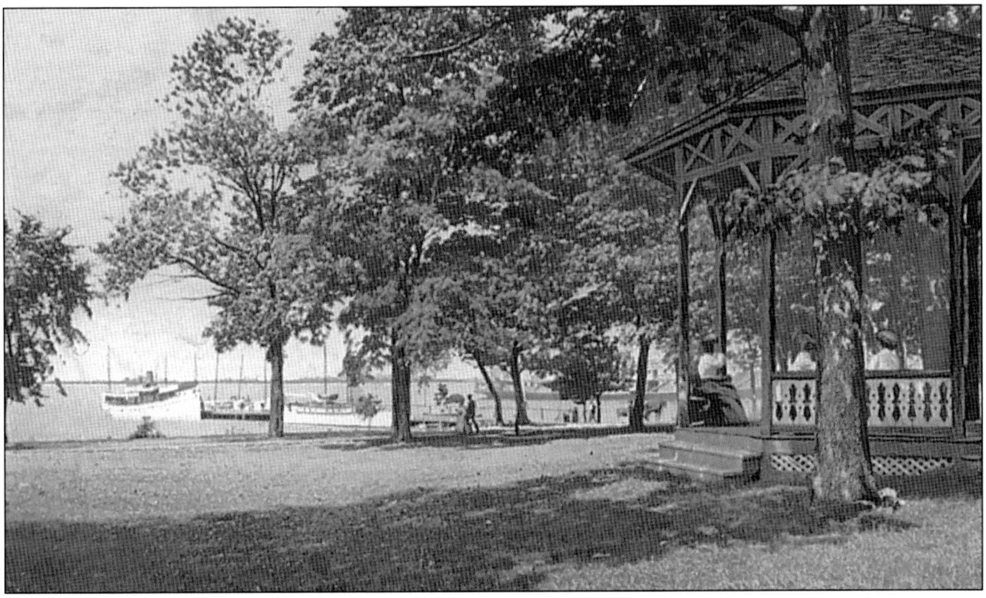

This 1904 scene shows the gazebo at Perry Park (now DeRivera Park). A steamship and two smaller boats are in the background, with women in Victorian garb looking on.

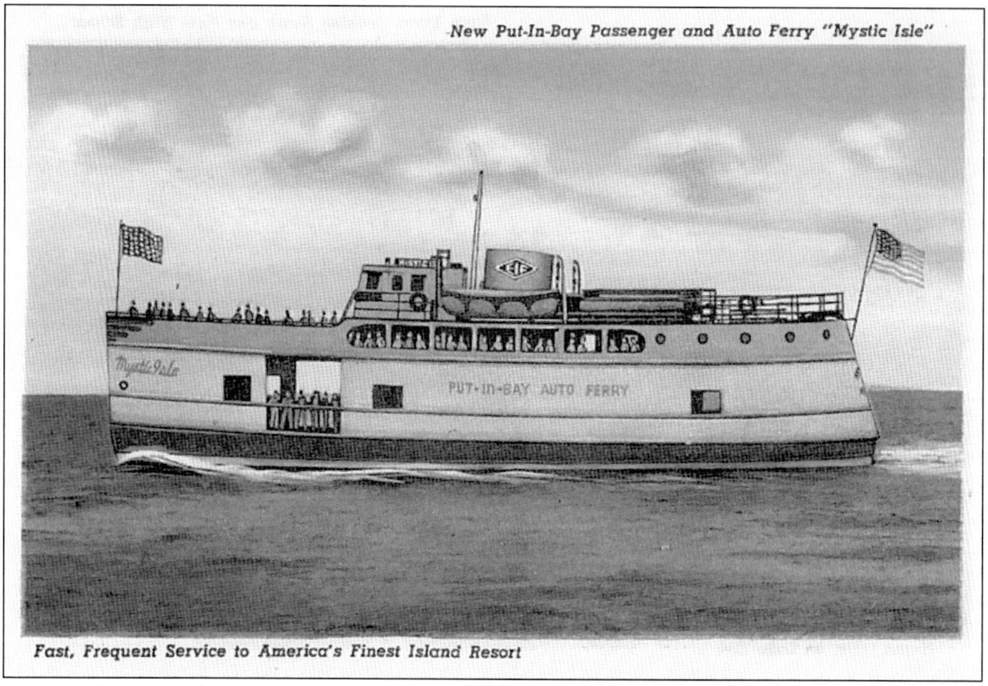

By the 1940s, with the opening of the Bay Bridge across Sandusky Bay, the automobile became the primary means of transportation to the Lake Erie resort region. Auto ferries replaced steamboats as the boat of choice to the islands.

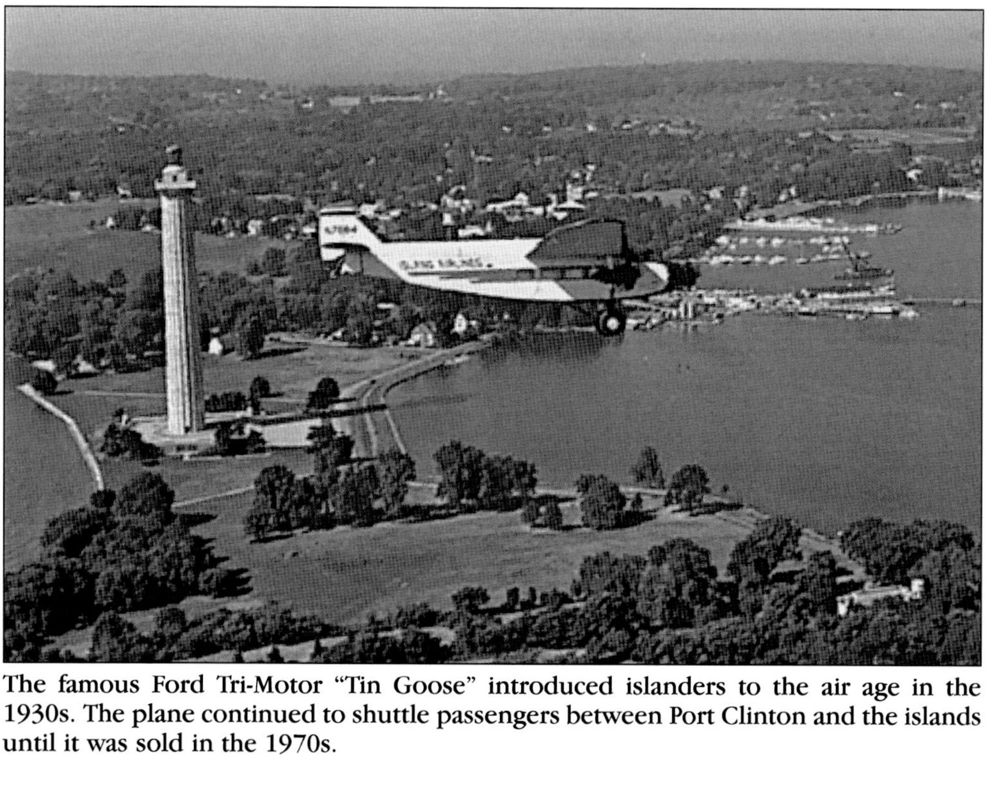

The famous Ford Tri-Motor "Tin Goose" introduced islanders to the air age in the 1930s. The plane continued to shuttle passengers between Port Clinton and the islands until it was sold in the 1970s.

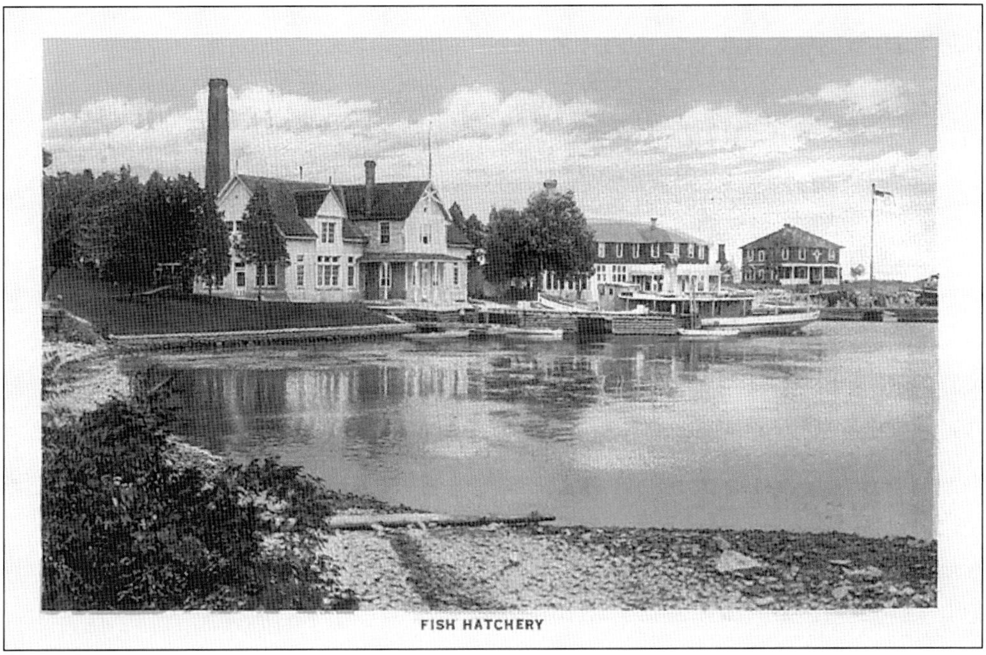

The fish hatchery was first established on Put-in-Bay in 1907, and burned to the ground on May 31, 1914. The current building, pictured here, was constructed later in 1914 and served over the years as a hatchery for whitefish, herring, pike, perch, salmon, and trout, until the hatchery operation shut down in the 1980s. Ohio State University now uses the building as a biological research lab.

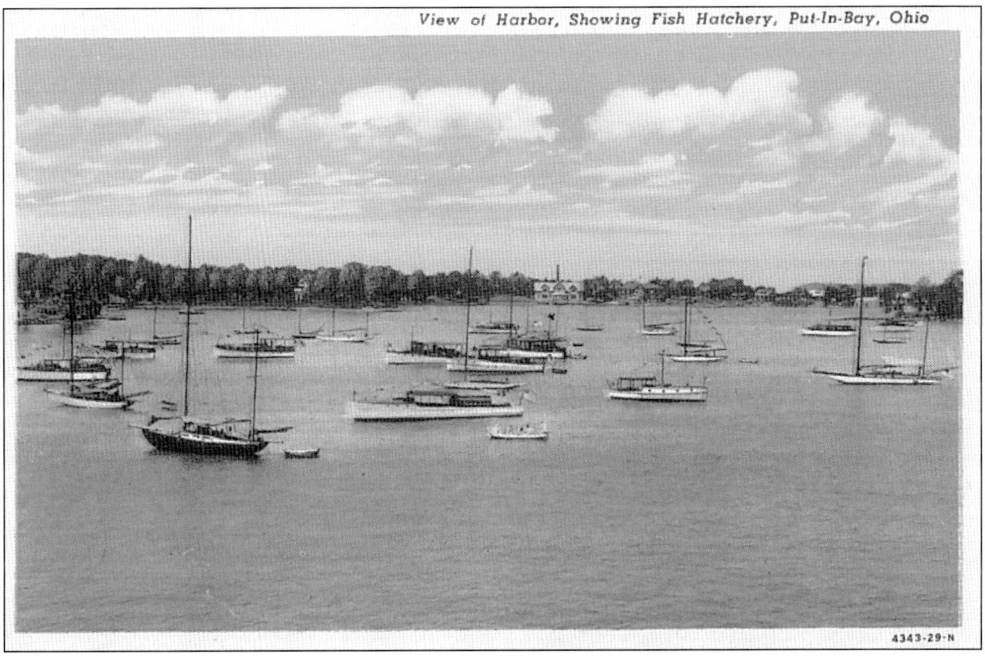

This harbor scene includes the fish hatchery across the bay.

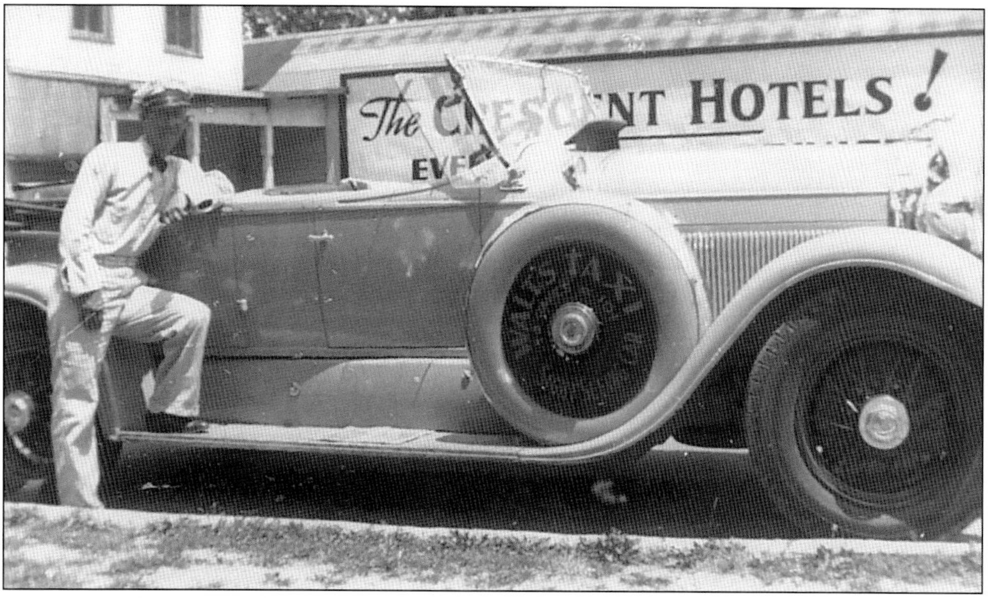

A taxi is shown in front of the Crescent Hotel, now a restaurant and bar in downtown Put-in-Bay.

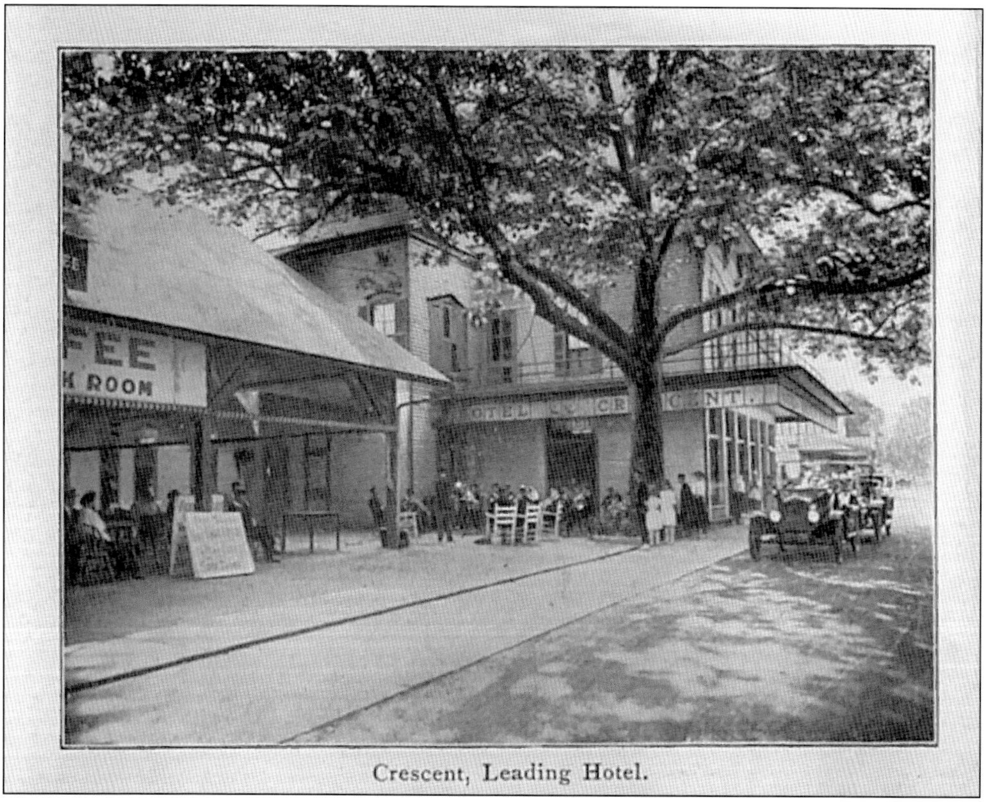

Crescent, Leading Hotel.

This view of downtown, circa 1915, shows the Crescent Hotel. It was built in 1871 and was originally called the Hunker House.

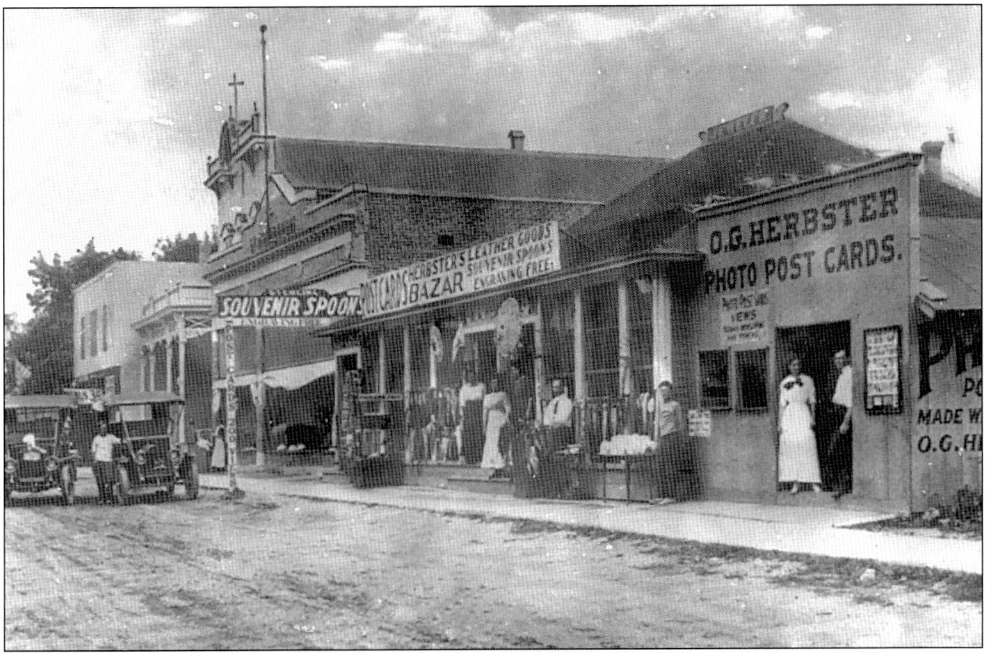

Downtown Delaware Avenue, Put-in-Bay, has changed surprisingly little from this scene around 1915. The postcard shop in the foreground was torn down in the 1980s due to deterioration. The site is now a shop that sells nautical artifacts. The other buildings are still standing.

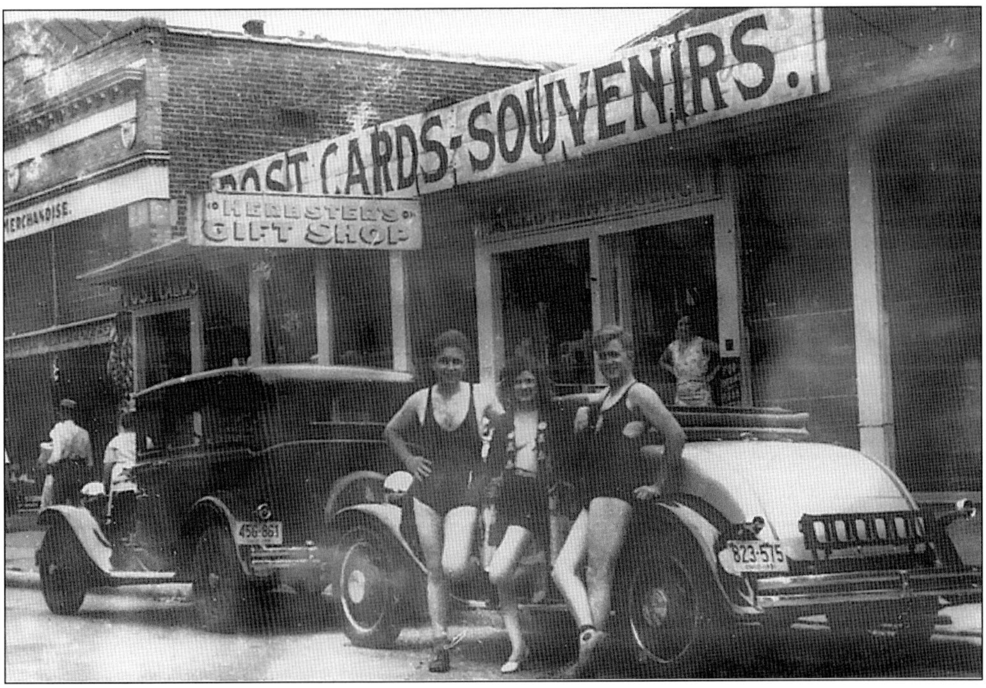

Many of the cards in this section are by H.A. Herbster, whose downtown postcard shop is shown here, along with male and female "bathing beauties."

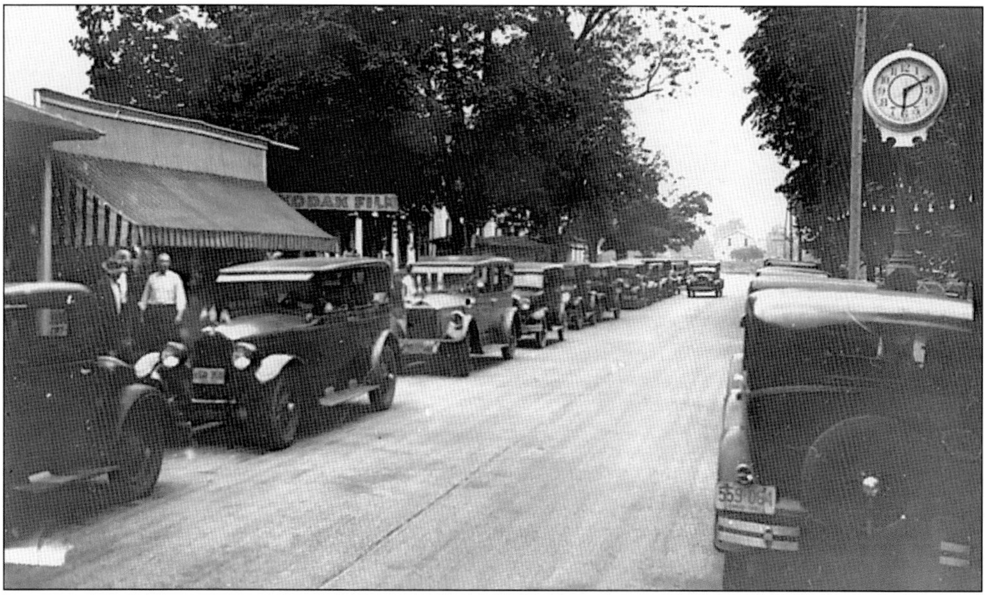

Downtown parking appears to be worse in this early scene than it is today. The clock on the right is still standing.

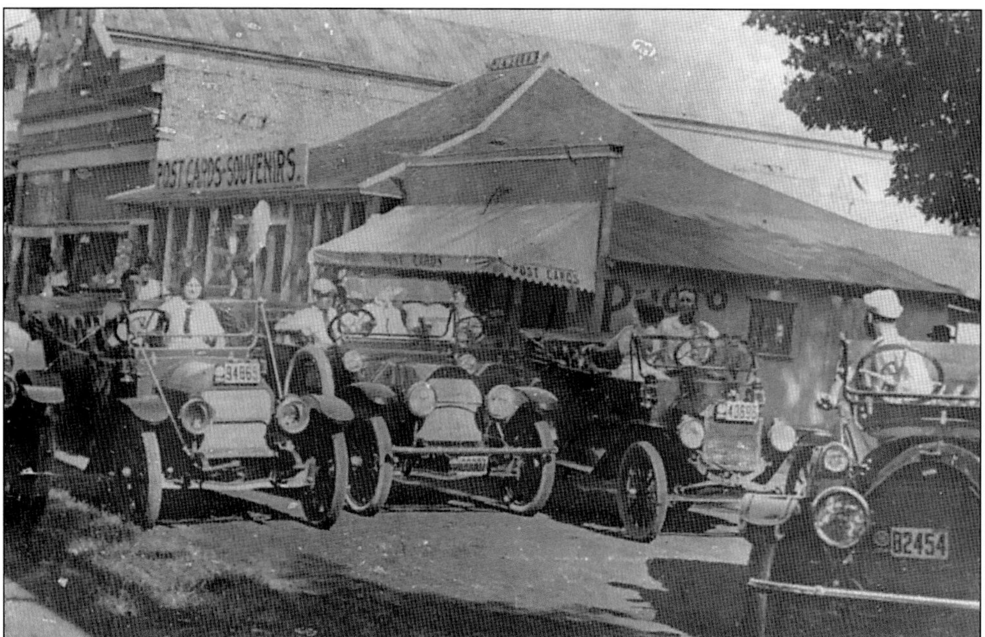

Is this a traffic jam or an auto race? The streets of downtown Put-in-Bay appear much more congested in this 1920s scene than they do today.

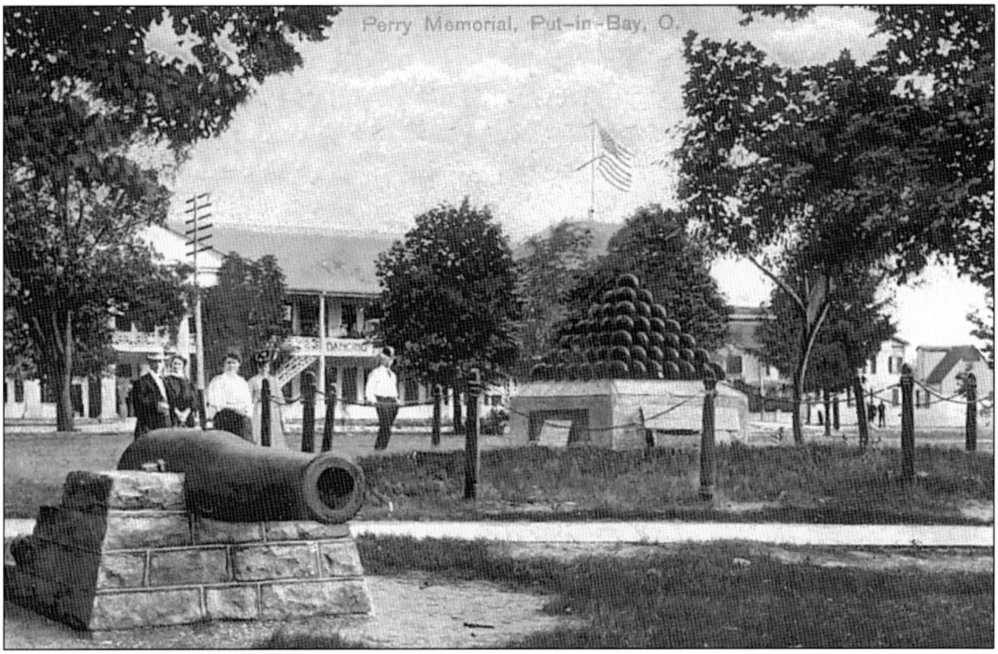

The Cannonball Monument in Perry Park was built on the original burial site of six officers (three American and three British) killed during the Battle of Lake Erie. When the monument was built in 1913, the remains were excavated and moved to the rotunda of Perry's Monument.

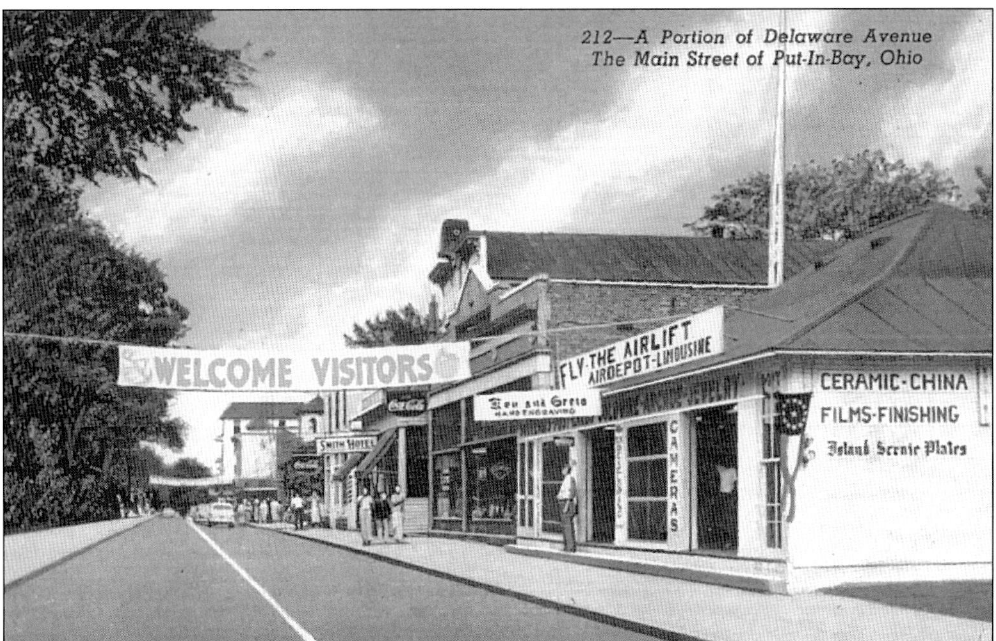

The second brick building in the foreground of this 1940s view is now Frosty's beer and pizza parlor. Behind it can be seen the top of what is now the Country House gift shop.

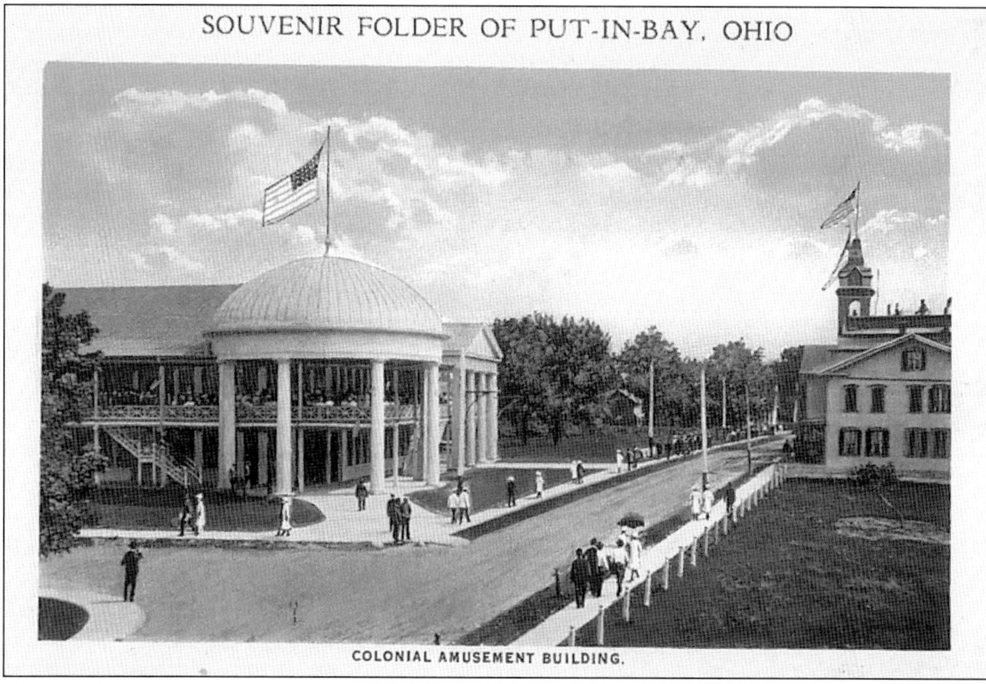

The Colonial, with its dance hall and bowling alley, was a hub of downtown entertainment until a raging fire destroyed it in 1988. The corner is now the site of the world's longest bar.

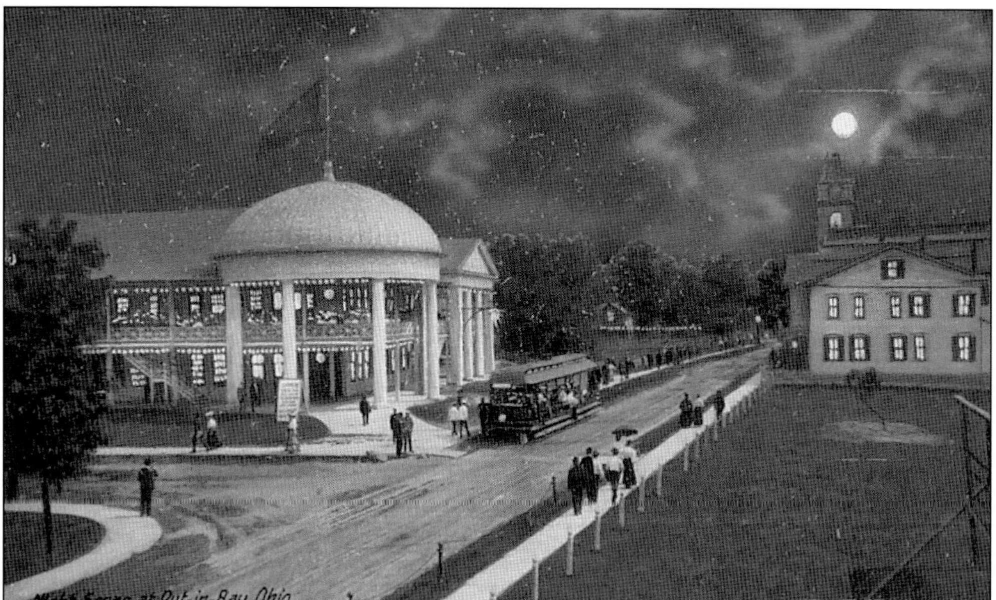

A close look at this night scene reveals many similarities to the daytime scene above—even a lady holding a parasol for protection from the sun! Postcard artists frequently created moonlit pictures by simply altering daytime shots. This postcard also includes the streetcar that brought guests directly from the Hotel Victory.

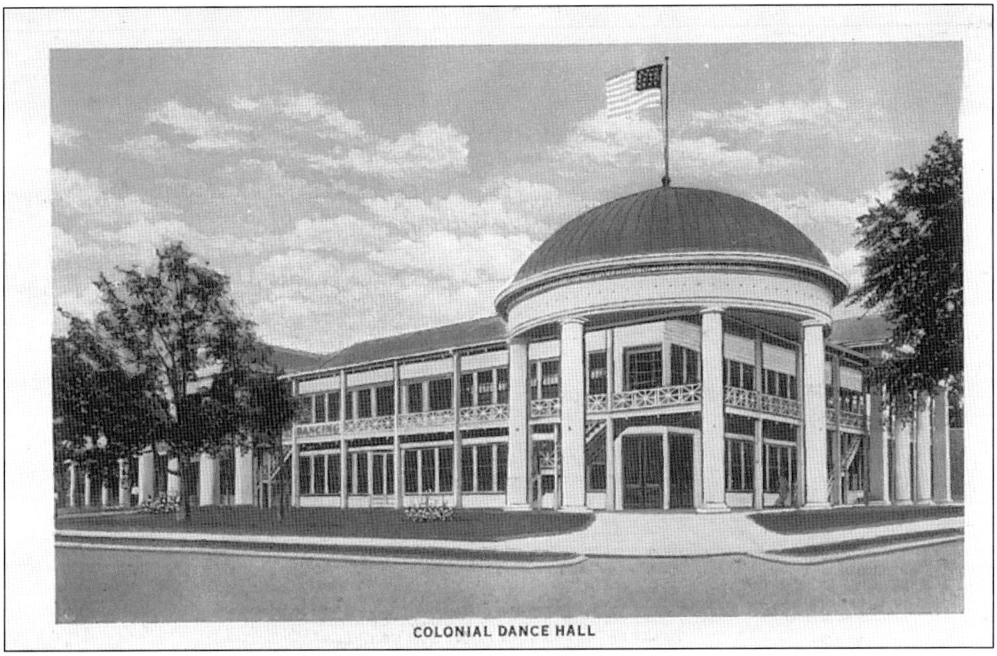

This stylized view of the Colonial shows the extent of this dominant structure in downtown Put-in-Bay. The corner is now the site of the world's longest bar.

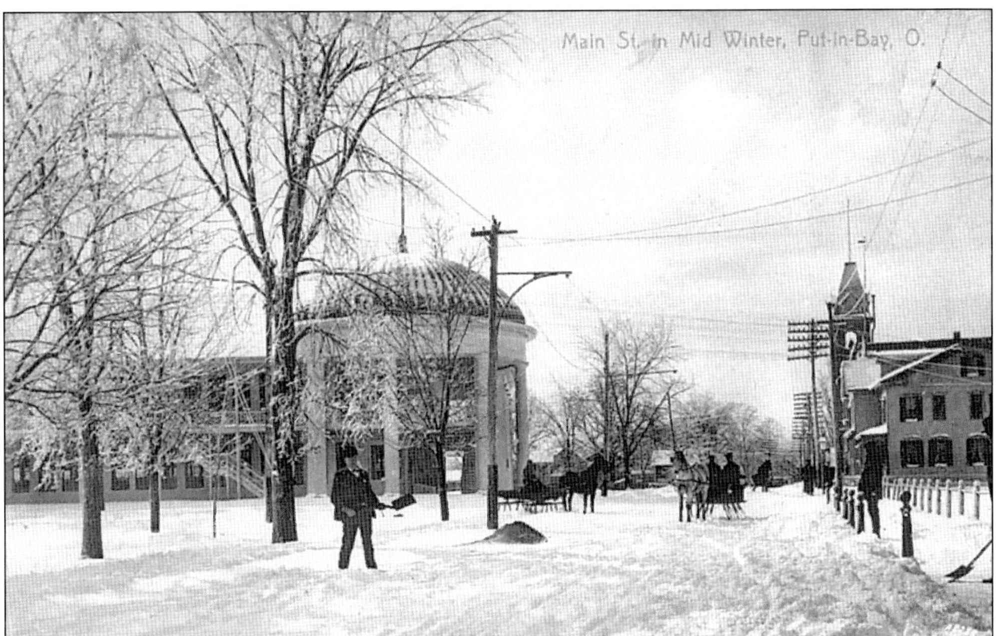

This winter view of the Colonial, looking down Catawba Avenue, offers an interesting contrast to the typical summer scene. Sleighs provided dependable transportation over snowy winter roads.

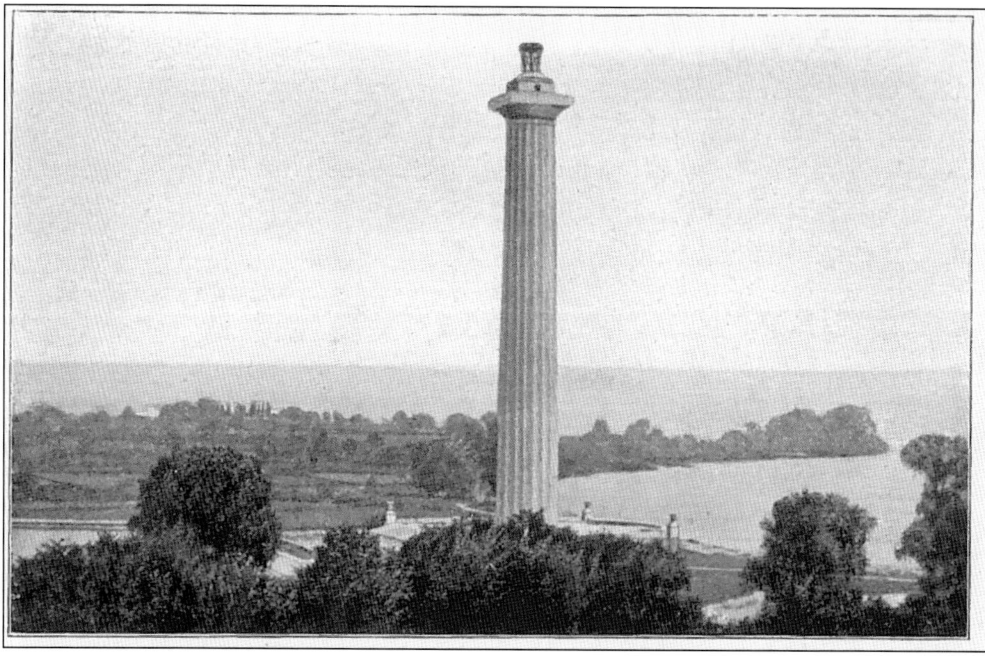

This card gives a good look at Perry Monument and the surrounding park around 1915. The description on the card reads, "The shaft is 335 ft. high and 45 ft. in diameter at the base... Dome contains 36 80-watt electric lights, shaft is built of Pink Granite Marble and concrete... Cost $850,000."

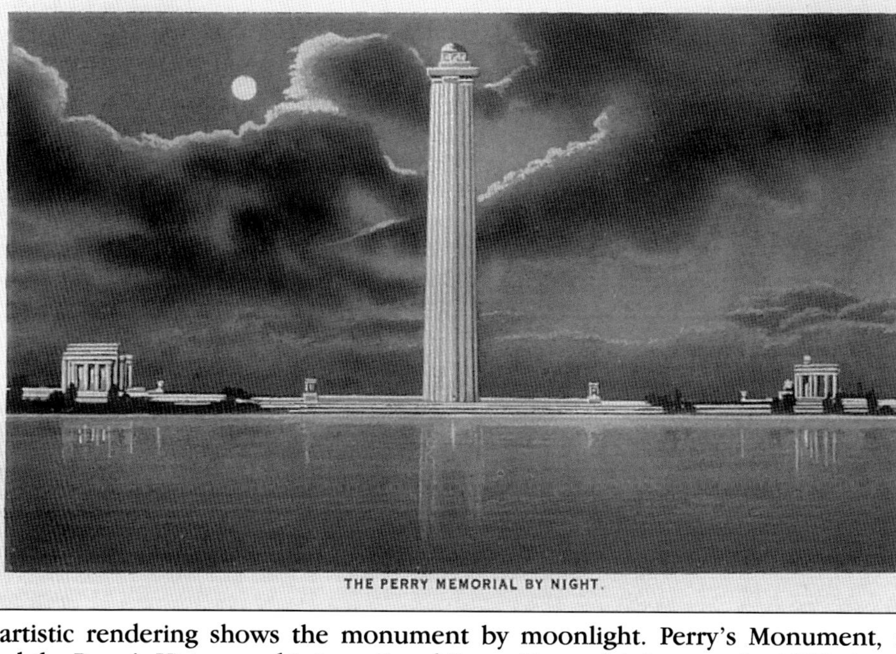

THE PERRY MEMORIAL BY NIGHT.

An artistic rendering shows the monument by moonlight. Perry's Monument, now called the Perry's Victory and International Peace Memorial, honors the 1813 victory of U.S. forces over the British Navy in the Battle of Lake Erie. The memorial, opened to the public in 1915, became a national monument on June 2, 1936.

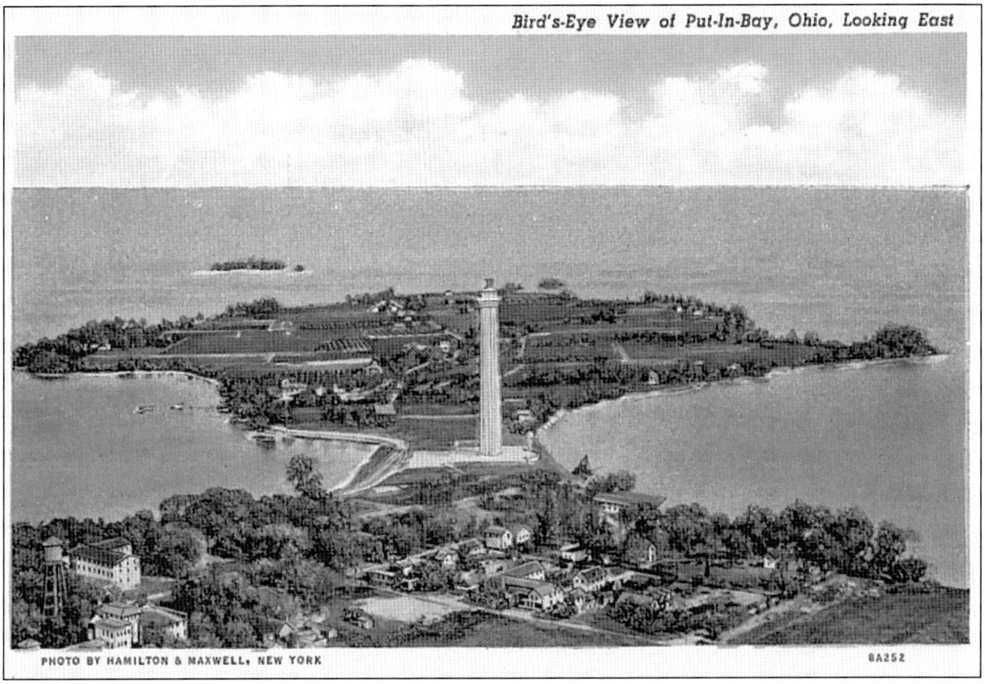

This bird's-eye view shows Put-in-Bay after construction of the Perry monument in 1915. Downtown Put-in-Bay, with the Beebe House at the lower left, can be seen in the foreground.

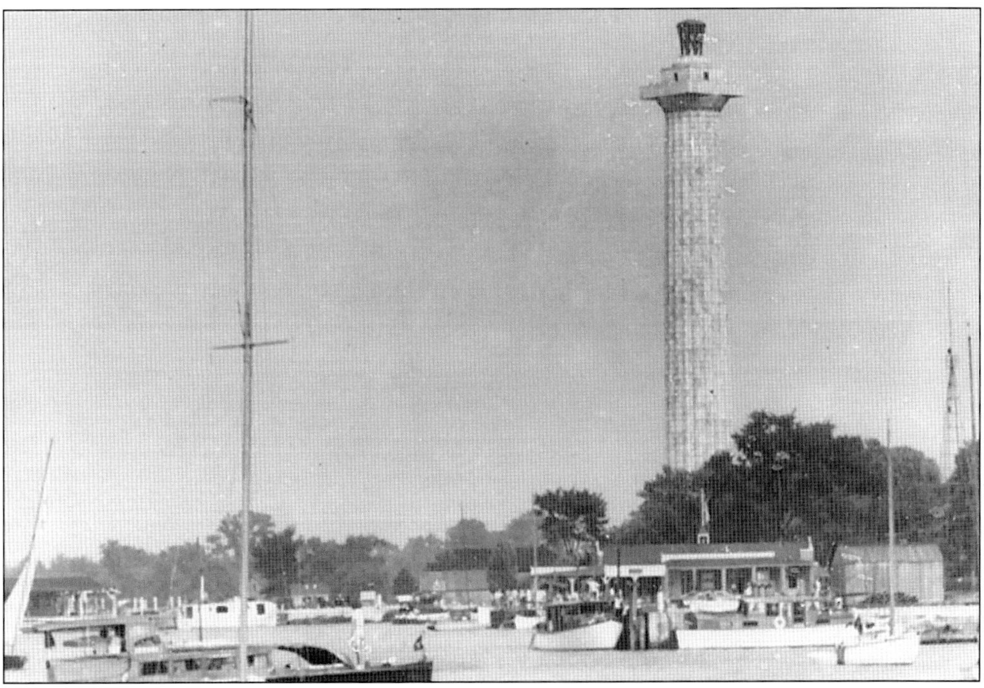

An early photograph postcard shows a busy day at Put-in-Bay harbor, with watercraft of all descriptions crowding the docks (a reminder of today's summer at the bay).

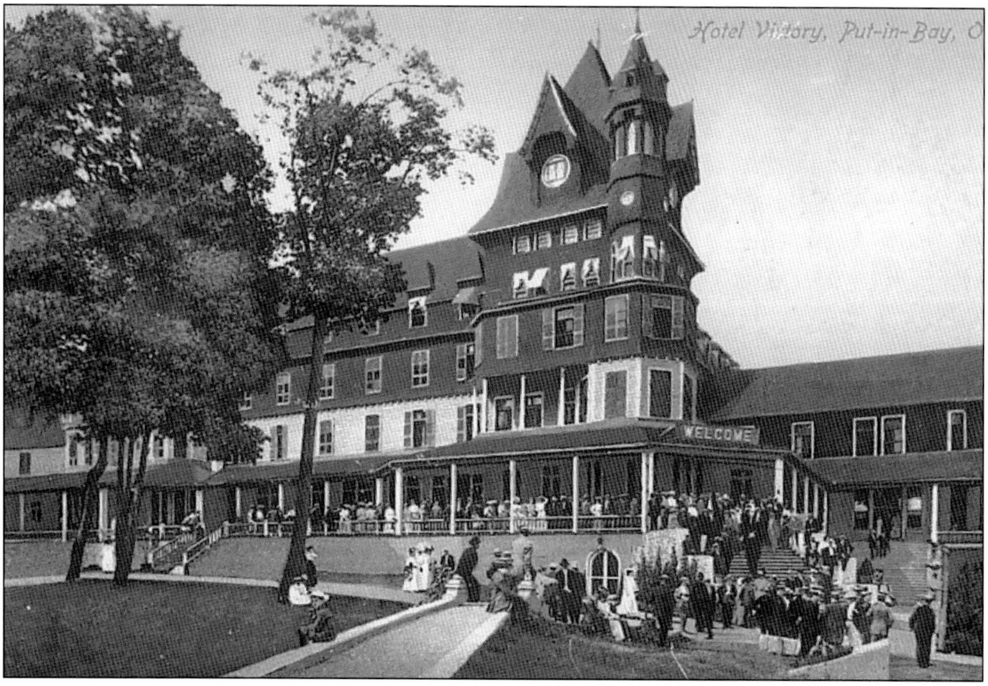

Guests line up at the Hotel Victory in its heyday. The huge hotel, the largest wooden structure in the world when it was constructed in 1897, contained 825 rooms and a dining room capable of seating two thousand people.

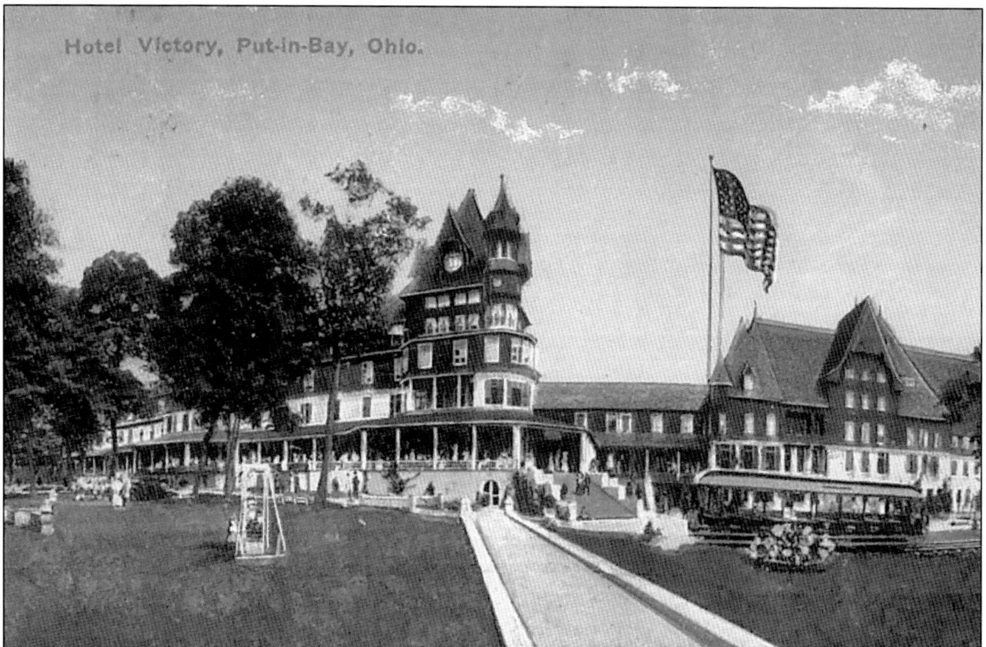

A sweeping view shows the fabulous Hotel Victory on a busy summer's day. The hotel, which despite its size and repute never made money, served thousands of guests through the years.

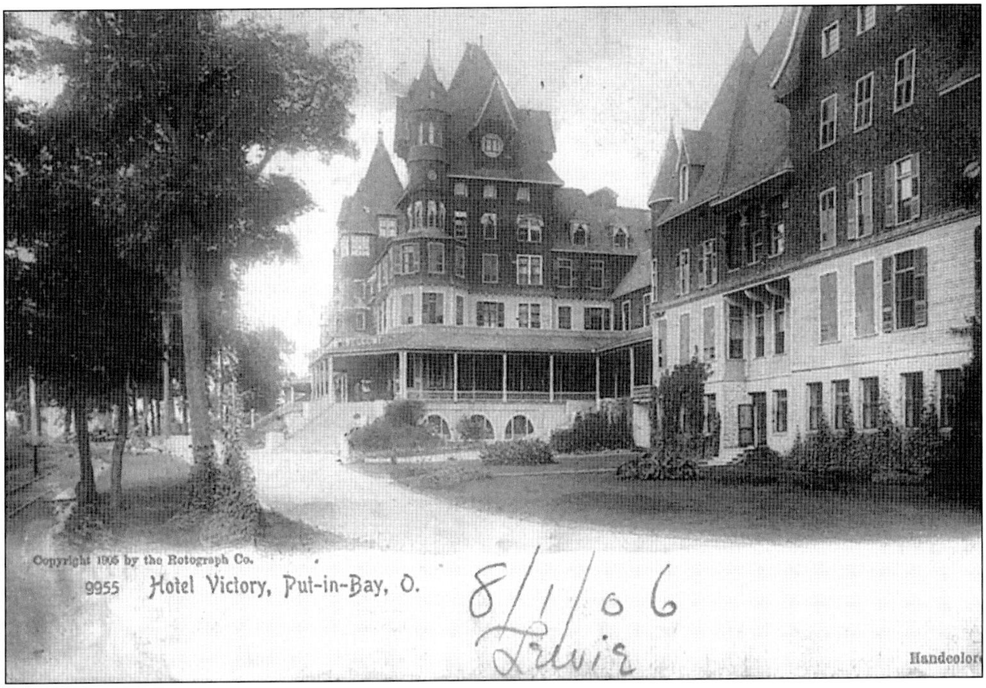

One hundred acres of grounds at the Victory featured a bridge, an electric fountain, gardens, and a boardwalk leading to the lake. An electric streetcar line (with tracks visible in the lower left) carried passengers from the hotel to Put-in-Bay village.

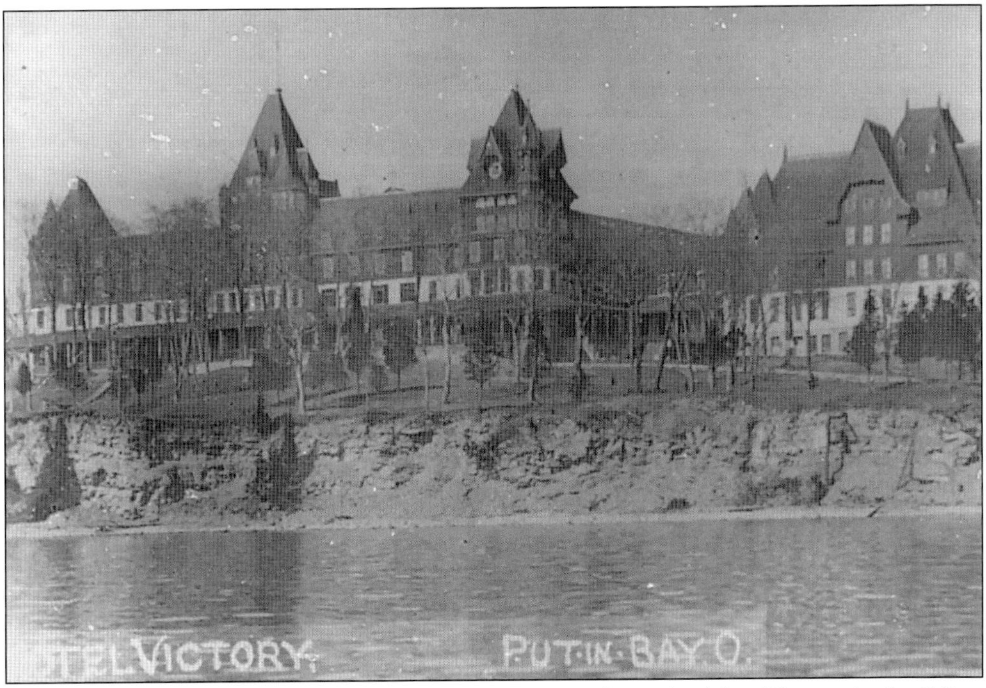

The huge size of the Victory is apparent in this view from the lake. The entire building burned to the ground in a spectacular fire in 1919.

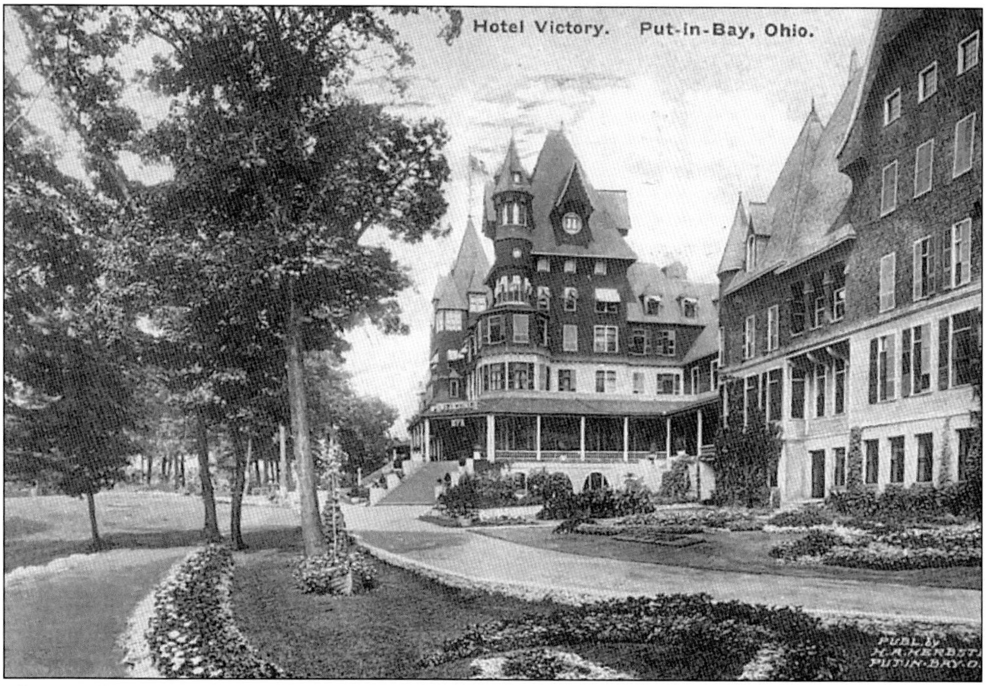

This card was postmarked August 16, 1919, two days after a spectacular fire destroyed the hotel. The card reads, "We were here yesterday and I see in the paper that this Hotel burned last night." H.R. Herbster, who made the postcard, had a shop in downtown Put-in-Bay.

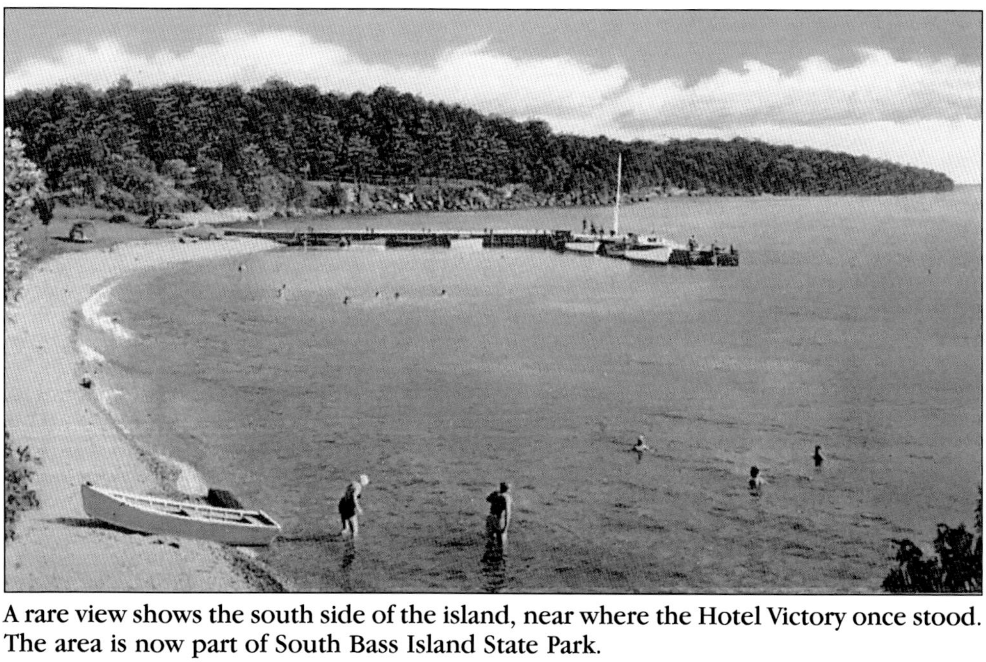

A rare view shows the south side of the island, near where the Hotel Victory once stood. The area is now part of South Bass Island State Park.

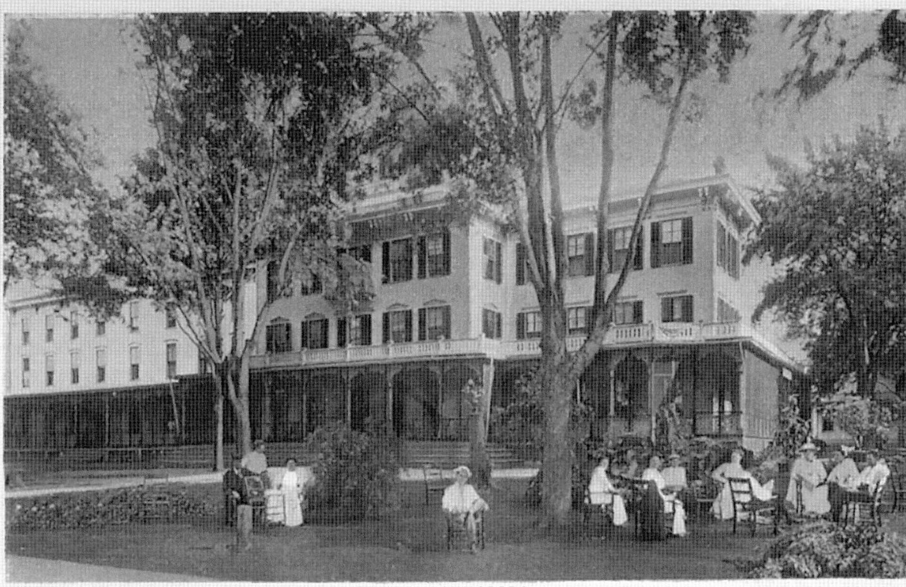

HOTEL COMMODORE.

The Hotel Commodore began its existence in the early 1860s as the Island House. It was later enlarged and called the Perry House, and was then sold in 1869 to Henry Beebe and renamed the Beebe House. In 1910, the hotel was bought by W.H. Reinhart and again became the Commodore. It burned to the ground on August 23, 1932.

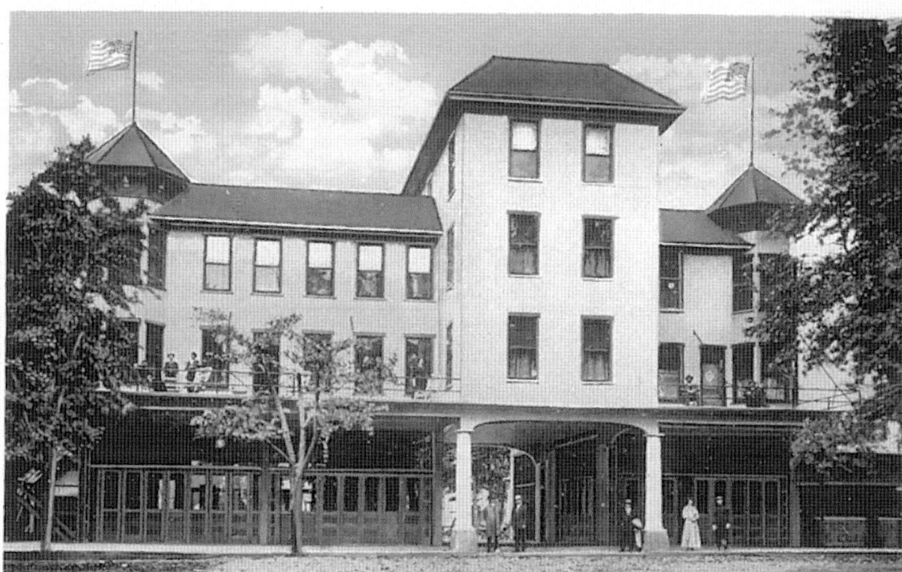

ANNEX, HOTEL CRESCENT.

This gives a good view of the Crescent Hotel in the 1920s.

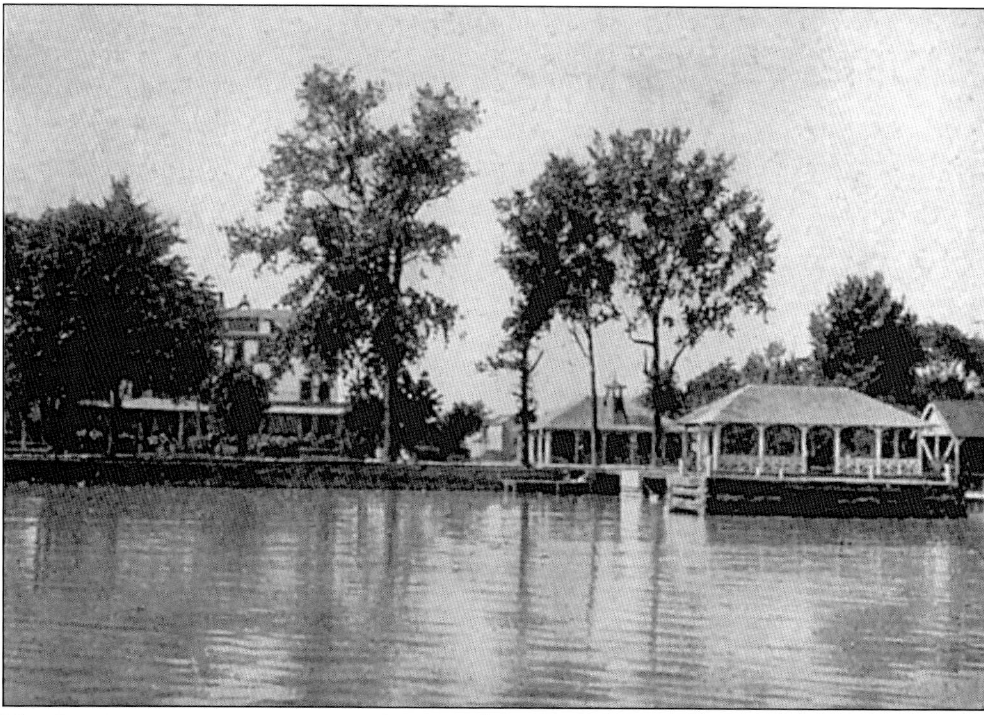

The Bay View House was created in 1906 when John S. Gibbons bought an existing hotel on Bay View Avenue, moved it closer to the waterfront, and added a third story. The hotel closed in 1972, but the adjacent Put-in-Bay Yacht Club is still in operation.

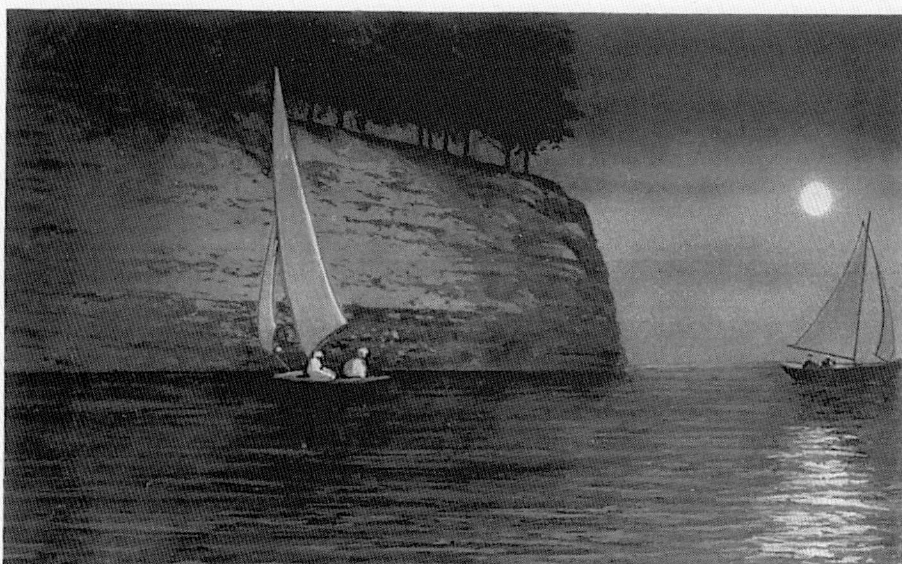

A MOONLIGHT SAIL.

The scenic cliffs on the south end of South Bass Island were a popular sailor's rendezvous.

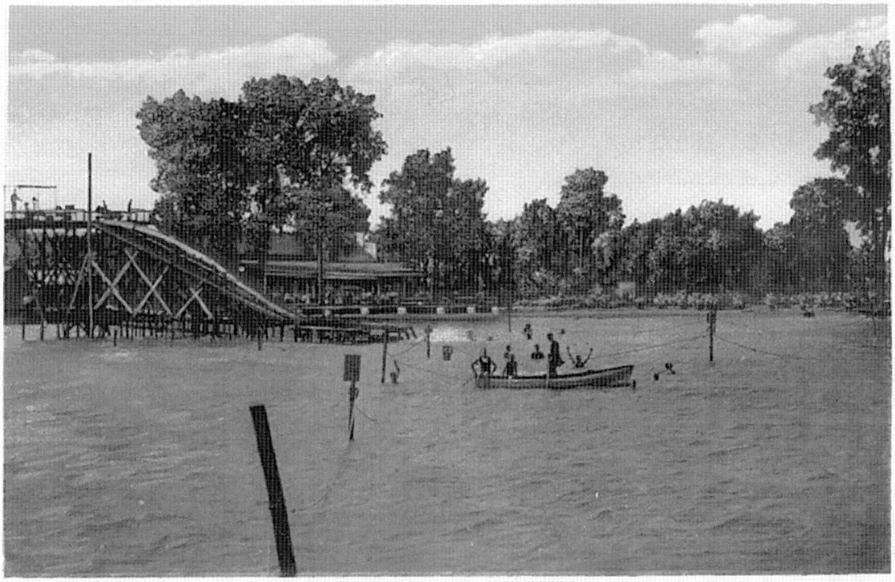

TOBOGGAN SLIDE AND BATHING BEACH.

Practically every Lake Erie island resort featured a bathing beach with bathhouse and toboggan. Put-in-Bay was no exception.

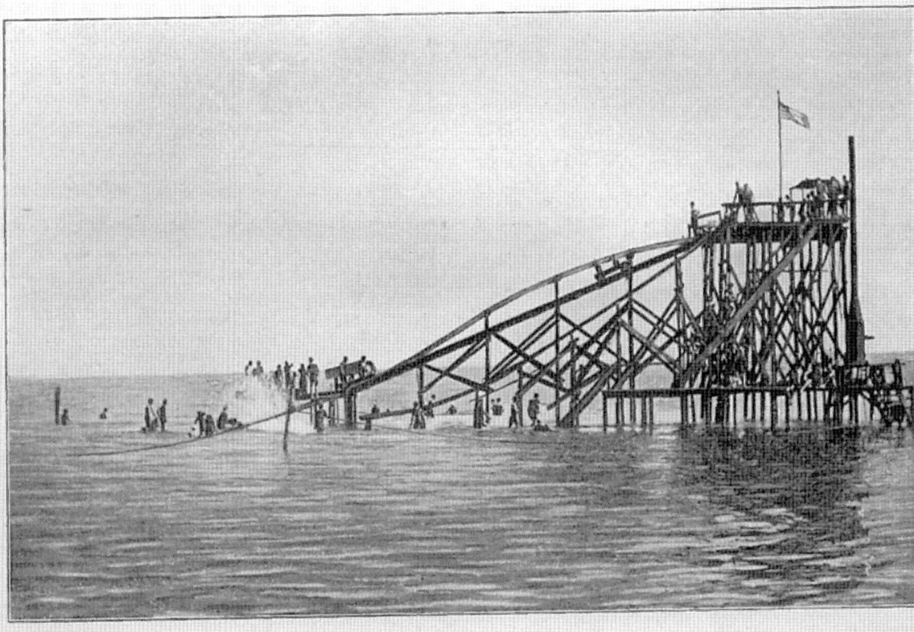

Water Toboggans at Deislers Bathing Beach.

The steep toboggan at Deislers Bathing Beach was a popular turn-of-the-century amusement. Two rival bathing establishments were located on the beach, which was described in the postcard folder as "a semi-circle of sand, bordered by clumps of willow and basswood, near the Victory Hotel."

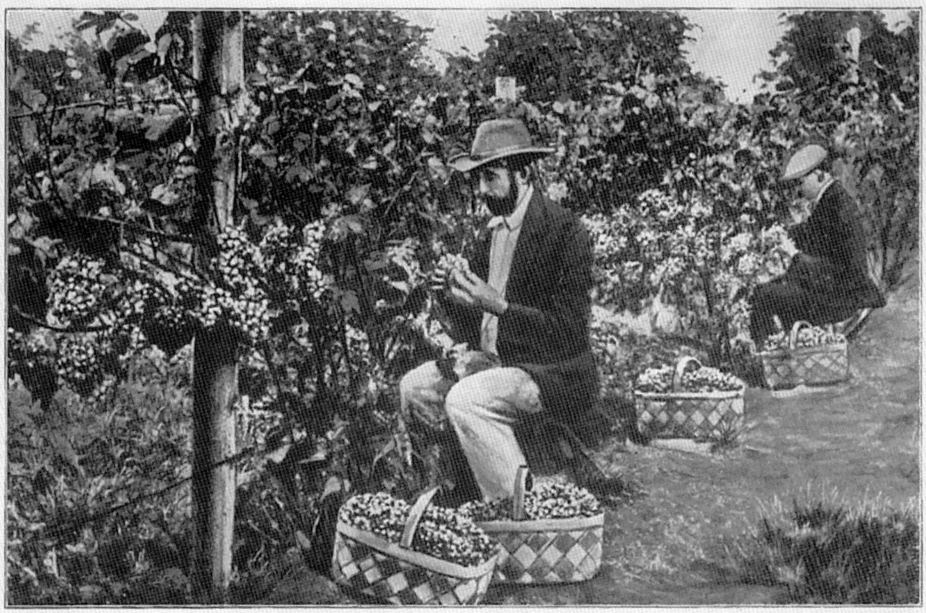

Grape Harvesting among the Islands.

Grape growing was a mainstay of the South Bass Island economy. The grapes were used primarily for winemaking. Until Prohibition, large wineries such as the Put-in-Bay Wine Company thrived on the island, along with numerous small wine cellars. Today the Heineman Winery, founded by German immigrant Gustav Heineman in 1901, is the sole survivor.

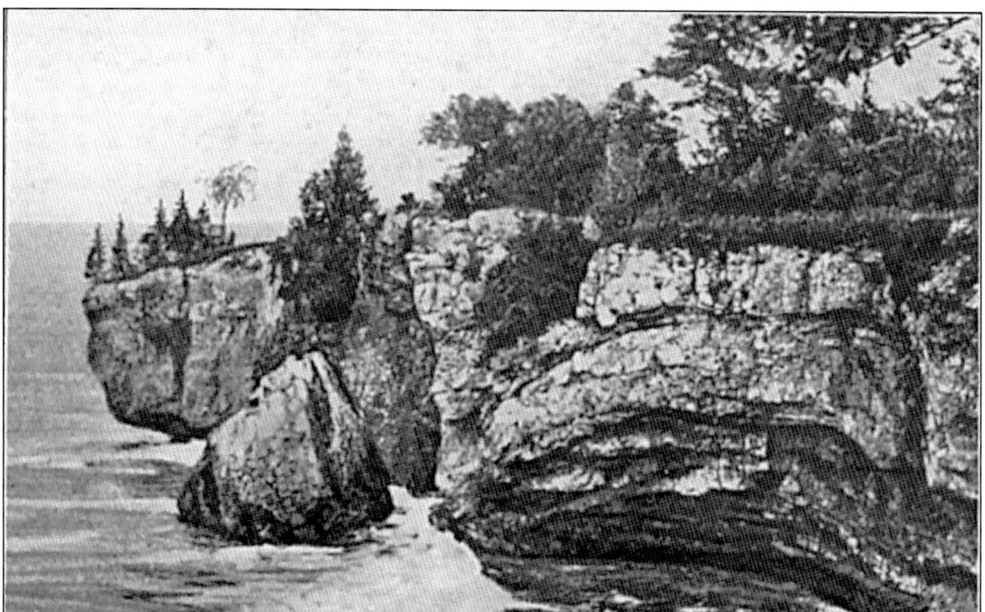

The bluffs on the west side of the island now feature homes offering fabulous lake views.

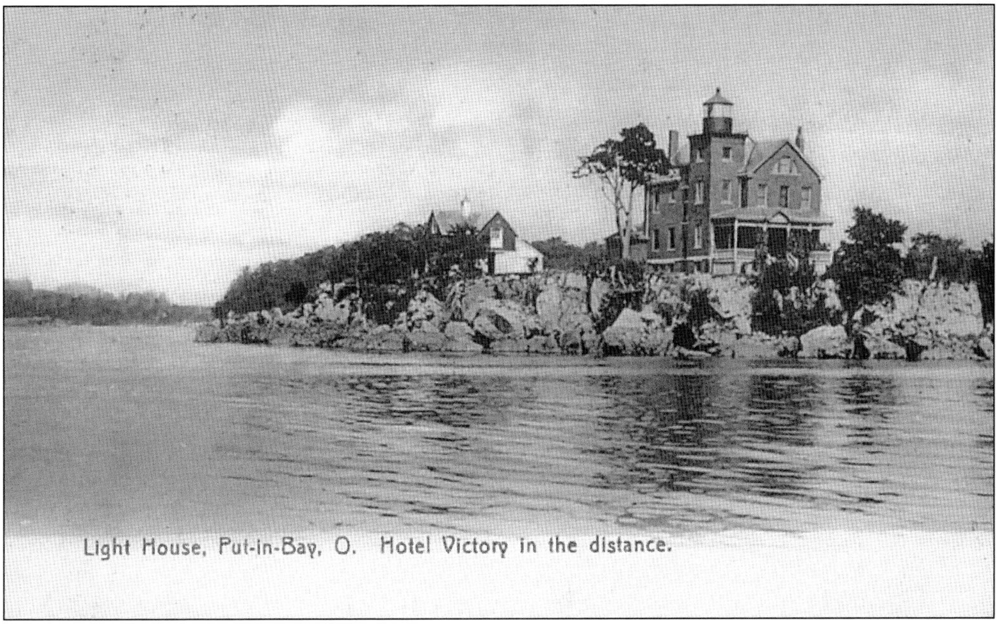

South Point Light is shown in this view. The Hotel Victory is barely visible on the left. The lighthouse was erected in 1897 to guide sailors past the rocky cliffs on the south shore of South Bass Island. Its beam was made automatic upon retirement of the lighthouse keeper in 1962.

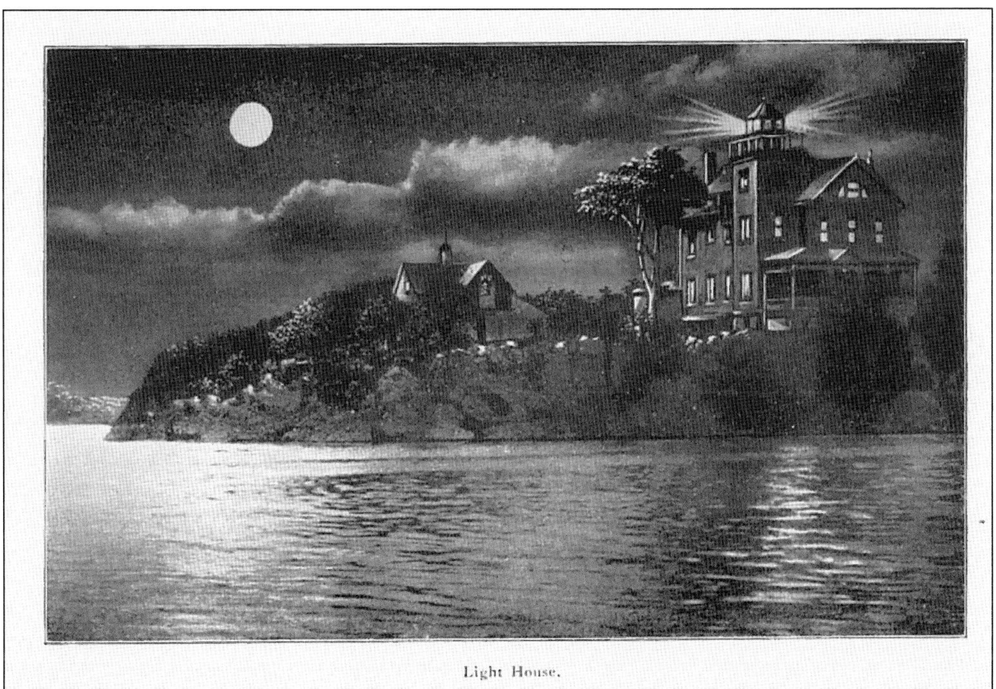

A moonlit night shows South Point Light ablaze, from the same viewpoint as the daytime scene above.

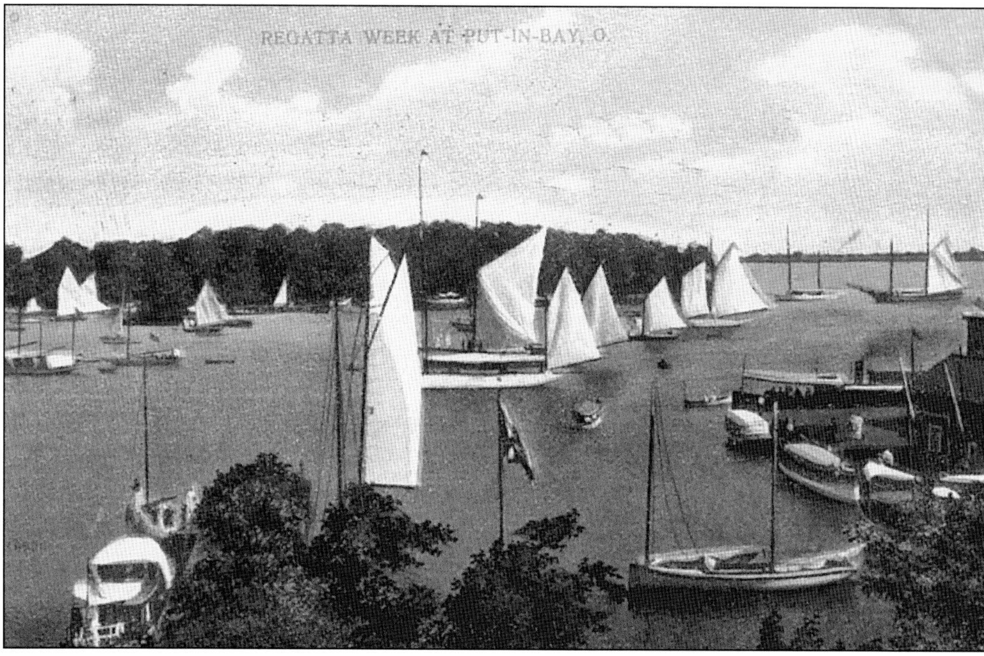

Here, early crafts (1908) race for the Cup during Regatta Week.

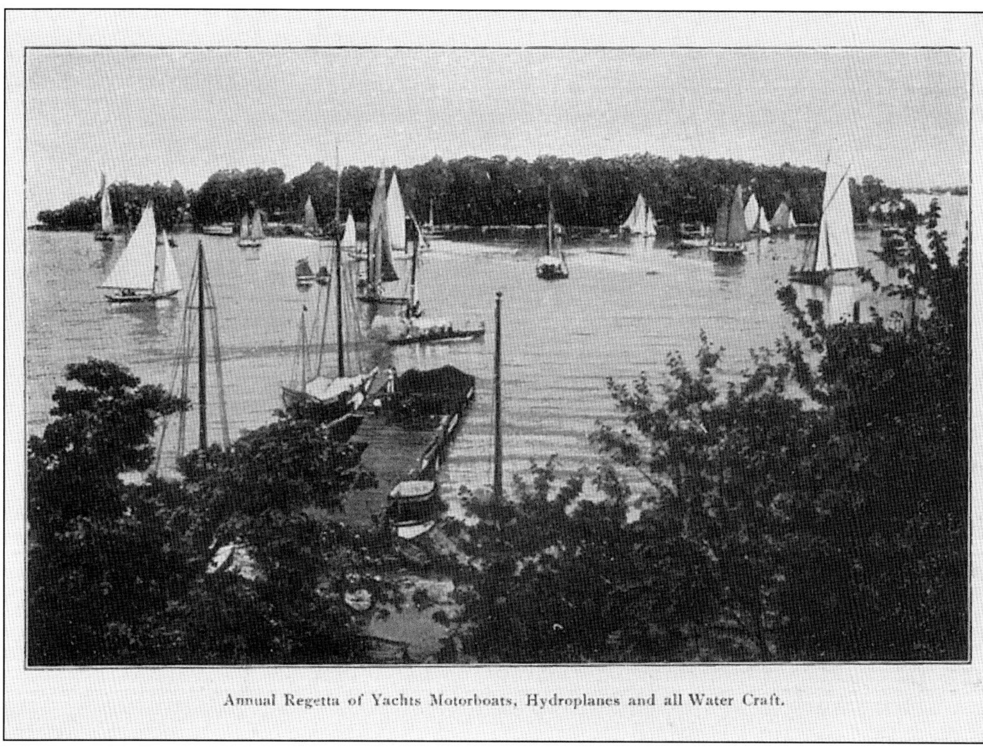

Yachts, motorboats, and hydroplanes all competed in the annual regatta.

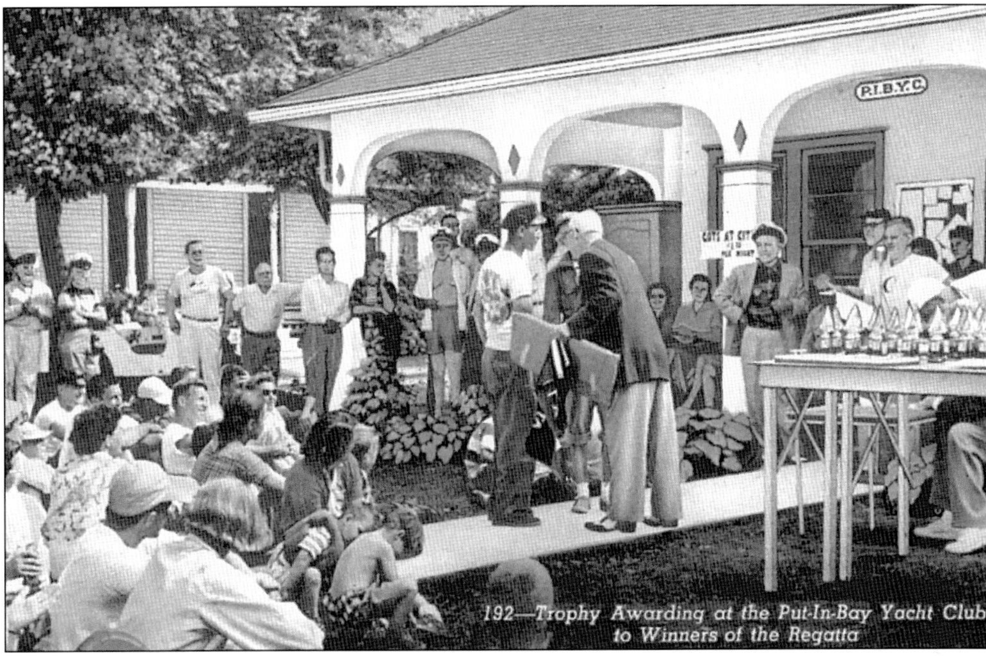

Regatta Week concludes here with the awarding of trophies.

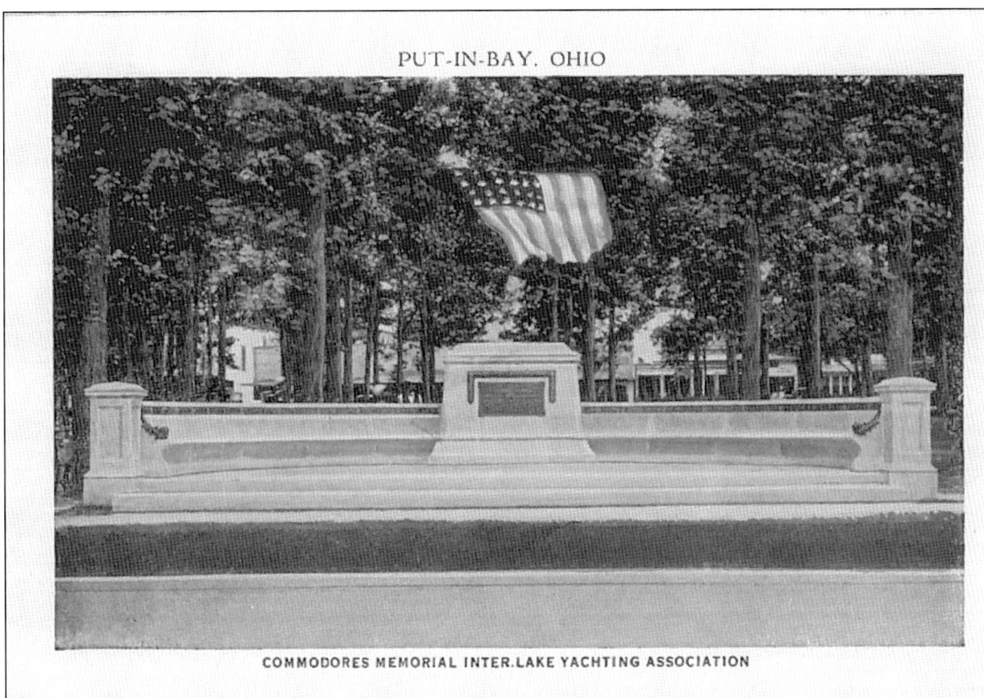

On February 13, 1885, Put-in-Bay business leaders met to found the Island Yacht Club, which became a charter member of the Inter-Lake Yachting Association. The annual I.L.Y.A. Regatta is a major event at Put-in-Bay every August. Part of Regatta Week is a memorial service held at Commodore's Monument in the park.

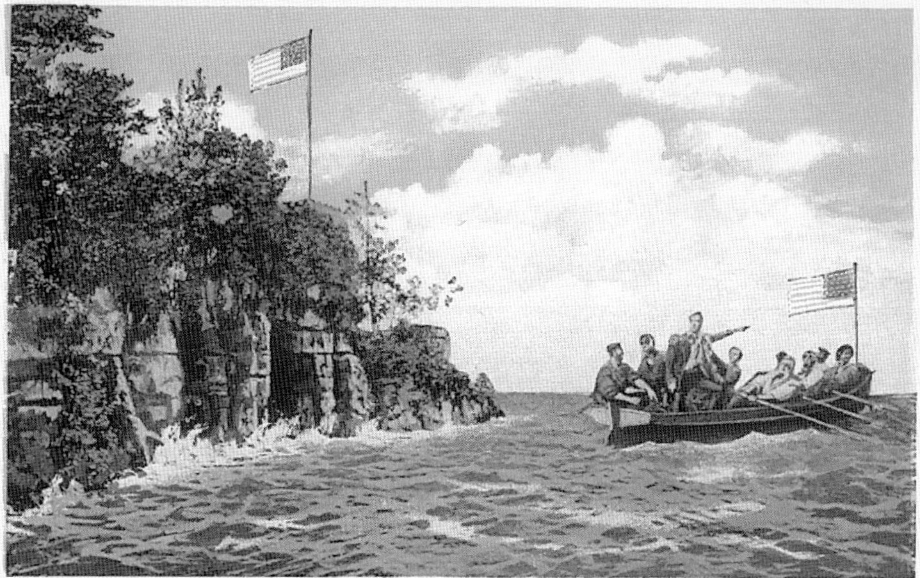

PERRY'S LOOKOUT. PERRY TRANSFERRING THE FLAG. THE NEEDLE'S EYE

The Battle of Lake Erie, fought in the summer of 1813, was a decisive event in the War of 1812. This card depicts Commodore Perry and his troops by Needles Eye at the tip of Gibraltar Island. It was Perry who penned the words, "We have met the enemy and they are ours."

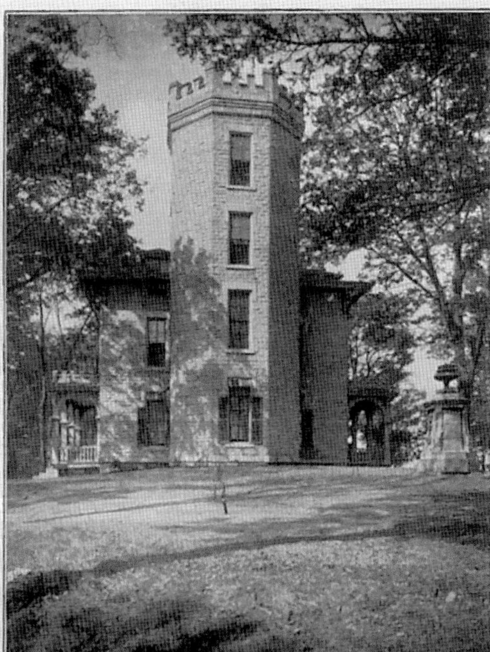

Cooke Castle, Gibraltar, O. Biological Department of the O.S.U.

Industrialist Jay Cooke built the castle-like structure on Gibraltar Island as a monument to Commodore Perry. Cooke bought the island from Jose DeRivera, a founder of Put-in-Bay, for $3,000 in 1864. He lived on the island in the spring and fall for many years. The castle still exists on the island, now part of Ohio State University's Stone Laboratory.

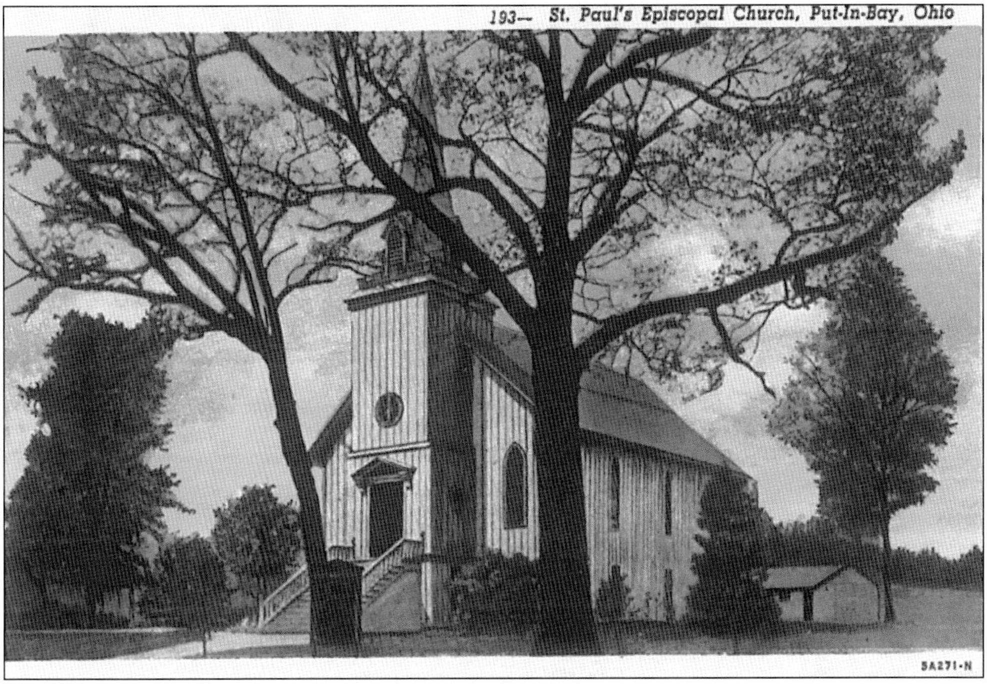

The Episcopal church on Put-in-Bay was built in 1865, funded by Jay Cooke. The church, one of two (along with a Roman Catholic church) on the island, is the oldest church in continuous use in the state of Ohio.

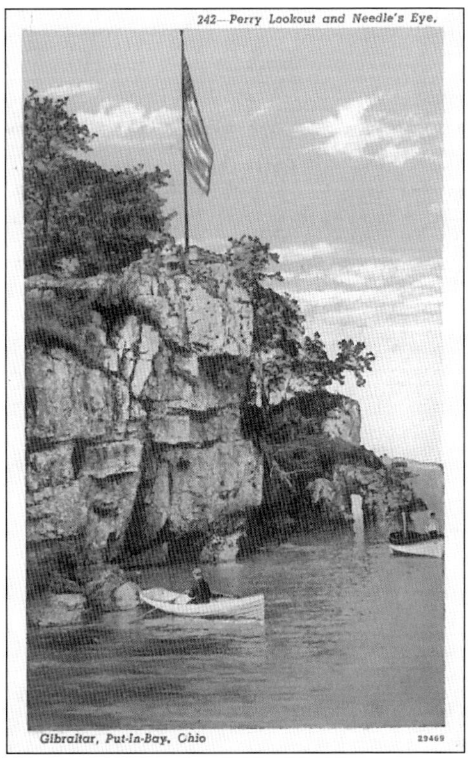

Cooke's Castle is located above Needle's Eye on Gibraltar Island. This is the spot where Commodore Perry watched and waited for the British fleet.

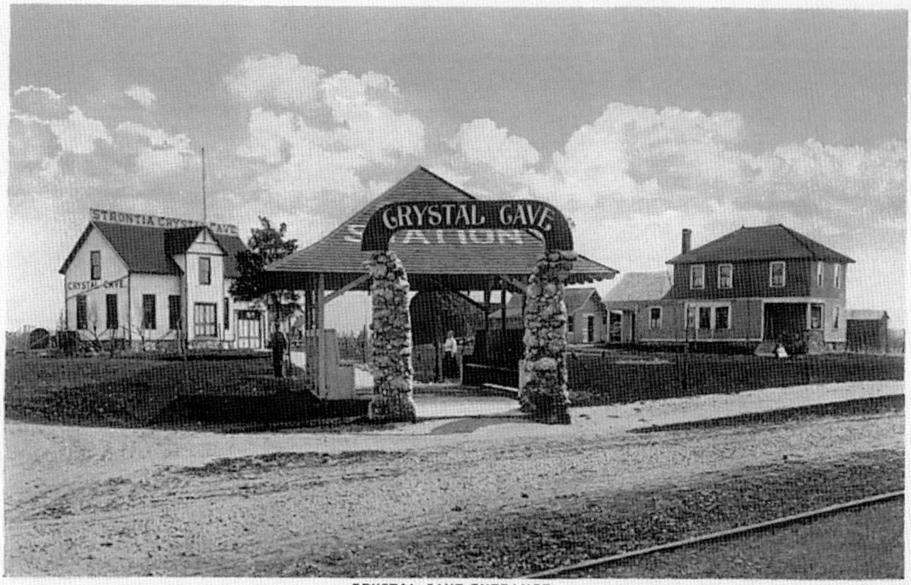

CRYSTAL CAVE ENTRANCE.

The entrance to Crystal Cave, "The most beautiful cave on the island," was a stop on the railway line from the Hotel Victory to downtown Put-in-Bay.

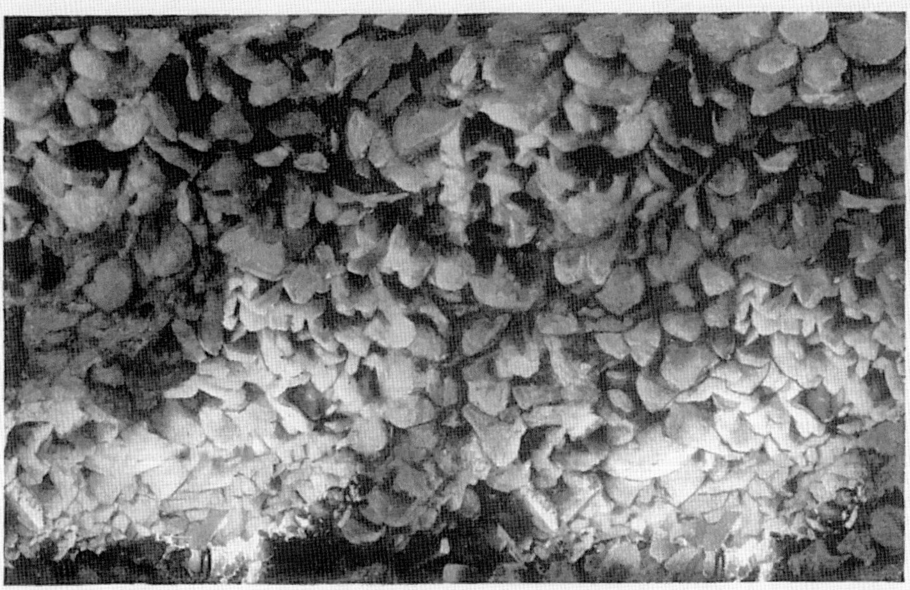

STRONTIA CRYSTALS. INTERIOR OF CRYSTAL CAVE

Strontia crystals, namesake of Crystal Cave, line the walls and ceiling of this natural wonder.

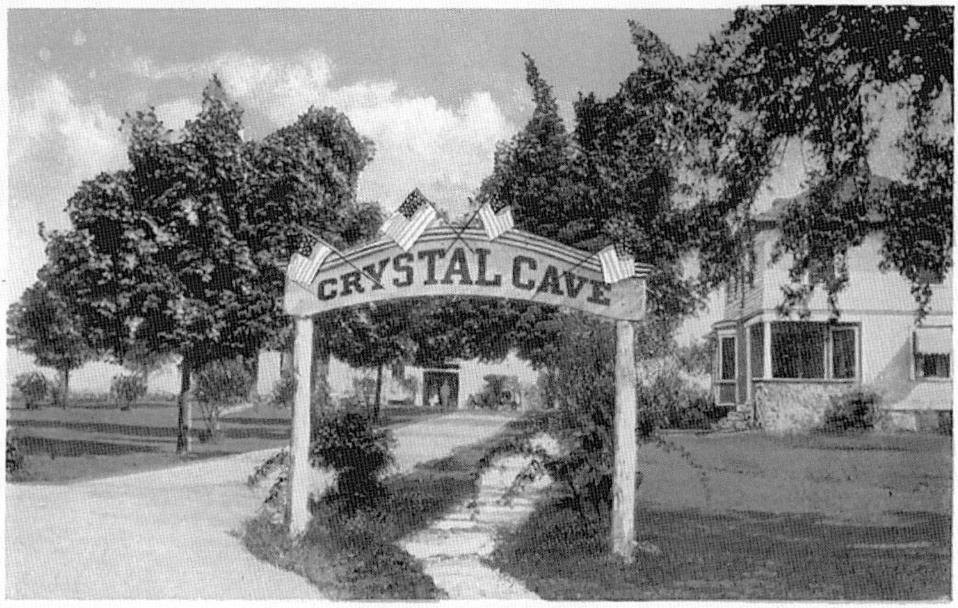

ENTRANCE TO CRYSTAL CAVE

Crystal Cave is one of some 30 natural caves on South Bass Island. Still open to the public today, the cave is a beautiful site, likened to the interior of a geode.

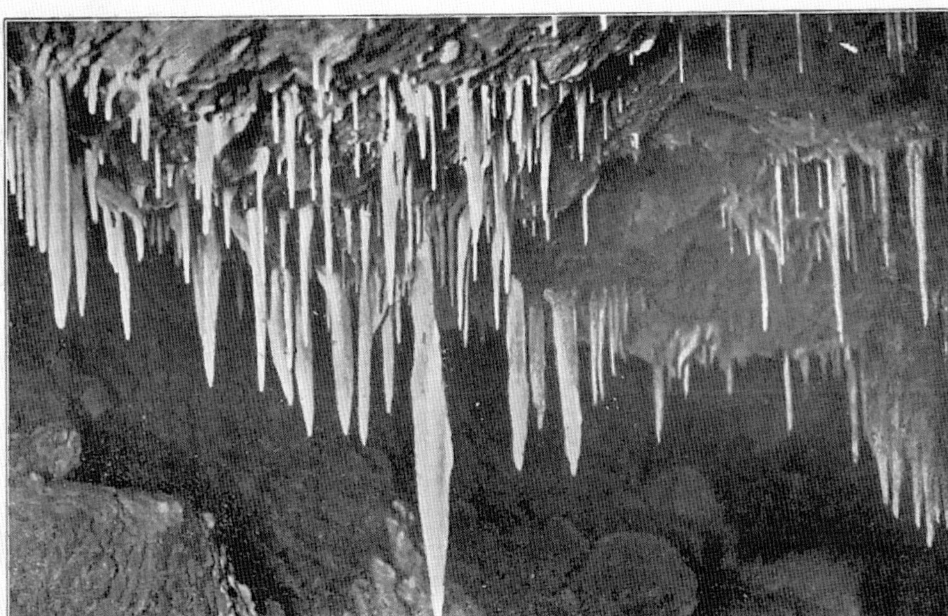

Group of Stalactite and Stalagmites showing in the Paradise Cave.

Paradise Cave was discovered in 1903 near Crystal Cave. It offered the best display of stalactites of any cave on the island. It was open to the public for many years, but was eventually closed and sealed.

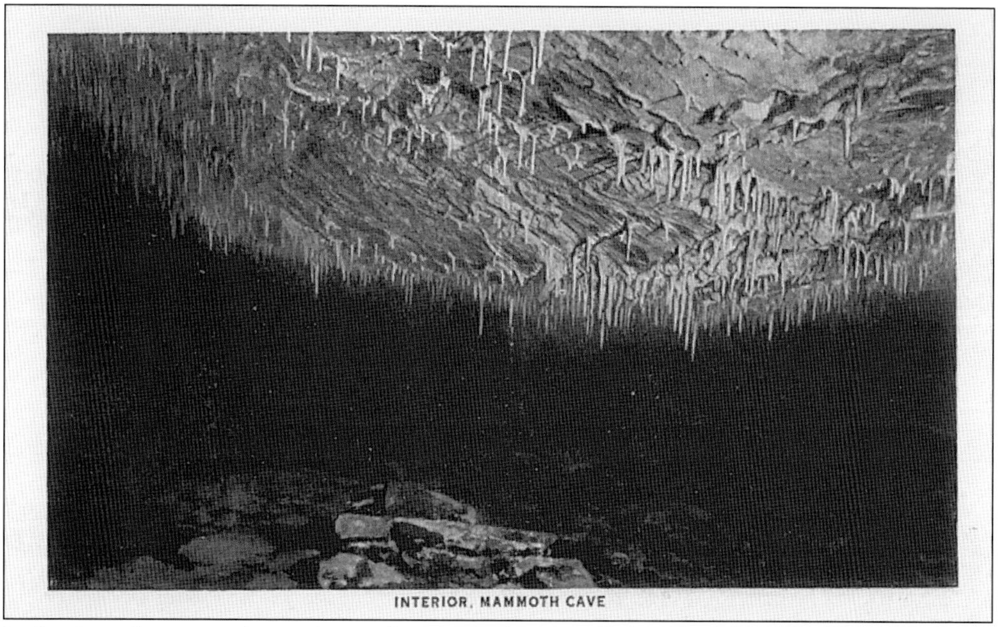

Stalactites decorate the ceiling of Mammoth Cave. Known since 1885, the cave was closed to the public due to safety concerns in 1955.

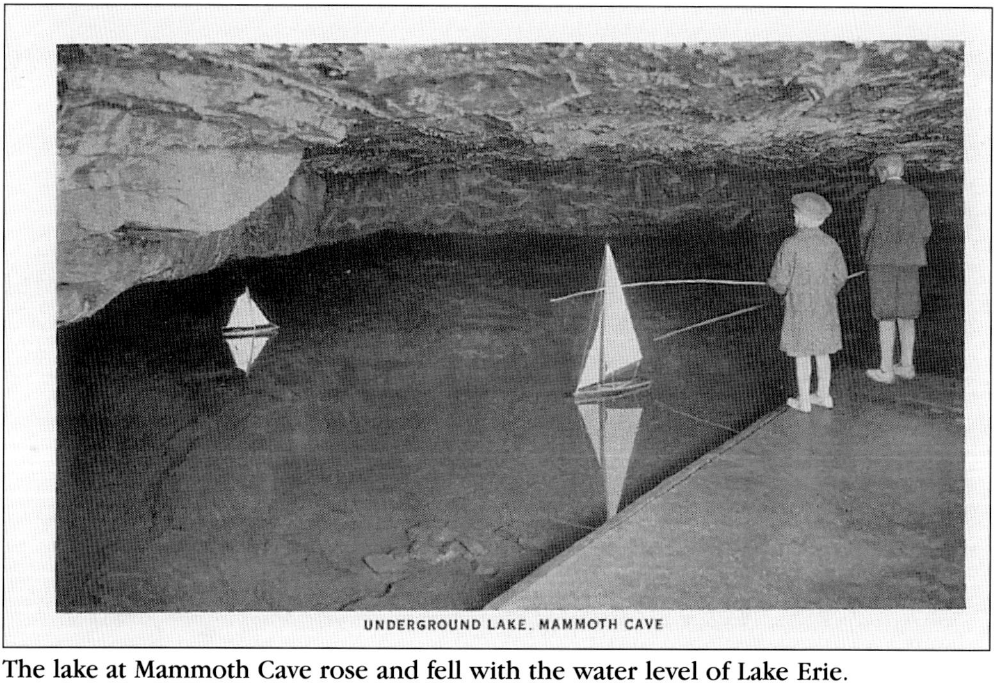

The lake at Mammoth Cave rose and fell with the water level of Lake Erie.

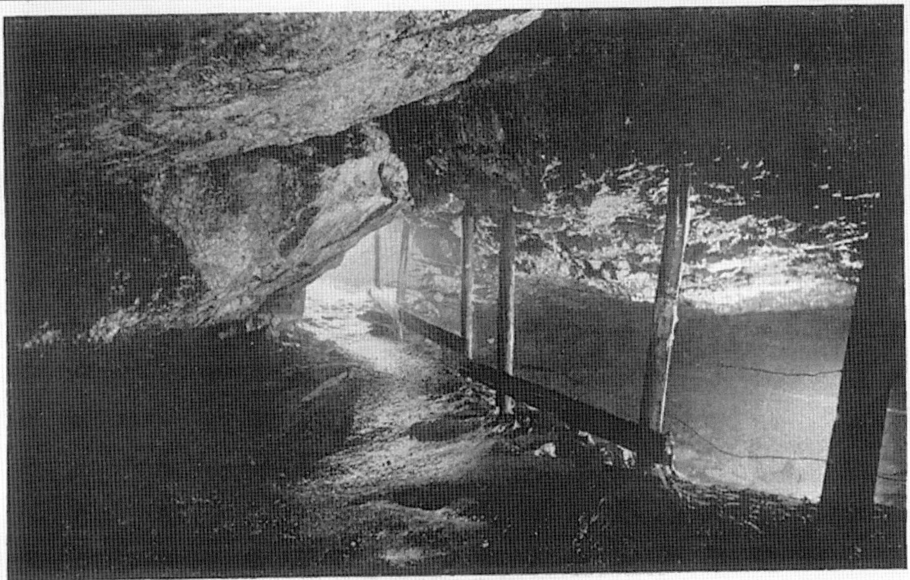
INTERIOR VIEW OF PERRY CAVE

Perry's Cave is said to have been used by Commodore Perry during the Battle of Lake Erie. Guided tours through the cave have been offered since the mid-1800s. The cave is one of two (along with Crystal Cave) on Put-in-Bay still open to the public.

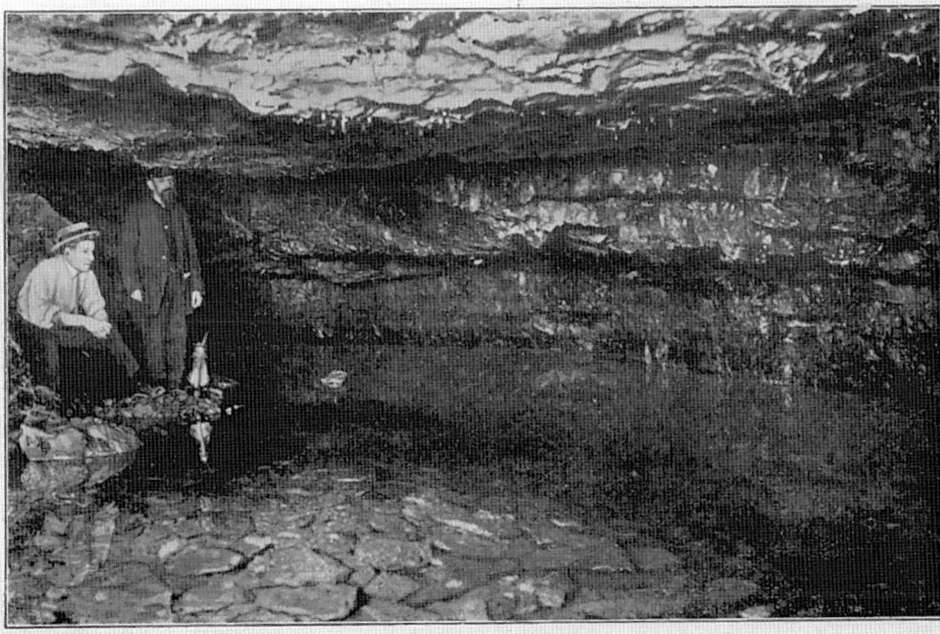
Scene in Perry's Cave. One of the great underground caverns of the Island.

The inside of Perry's Cave can be seen in this view circa 1915.

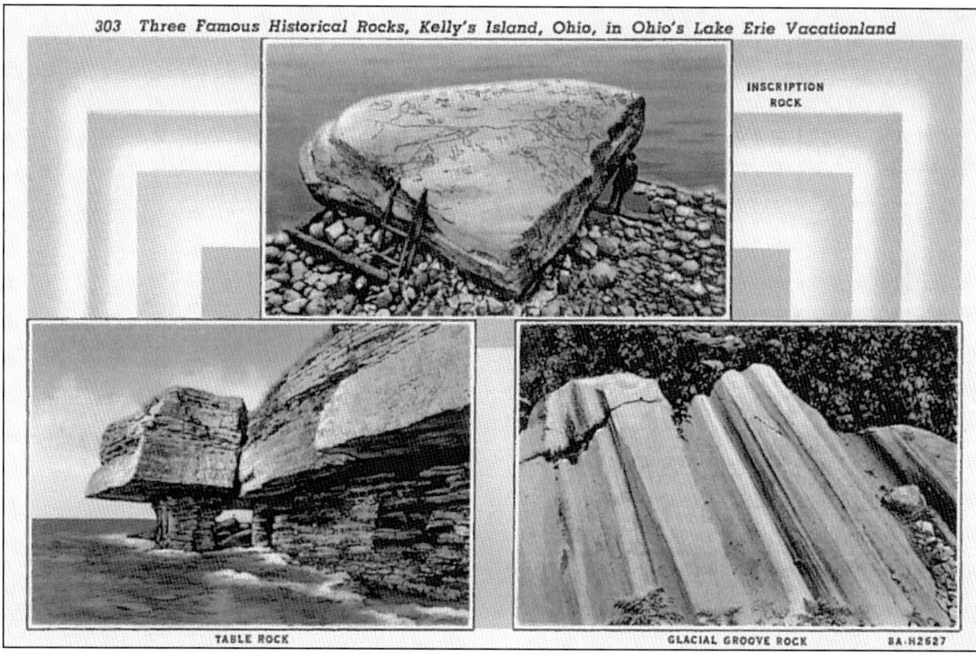

Inscription Rock, thought to be inscribed with hieroglyphics from an ancient Indian tribe, in addition to Table Rock and glacial grooves dating to the Glacial Age, all remain popular tourist attractions on Kelleys Island. Today, the markings on Inscription Rock have been largely obliterated due to wear. A fence now protects the artifact.

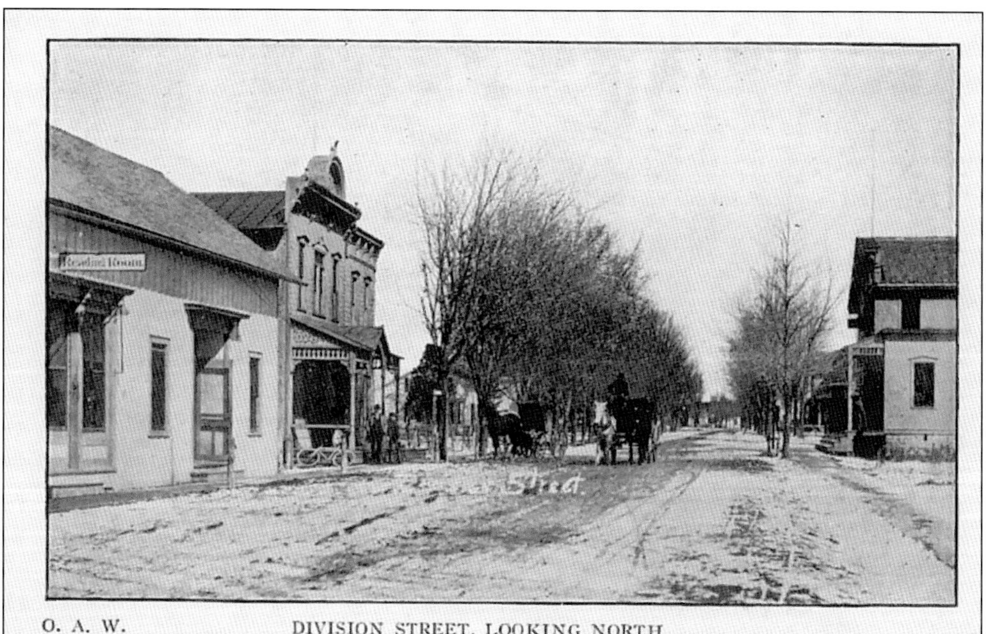

This off-season view of Division Street on Kelleys Island includes downtown stores that are still in use.

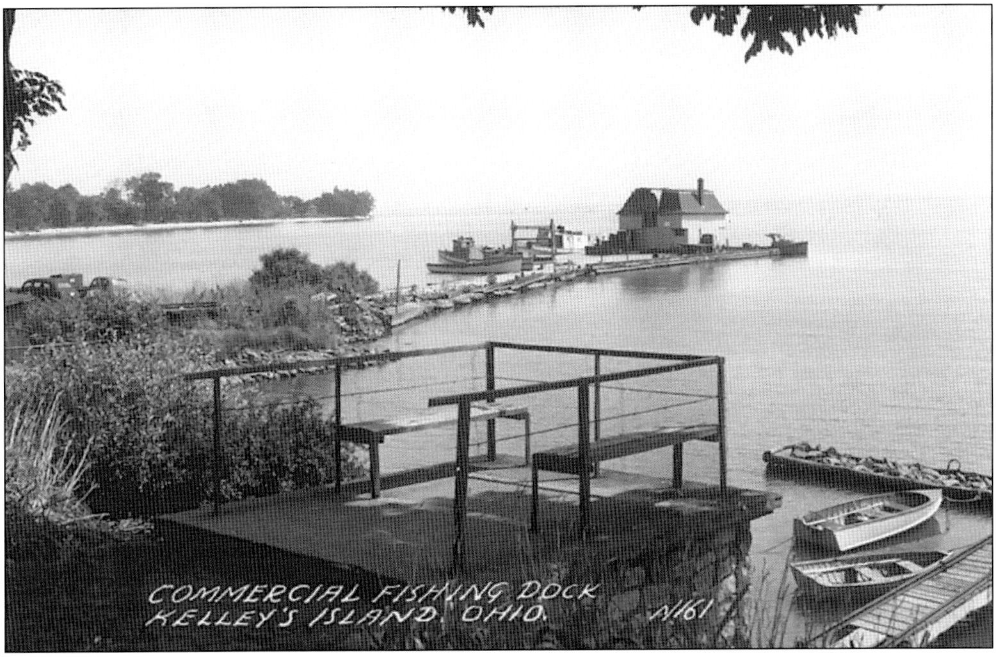

This rare view of the shore at Kelleys Island shows fishing boats docked near Inscription Rock.

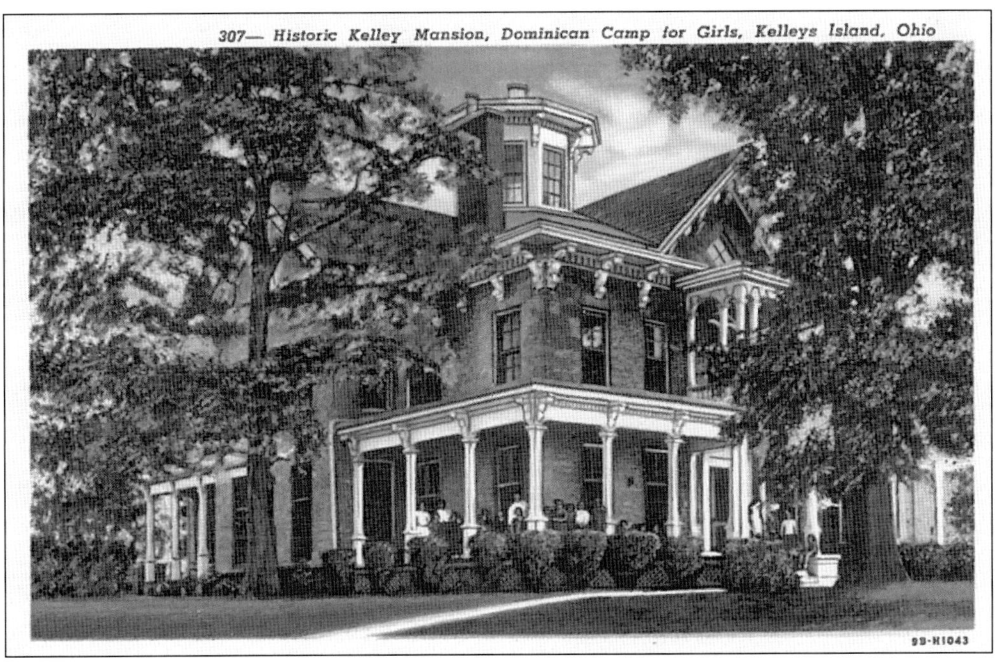

The Kelley Mansion, one of the island's more distinctive landmarks, was constructed in the mid-1860s from locally quarried limestone. It was built for Addison Kelley, son of Kelleys Island namesake Datus Kelly. The house features carved wood, stained and etched glass, and an exquisite spiral staircase leading to an enclosed widow's walk. The mansion is now a popular bed and breakfast inn.

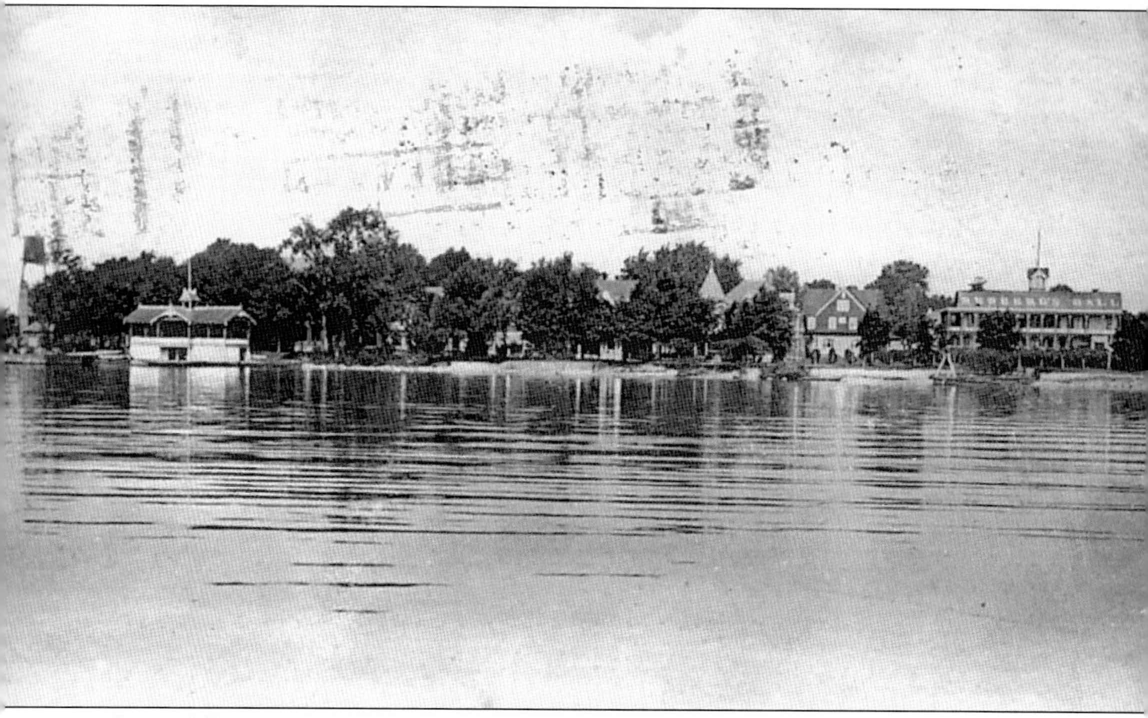

The Middle Bass Club, on Middle Bass Island, was described in *Sketches and Stories of the Lake Erie Islands* (1900) as follows: "In addition to the magnificent club house with massive tower and wide, cool verandahs, the grounds also contain a handsome pavilion and boat house, a Gothic chapel in which religious services are conducted, and a large and elegant hall, at which are held club parties and entertainments. The club consists of two hundred members, limited to that number, and represents some of the most influential families of Toledo, Cleveland, Cincinnati, Springfield, Dayton, Chicago and other cities." The Island is now owned by Meier's Wine Cellars and is home to the historic Lonz Winery, once Golden Eagle Wine Company, which was one of the largest wineries in the United States in the 1800s.

Four

Lakeside and the Marblehead Peninsula

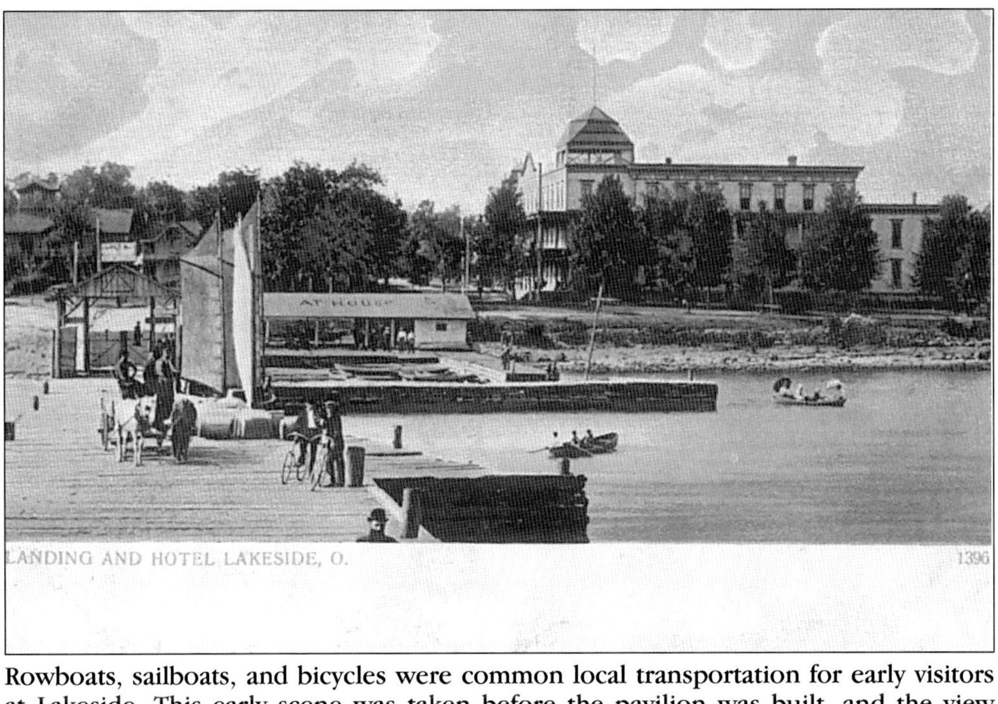

Rowboats, sailboats, and bicycles were common local transportation for early visitors at Lakeside. This early scene was taken before the pavilion was built, and the view of Hotel Lakeside reveals the existence of second floor balconies now long gone. The hotel has hosted such prominent guests as Presidents Rutherford B. Hayes and William McKinley.

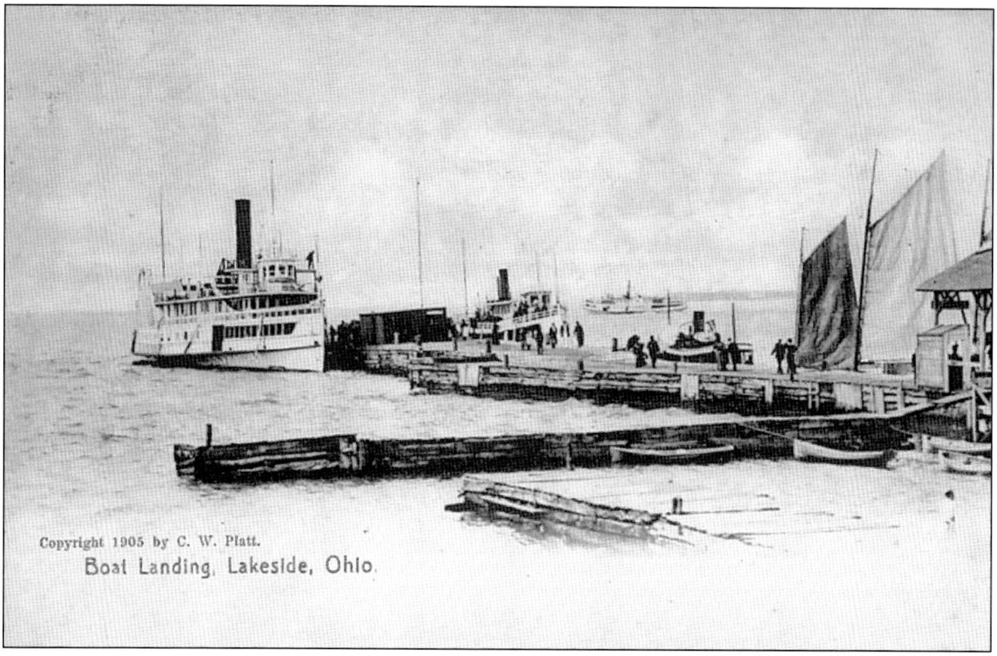

The steamer *Metropolis*, which ran from Toledo during the period 1895 through 1901, is competing for dock space with three other steamboats and a pair of schooners.

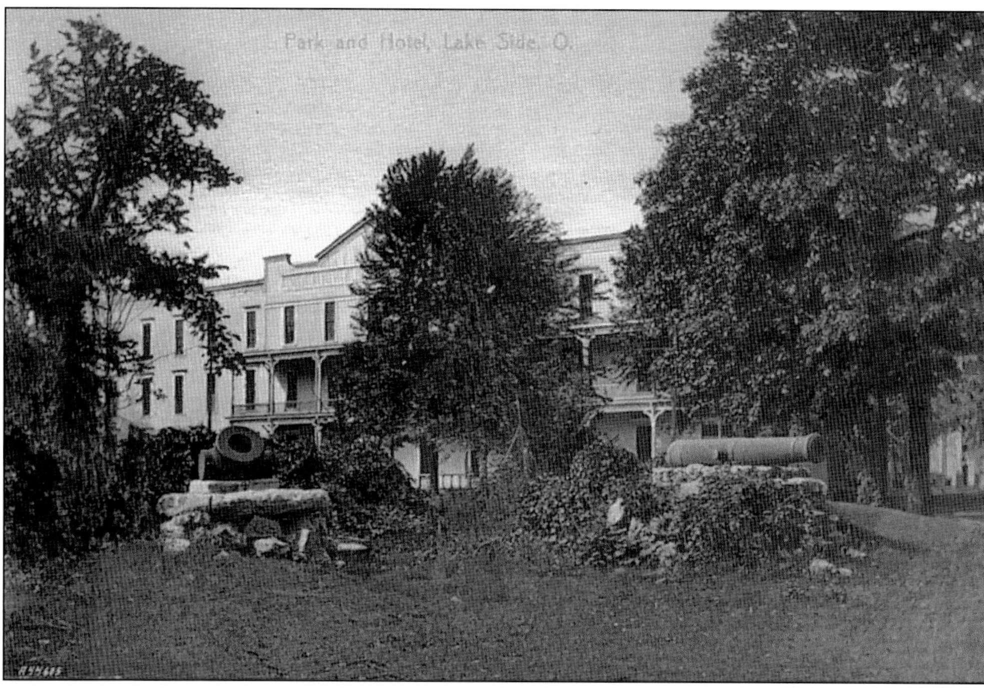

An early (1908) view of Hotel Lakeside shows the commemorative cannon on the front lawn. The first unit of the hotel was constructed in 1875, and major additions were built in 1879 and 1890. The 1890 wing has since been removed, so the present hotel was in reality completed in 1879.

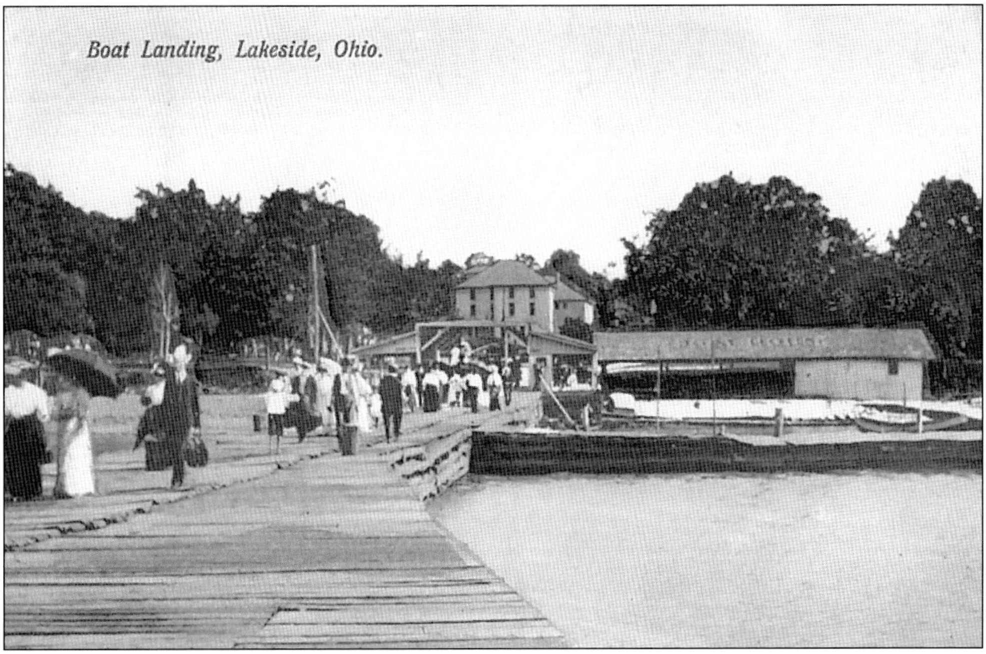

The planked boat landing at Lakeside was a busy scene, as passengers with luggage hurried to catch a departing steamer. The pavilion at the foot of the pier did not exist yet in this pre-1909 scene. The boathouse is on the right.

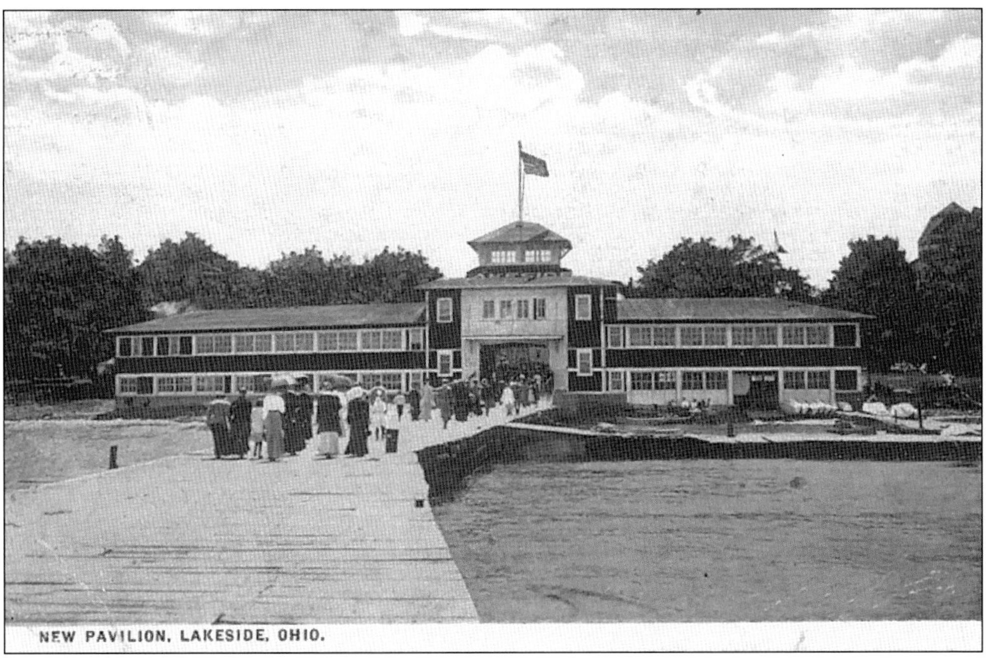

The pavilion is shown here shortly after construction in 1923. The building housed a restaurant, arcade, bowling alleys, and a barbershop before it was torn down in the 1950s. It has been splendidly reconstructed in a similar style, and today houses shops, a deck for sunning, and a bell tower with musical chimes.

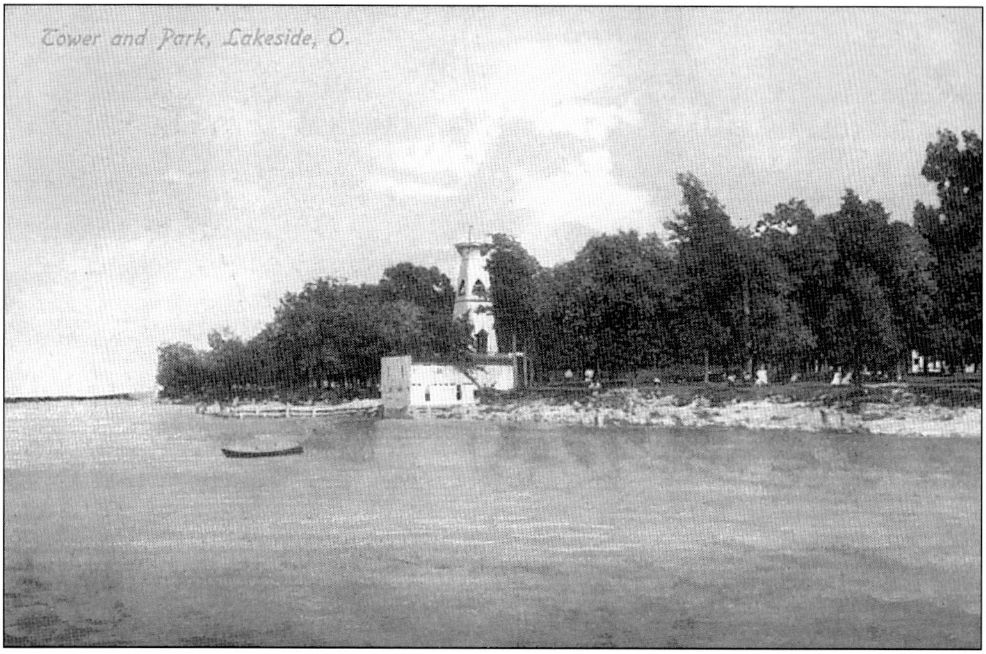

The original bell tower, constructed in the 1880s, called the devout to services and events.

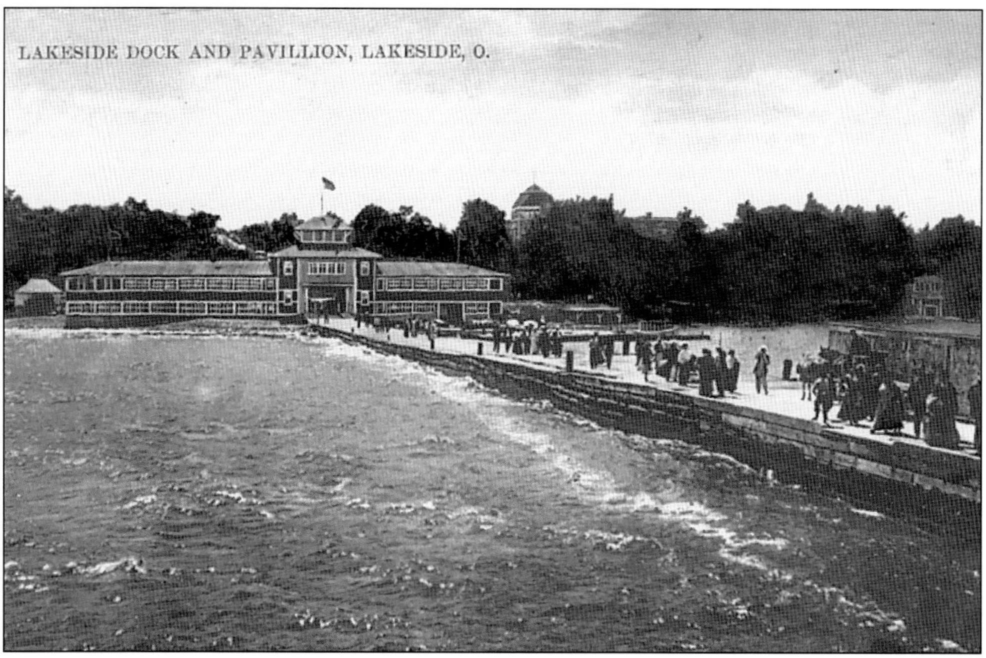

The famous pavilion and pier were the major entryway to Lakeside, the Chautauqua of Lake Erie. The pavilion has been reconstructed to its original splendor. Hotel Lakeside can be seen above the trees in the background.

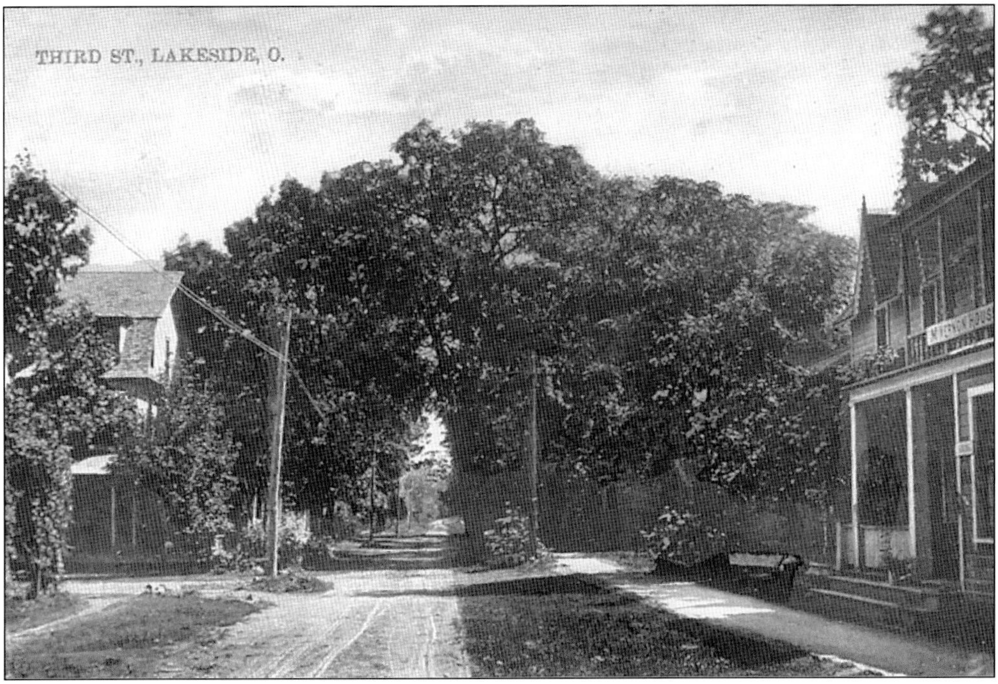

Wagon trails rut the sandy roads of early Lakeside. The Inn, with gingerbread trim, was a forerunner of the quaint bed-and-breakfast inns that dot today's Lakeside.

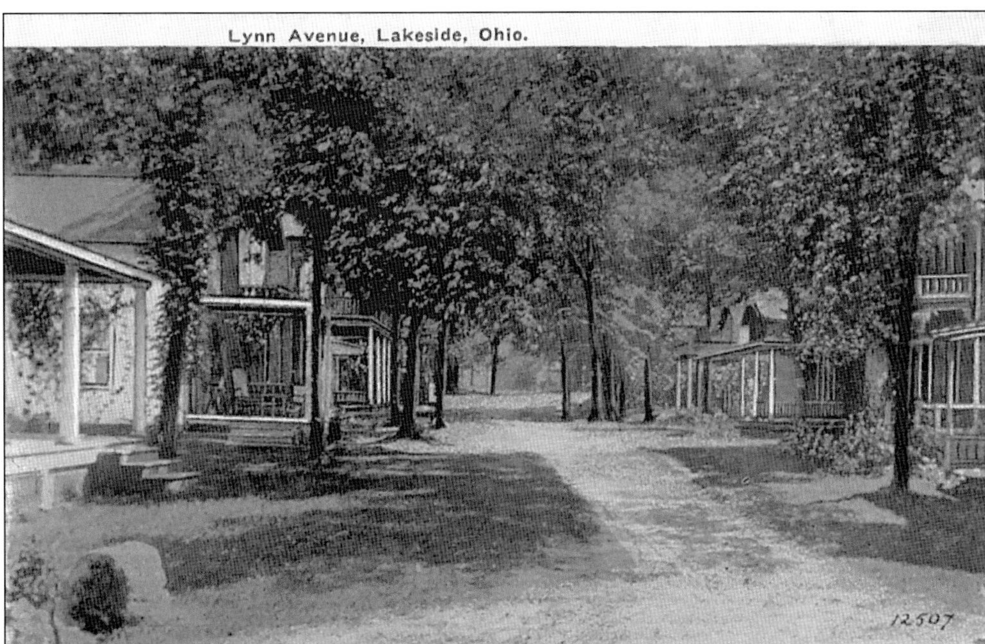

The shady streets of Lakeside (Lynn Avenue was little more than a path in this 1925 view) are bordered by "Lakeside cottages," most with gingerbread trim.

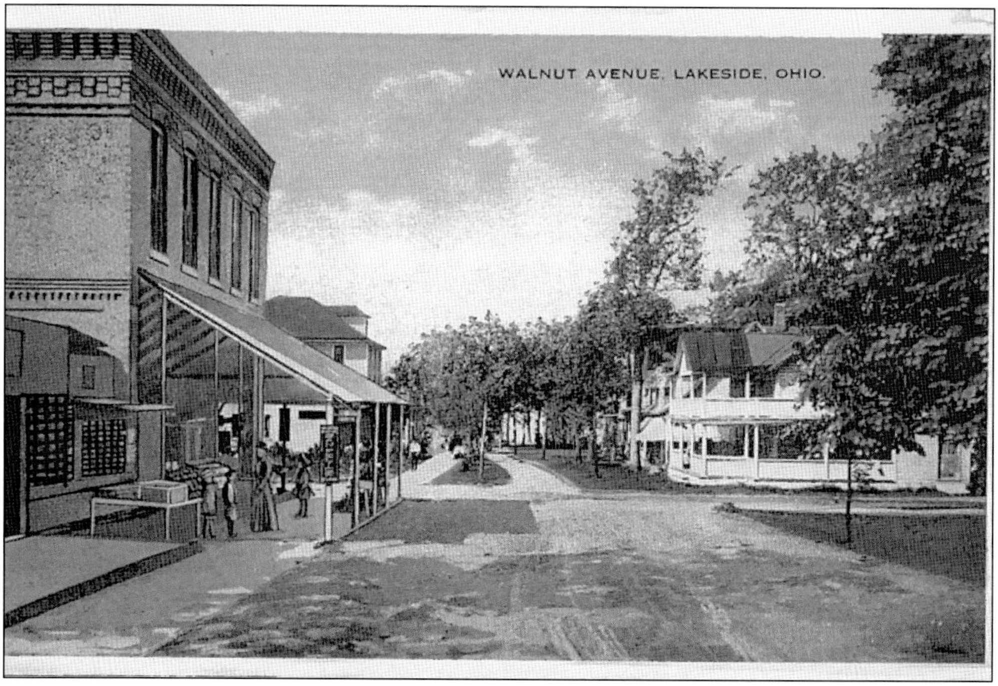

Walnut Avenue, Lakeside's main street, is shown here in 1919. The entire community has retained the charm that is evident in these early scenes.

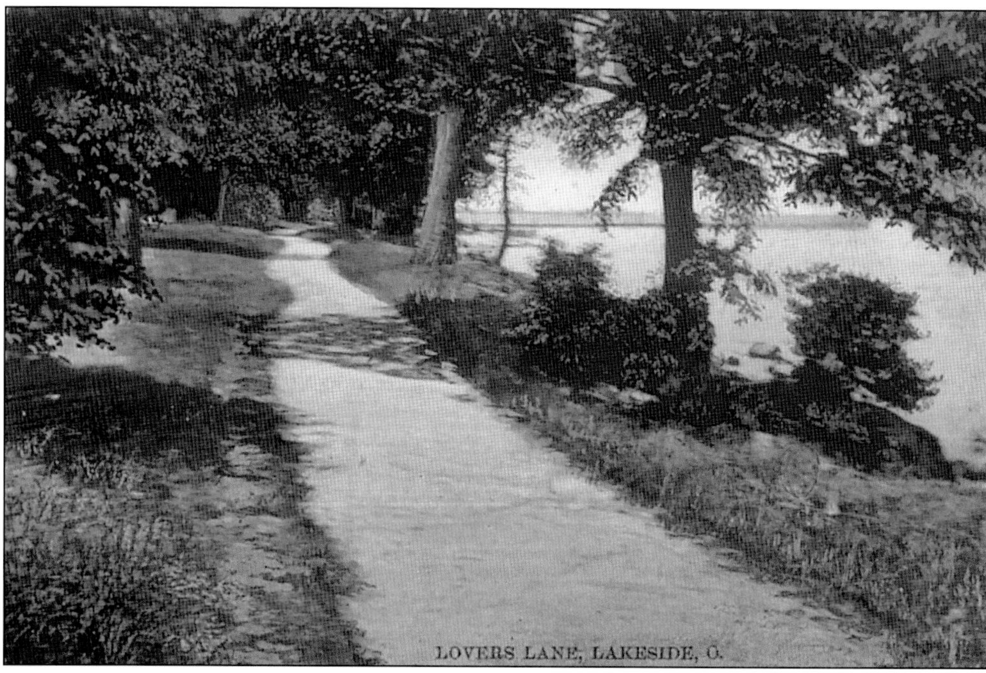

The beautiful shoreline walk at Lakeside was known as Lovers' Lane, a somewhat daring title for this devout religious community in 1912.

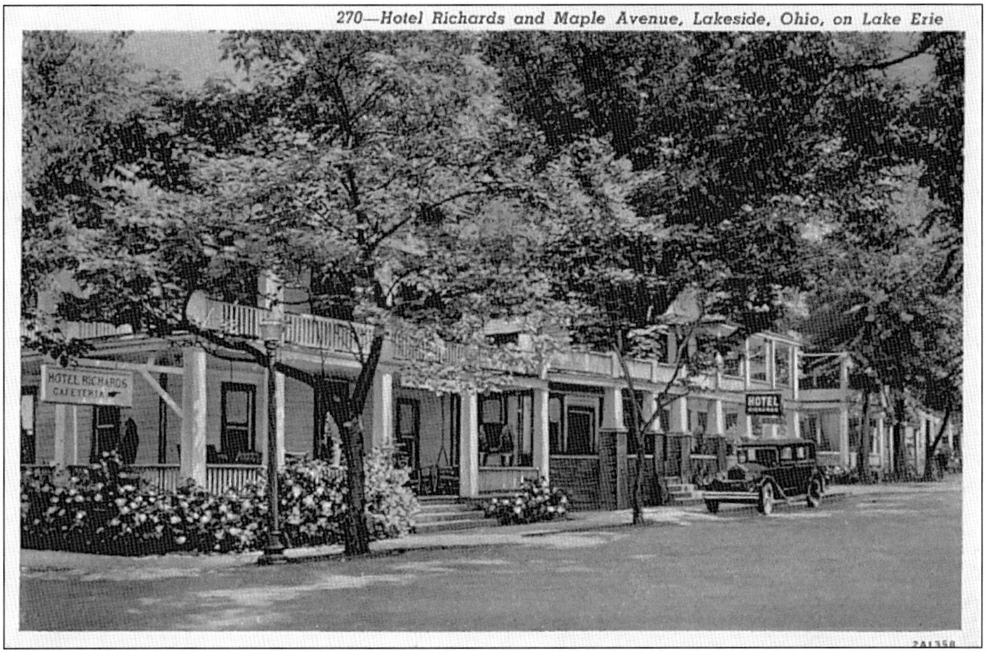

The Hotel Richards, built in 1885, later became known as Poor Richard's Inn, and is now called the Same Time Next Year B&B. In 1900, the rates were $1 a day, including board. In 1931, with the addition of hot and cold running water, daily rates were raised to $1.25 for a single room.

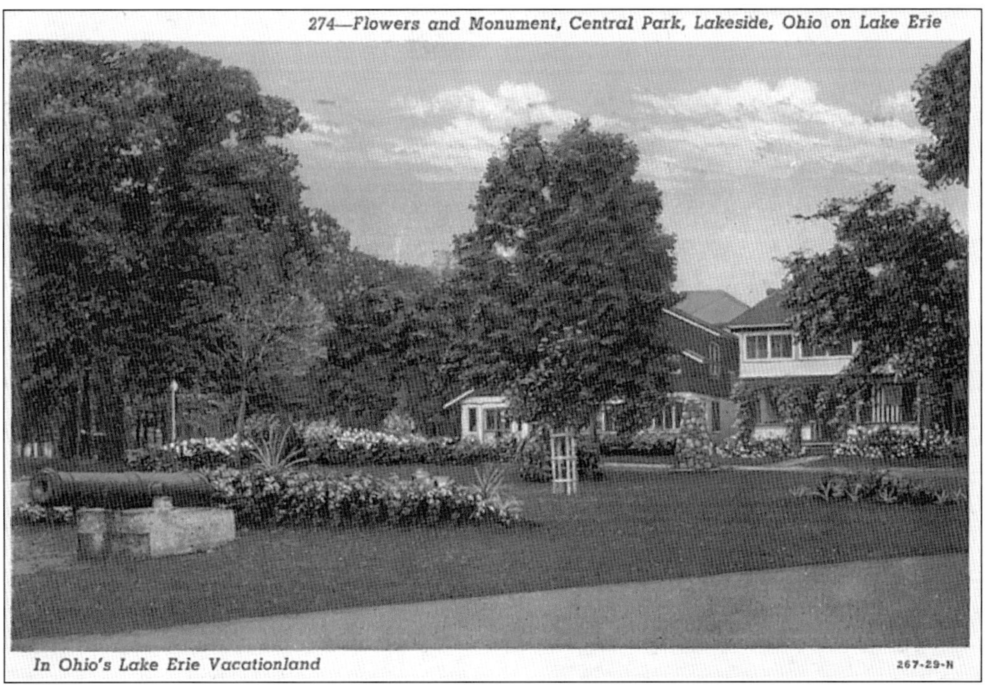

Central Park in Lakeside shows off its summer finery with flowers and shade trees abounding.

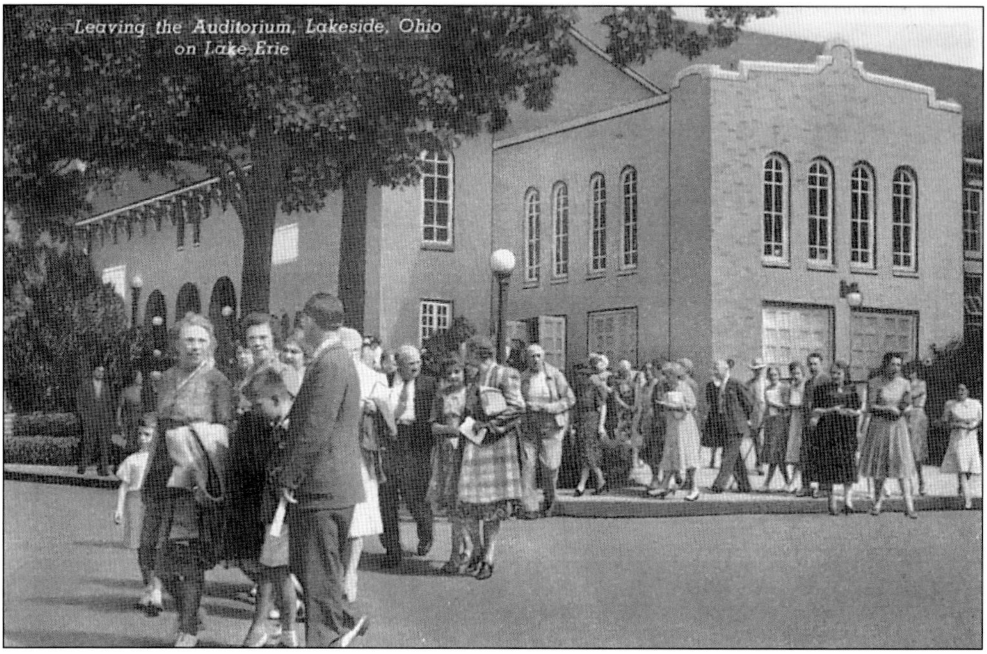

In this image, worshippers leave Sunday services at Hoover Auditorium, which seats three thousand people. The center of Lakeside spiritual and entertainment programs, the auditorium was constructed in 1929 and named for A. L. Hoover, longtime General Manager of Lakeside.

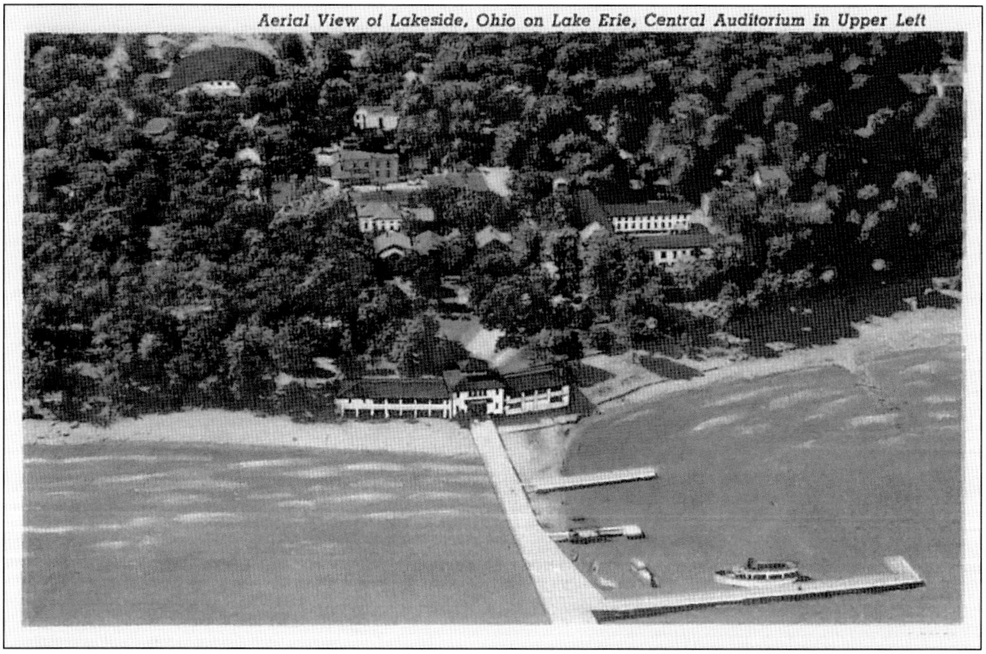

This bird's-eye view of Lakeside shows the old pavilion (now reconstructed). The Hotel Lakeside is among the trees to the right, and Hoover Auditorium is visible in the upper left.

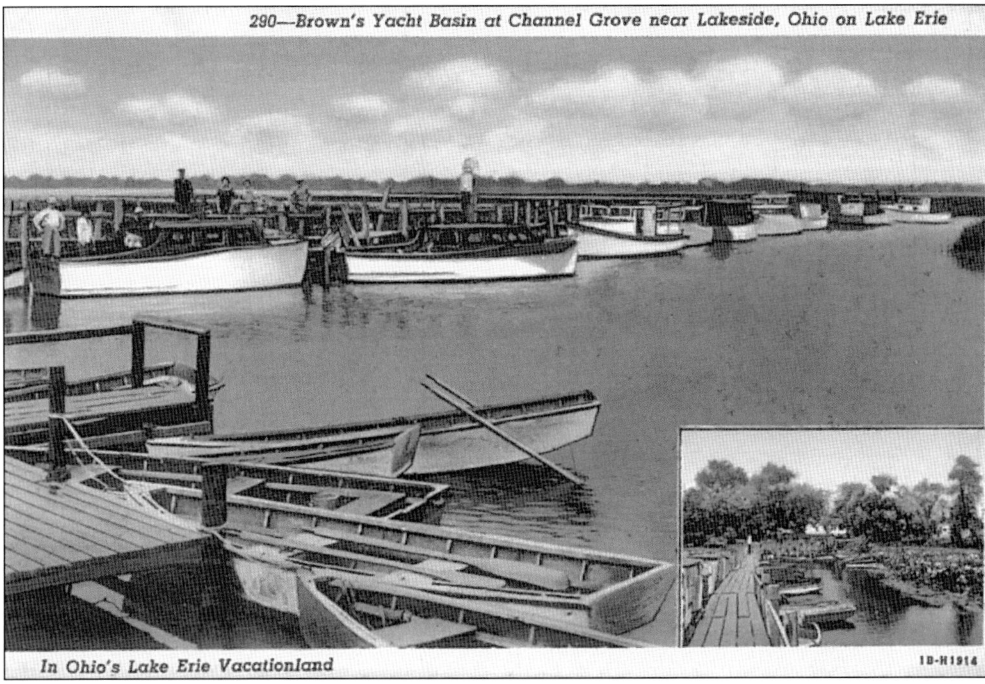

Brown's Yacht Basin near Lakeside was a popular "tying up" spot for motorcraft and rowboats. The card mentions that the marina was "At entrance to Sandy Beach, one of the finest beaches on Lake Erie."

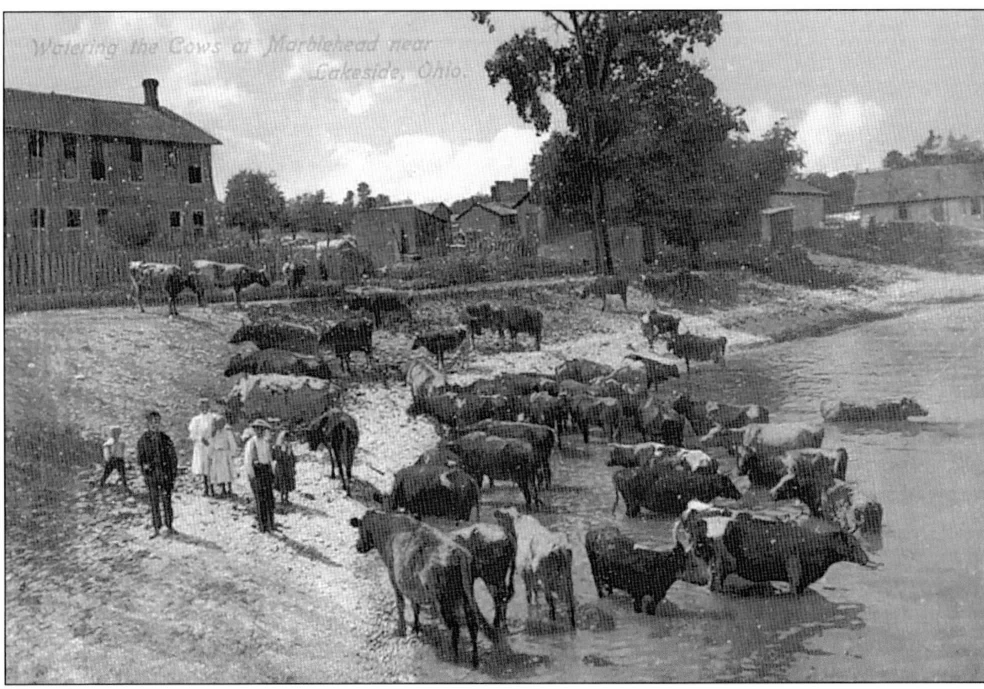

Cows would be a rare sight along today's lakeshore.

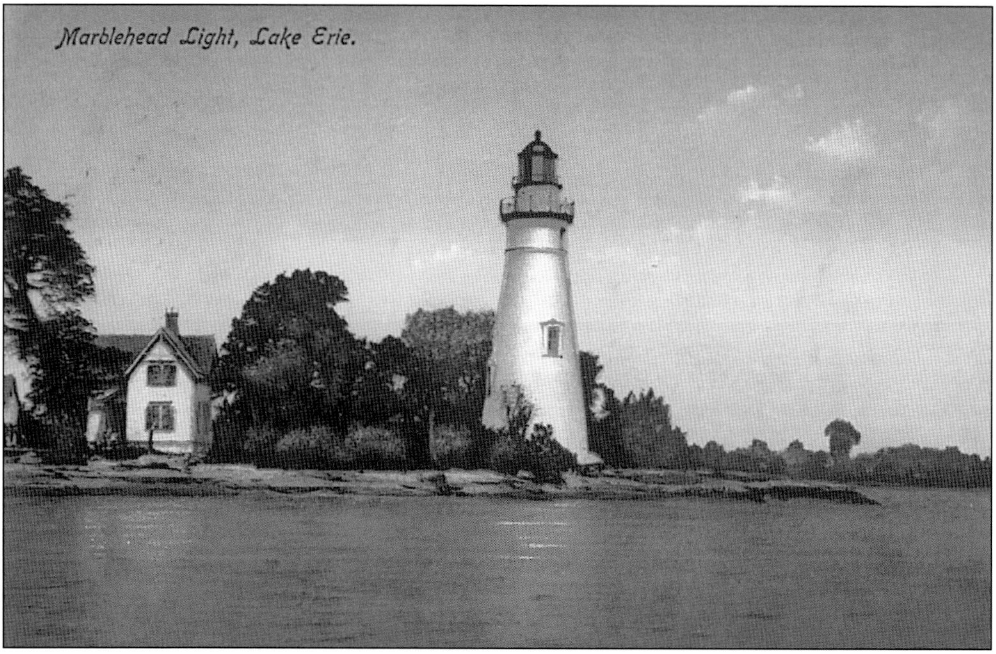

The famed Marblehead Lighthouse, oldest operating lighthouse on the Great Lakes, dates to 1821. The keeper's house, built in 1880, can be seen on the left. The original keeper's house, built about a mile away in 1822 (facing Sandusky Bay), has been restored and can be visited on selected summer weekends.

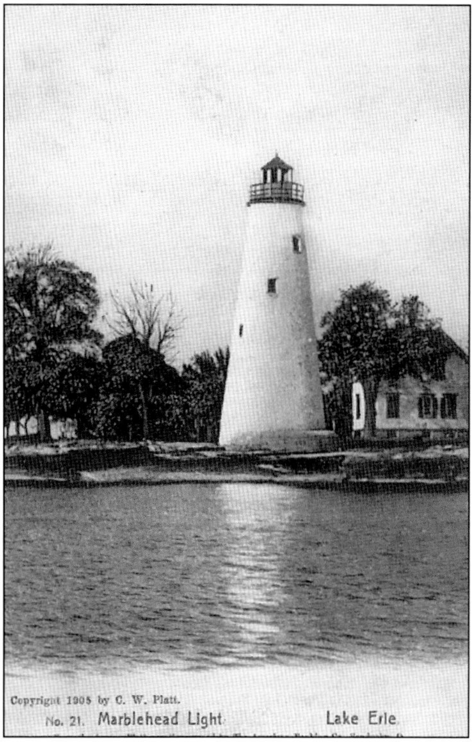

This early view shows the lighthouse as it appeared in the 1800s, a 50-foot tall structure built of locally quarried limestone. A Fourth Order Fresnel lens, which had been installed in 1858 and replaced in 1897, is shown here.

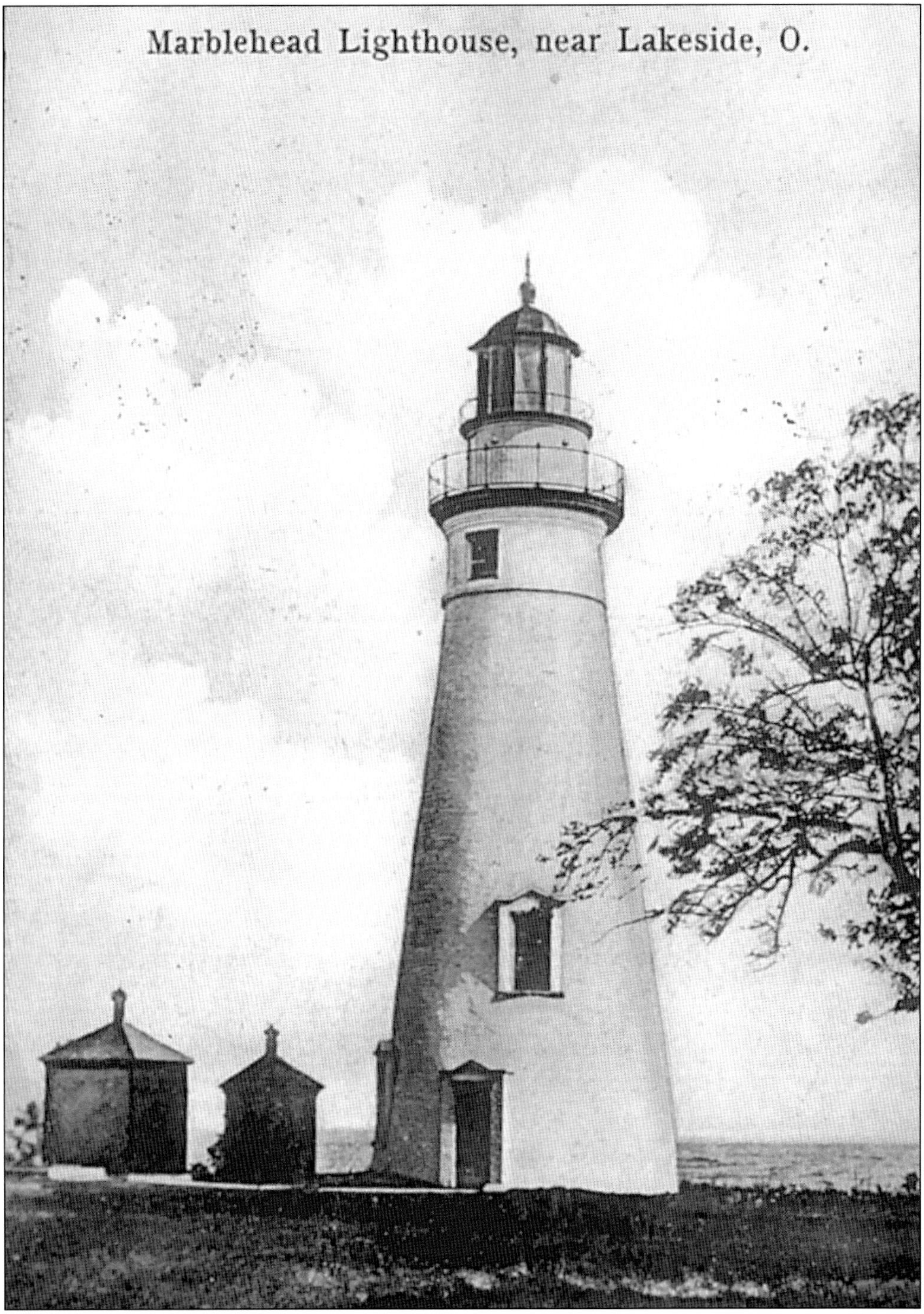

The lighthouse assumed its classic look of today after the addition of the larger third-order lens and 15 feet of height in 1897. The small structures on the left held oil that was used to fuel the lantern atop the lighthouse. The lamp was converted to electrical power in 1923.

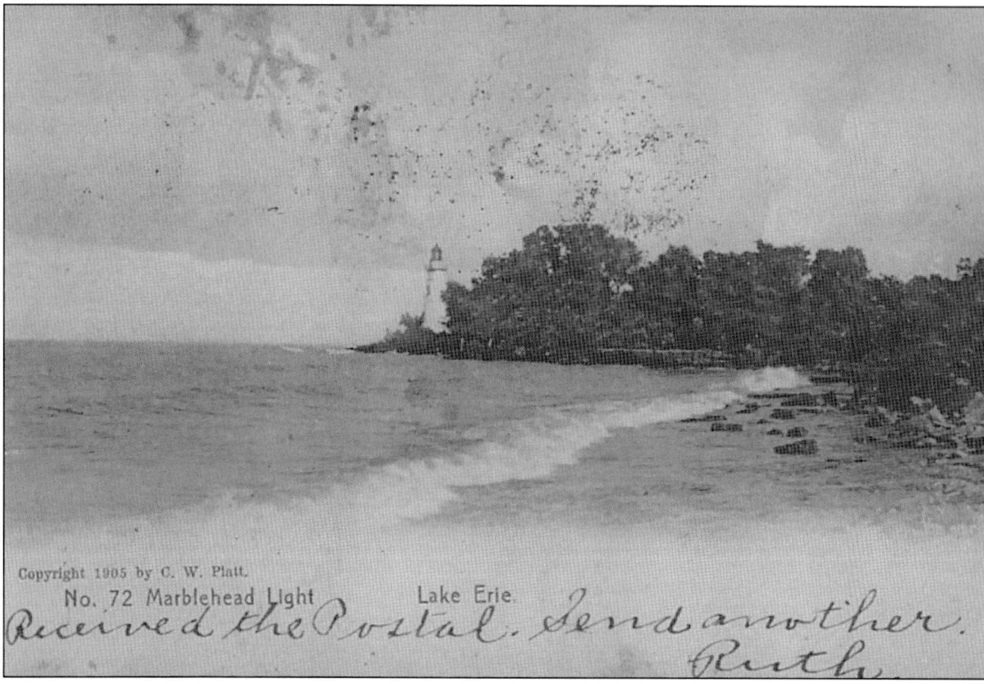

Marblehead Lighthouse, standing at the tip of Marblehead Peninsula on the passageway between Lake Erie and Sandusky Bay, has guided many a sailor past the rocky shoreline. This card carries a simple but direct message, "Received the postal. Send another."

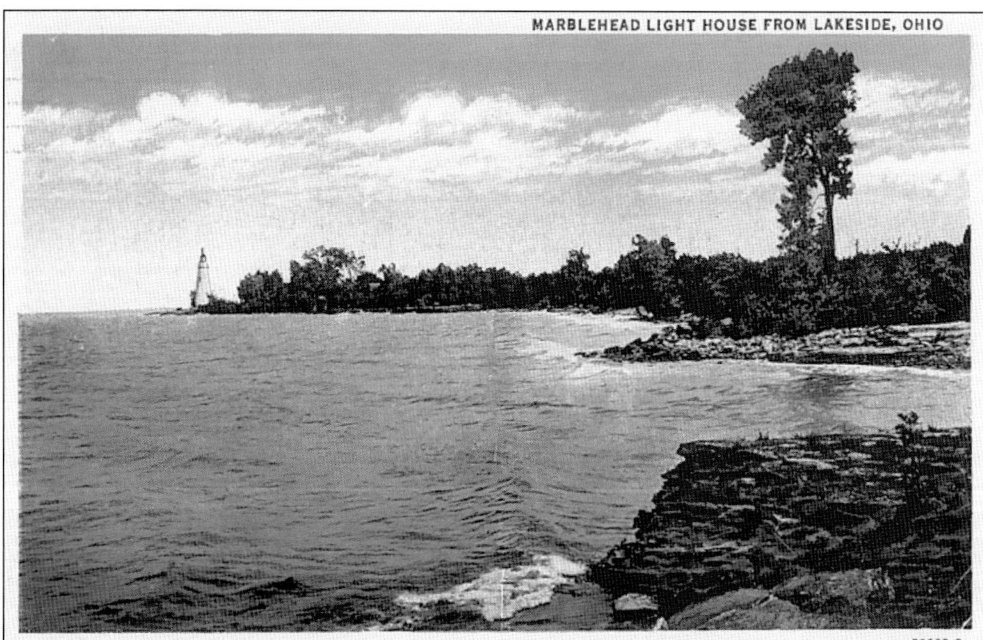

This postcard, dated 1939, is essentially the same as the 1905 card above, and the scene even today remains unchanged.

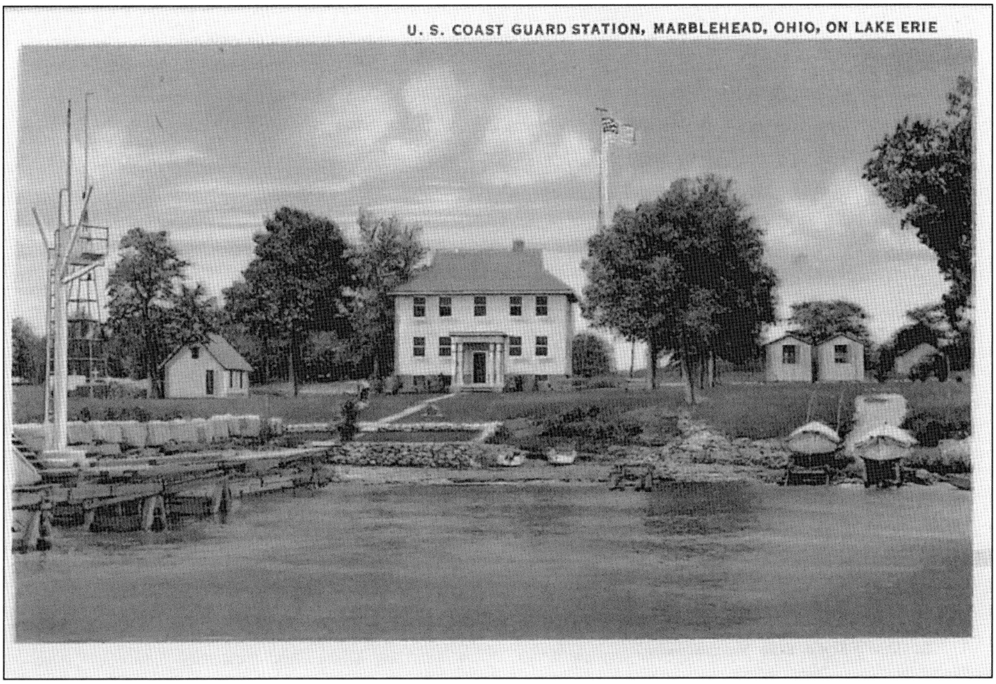

The Coast Guard station was located in the town of Marblehead. Today, Marblehead boasts a new facility as well as the landing for a Kelleys Island ferry.

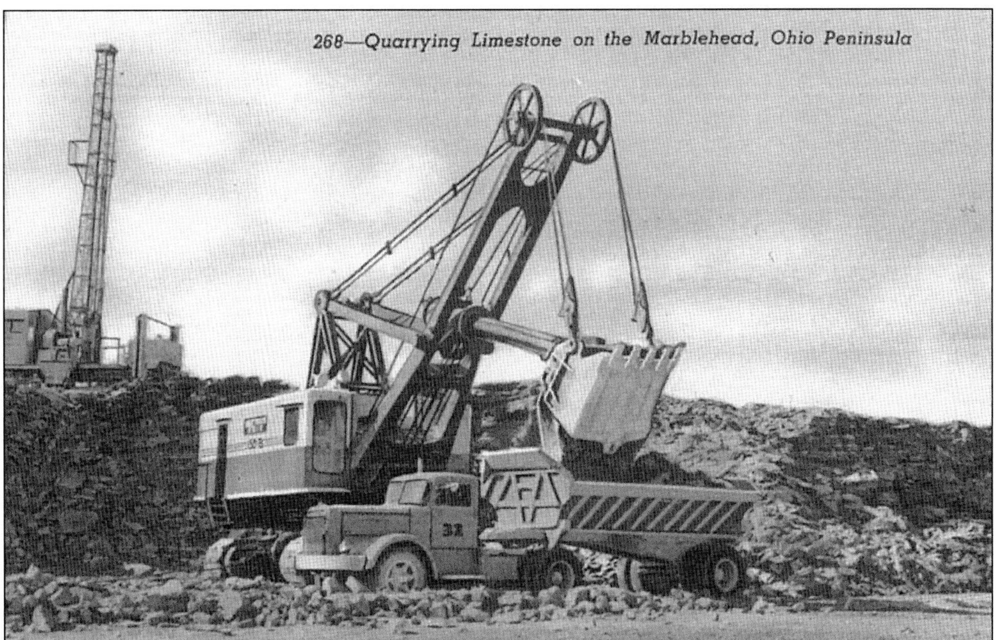

Limestone quarrying has been Marblehead's major industry since the 1830s. Quarrying was at its peak from around 1900 to the 1930s, when more than 1,300 people worked in the quarries. The industry is still active today, and the limestone loaders and conveyors work side-by-side with the boats ferrying tourists to Kelleys Island.

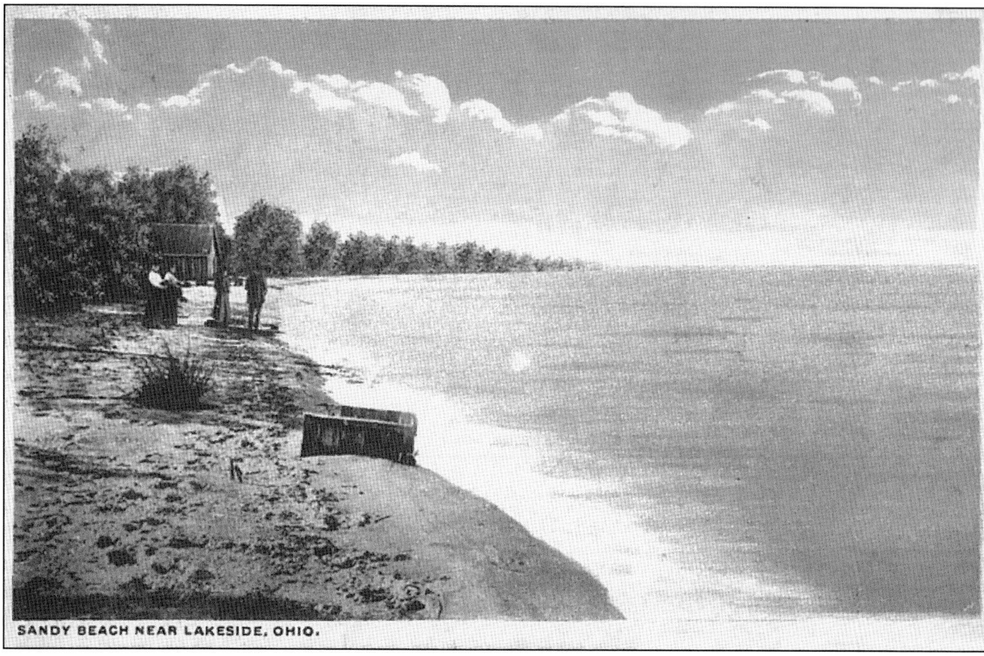

This stretch of sandy beach near Lakeside on Marblehead contrasts with the rocky shores that border the Lakeside grounds.

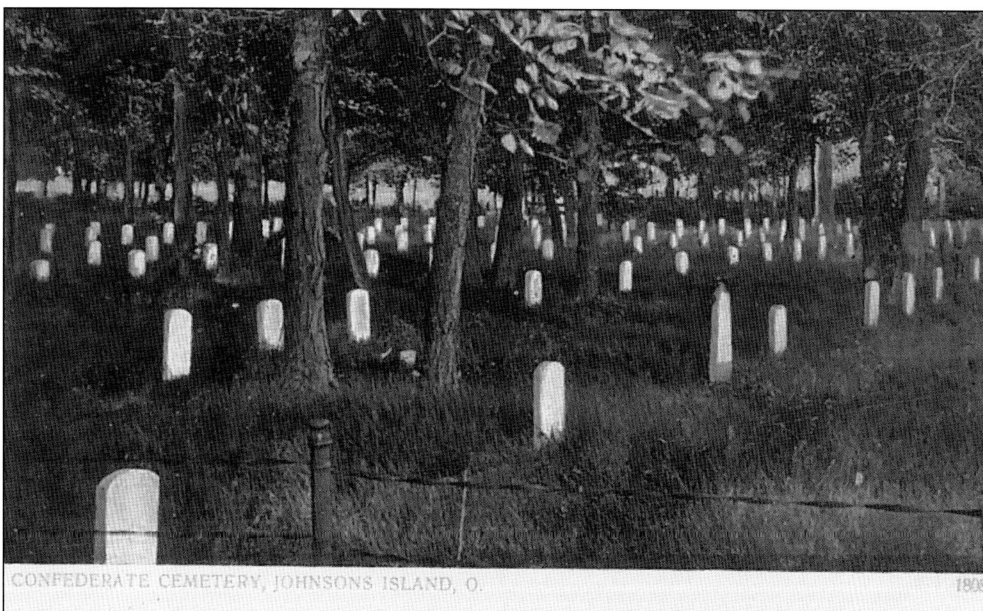

During the Civil War, Confederate officers captured by Union troops were taken to the prison on Johnson's Island off Marblehead. Conditions were harsh for the southerners during the long Ohio winters, and a number of the prisoners perished. Today the Confederate Officers Cemetery, on the prison site, is maintained by the Daughters of the Confederacy and looks much the same as it did in this view from 1906.

Five

Vermilion, Sandusky, and the Firelands

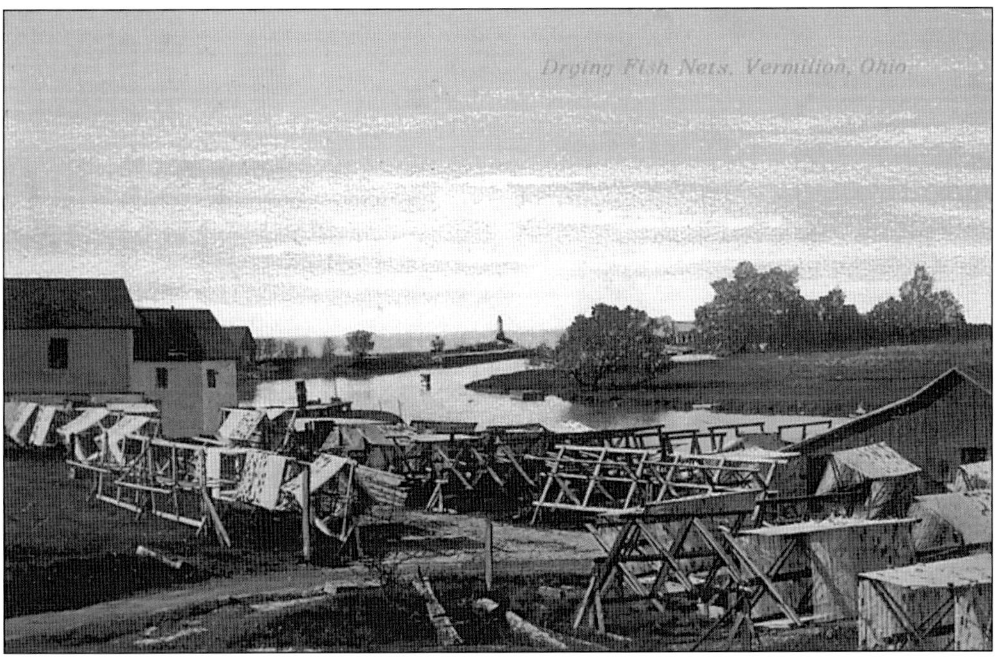

Vermilion began as a fishing village in the 1820s, and the fishing industry anchored Vermilion's economy into the 1930s. During the prime years of 1890 until 1945, a number of commercial fish companies operated out of Vermilion. The last, Kishman's, closed in the early 1980s. In this 1912 scene, fishnets dry along the Vermilion River.

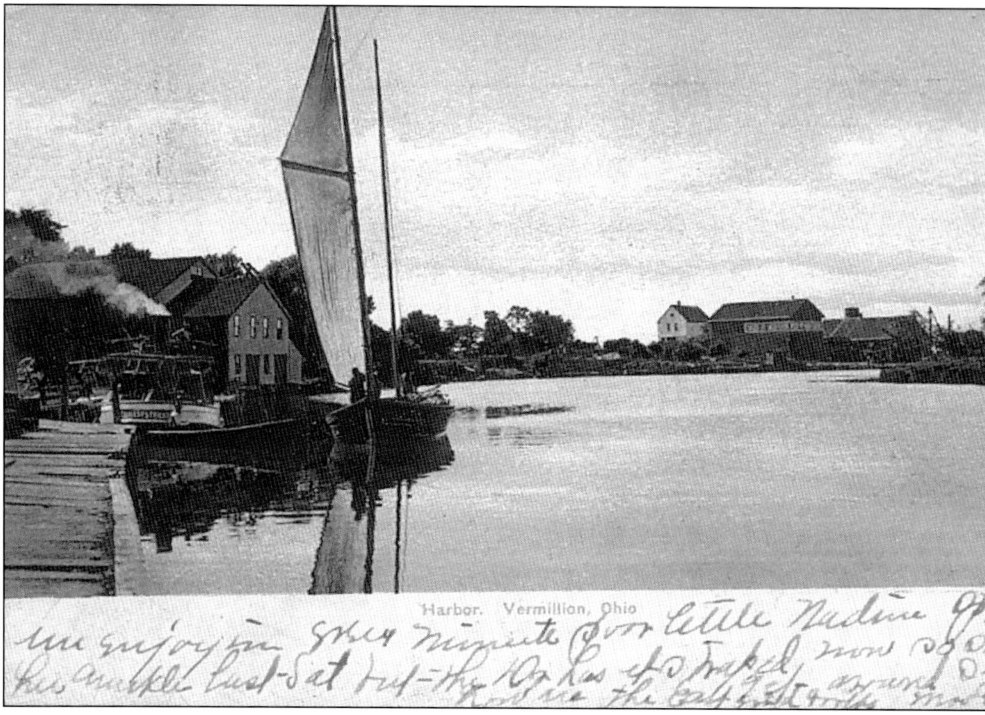

This view shows the Vermilion harbor in 1909. The steam tug emerged around 1900 as the champion in harvesting perch, pickerel, whitefish, herring, trout, and other delicacies from the lake. The tug *Charles P. Stricker*, visible at left, dates to 1892 and was part of the fleet of the Edson Fish Company.

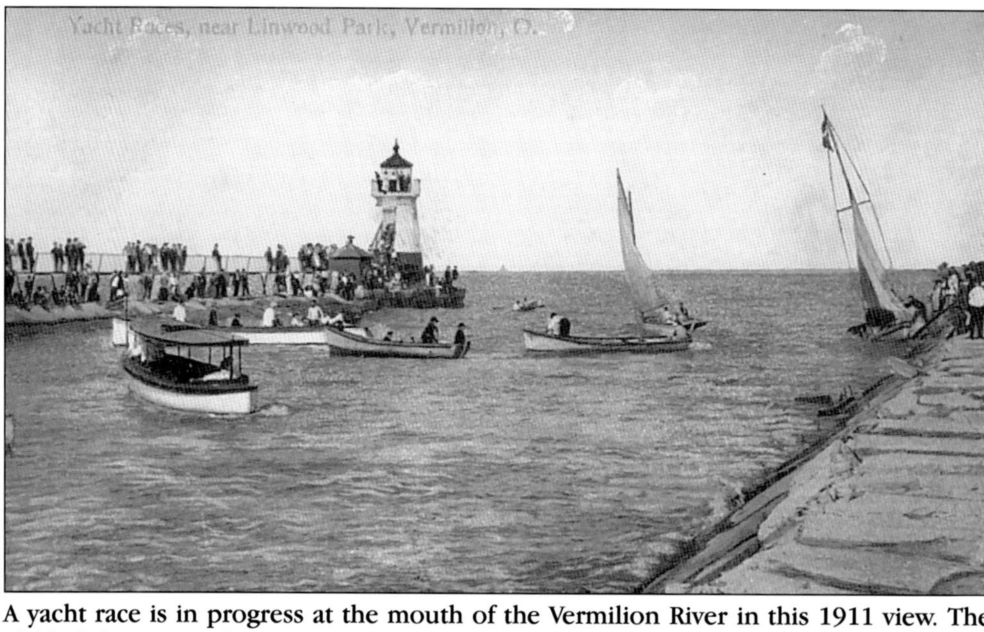

A yacht race is in progress at the mouth of the Vermilion River in this 1911 view. The old lighthouse on the pier was originally built in 1847, rebuilt in 1859 and 1877, and dismantled in 1929. A replica stands today at the Inland Seas Maritime Museum.

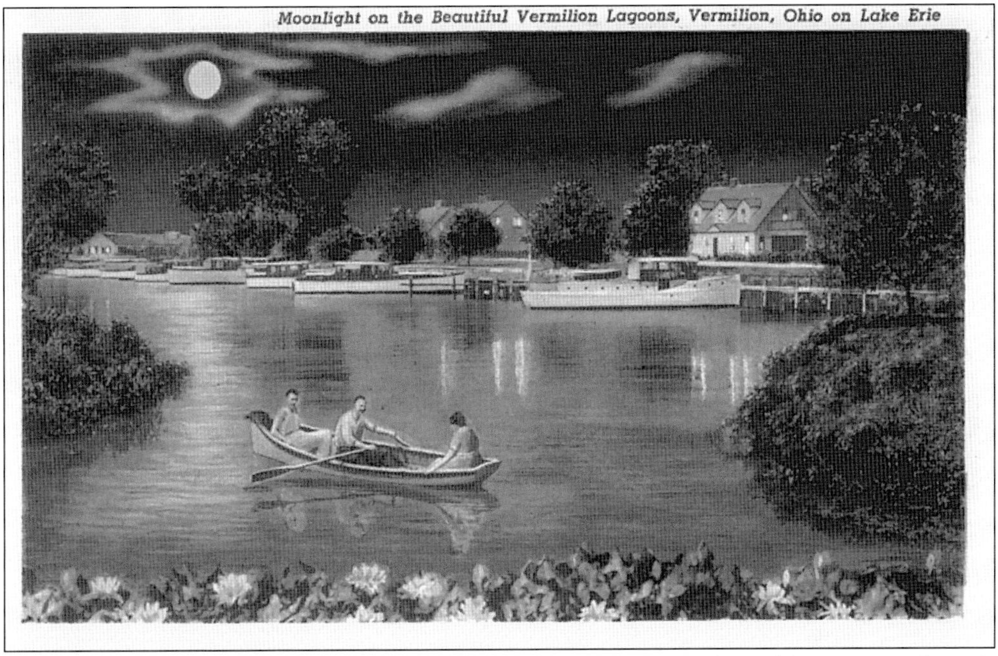

The Vermilion Lagoons feature New England-style white, clapboard houses, each with a dock, set on a network of picturesque waterways. The Lagoons project was begun in 1931 by Cleveland contractor Louis Wells as a means of keeping his workmen busy during the Depression. The lagoons were dredged and many of the homes were built during the 1930s. Today's residents of this exclusive area would be amused to know that the original homebuyers were often referred to as "swampdwellers," and were thought to be somewhat loony for wanting to live on these canals.

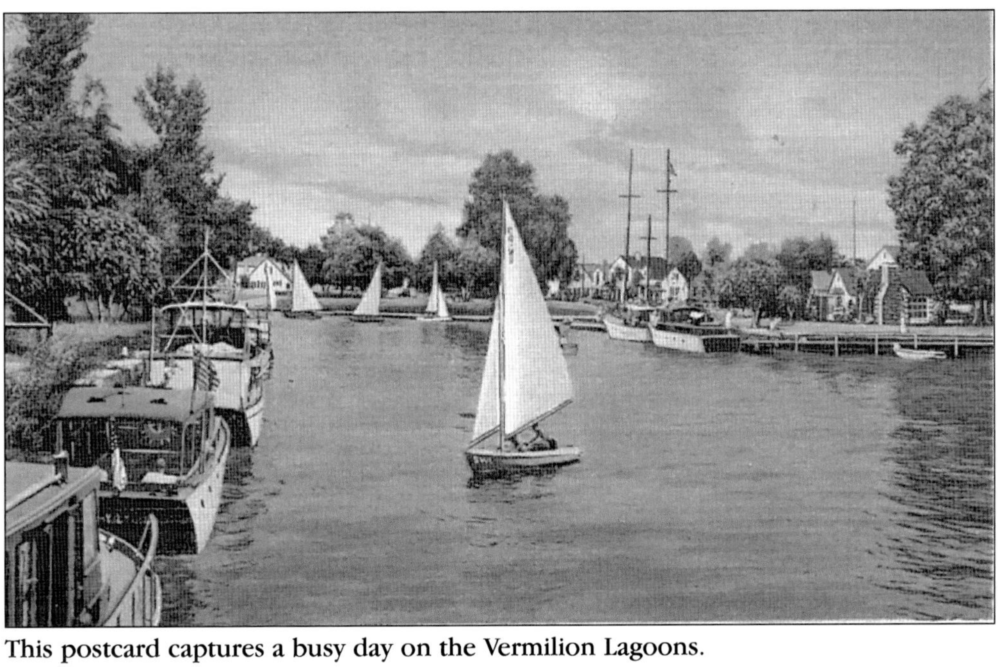

This postcard captures a busy day on the Vermilion Lagoons.

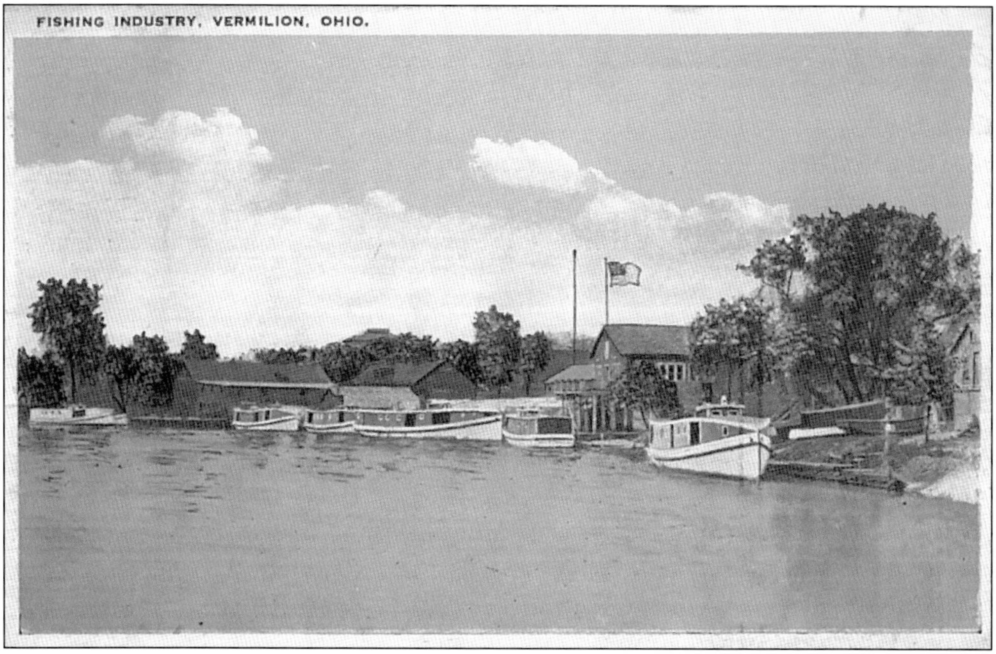

The abundance of fish in Lake Erie made fishing the livelihood of a great portion of the Vermilion population until well into the 1930s. In this 1925 scene, fishing boats are docked at the Kishman Fish Company, the large building at the left.

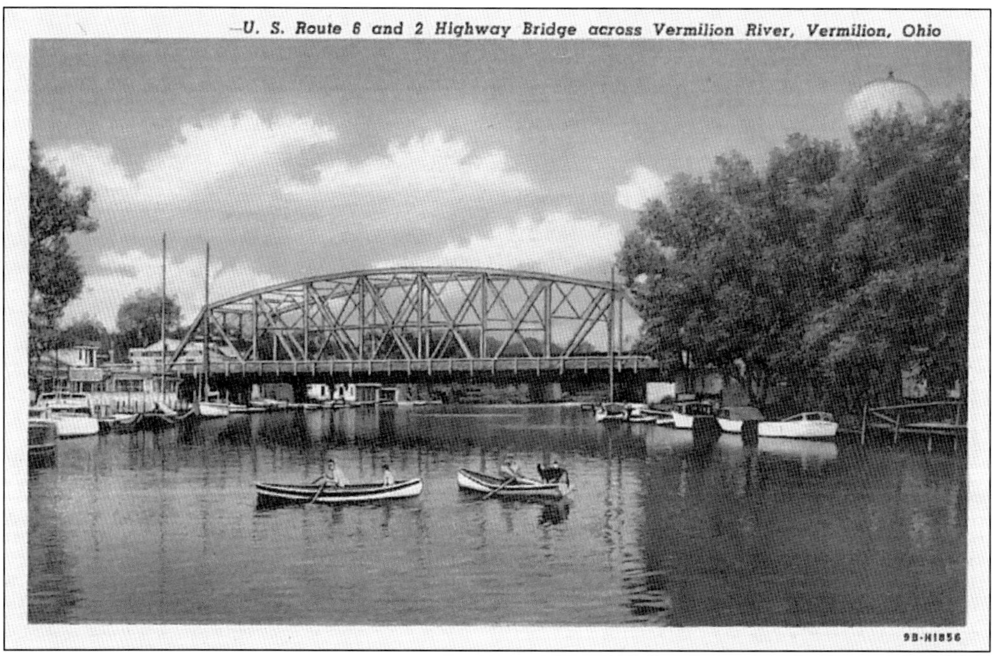

Canoers paddle in front of the old iron bridge spanning the Vermilion River. McGarvey's Restaurant is located at the far left.

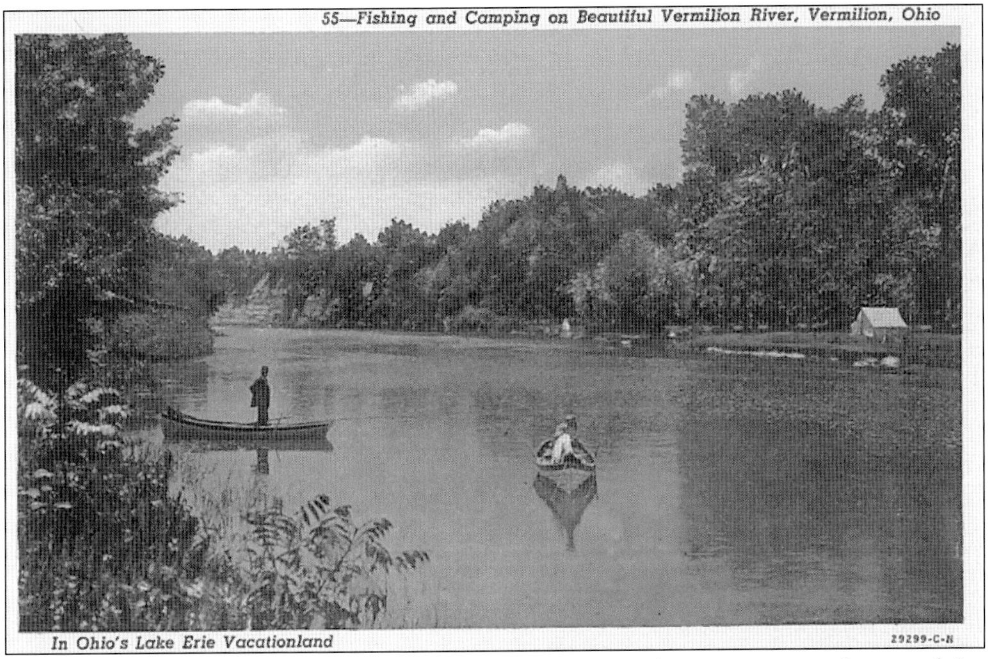

Fishing was a popular pastime on the Vermilion River. The picturesque shores of the river feature cliffs alternating with flat "bottomlands."

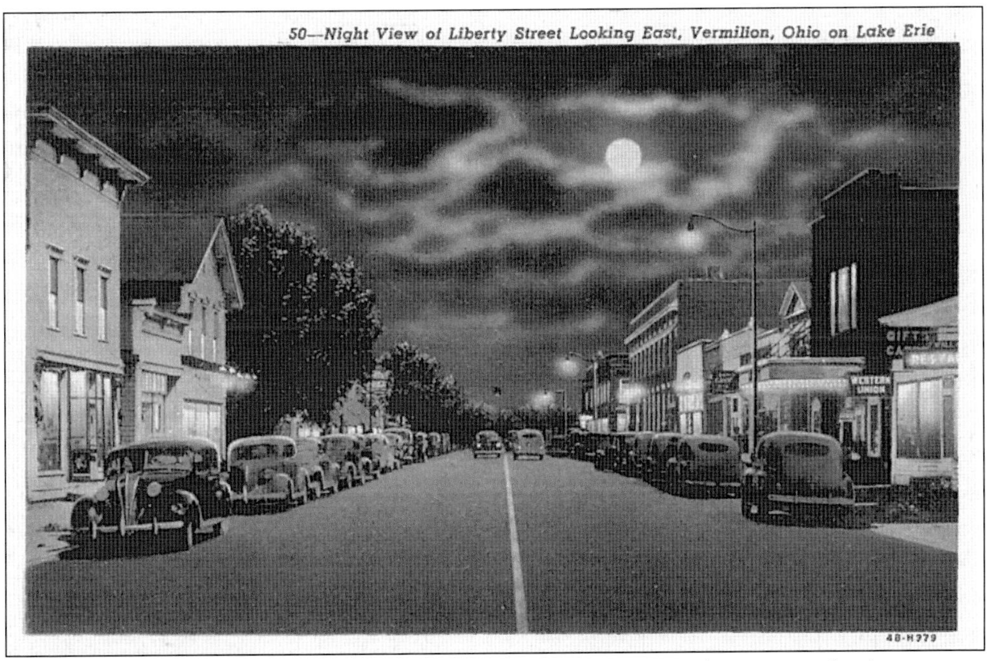

Downtown Vermilion was aglow in this moonlit 1940s view looking east down Liberty Street.

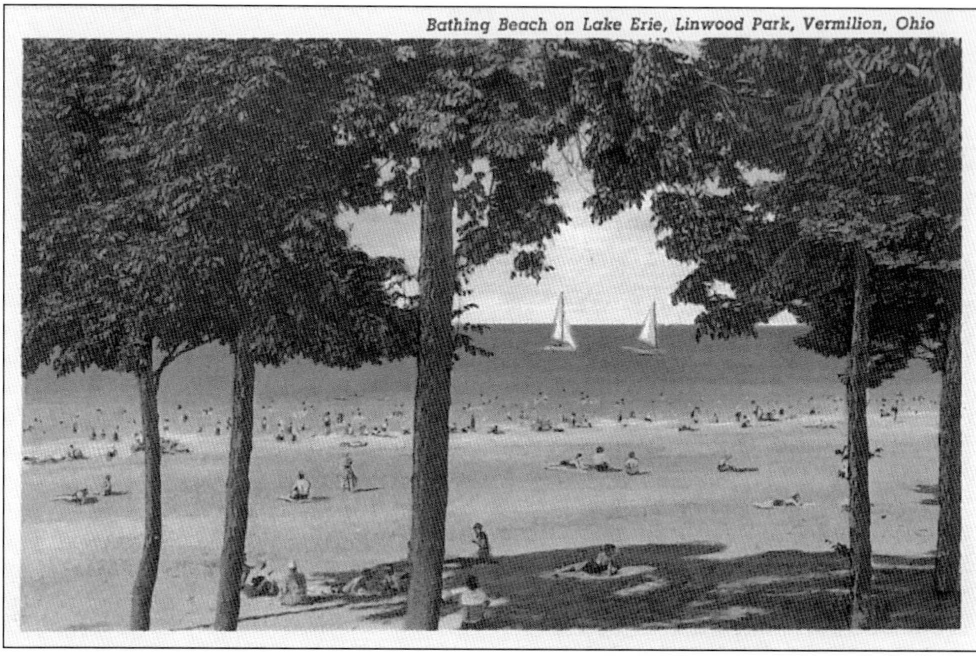

Linwood Park, named for its Linden trees, dates to 1884 when it operated as a summer family resort. The wide sandy beach, delightful summer cottages, and shady grounds continue to attract those seeking peaceful, religious-oriented vacations. The grounds have been described as "A Suburb of Heaven," and even as "Heaven Itself."

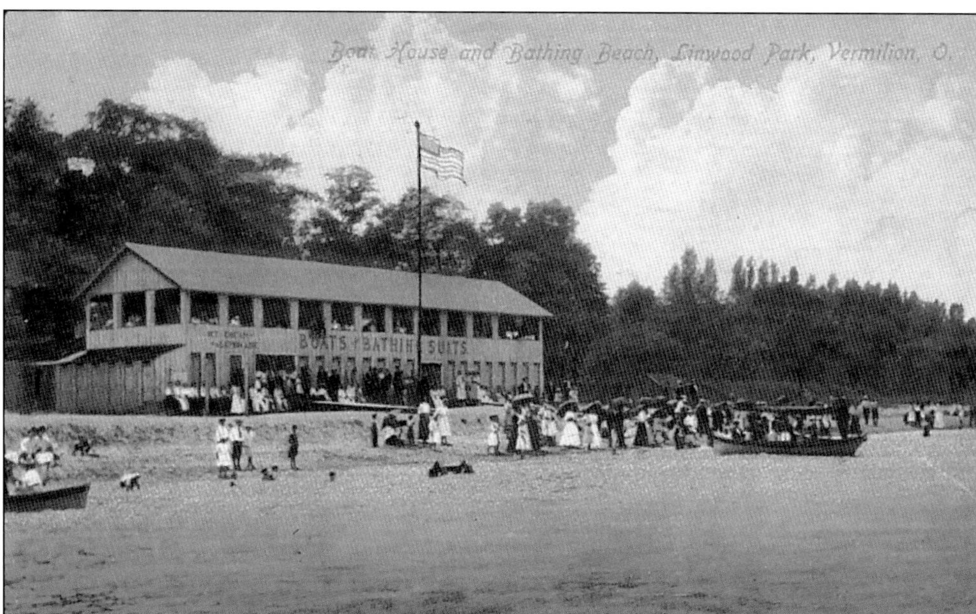

This 1909 scene shows the bathhouse and bathing beach at Linwood Park, with vacationers formally dressed in skirts and trousers.

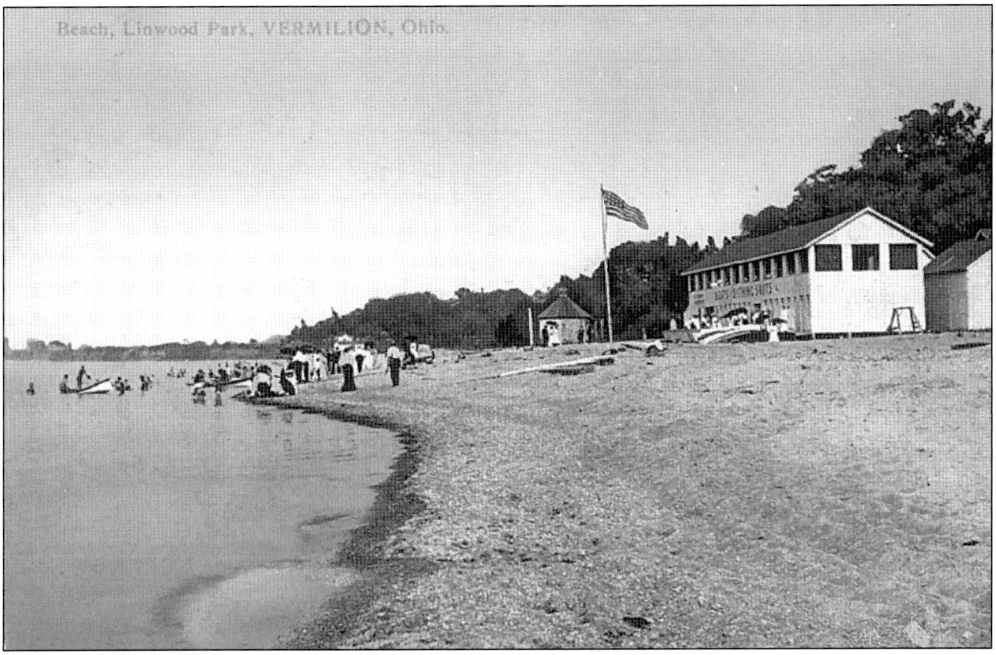

The message on this postcard from Linwood Park reads, "Going for a launch ride now, then bathing & rowing & dancing. Jolly time."

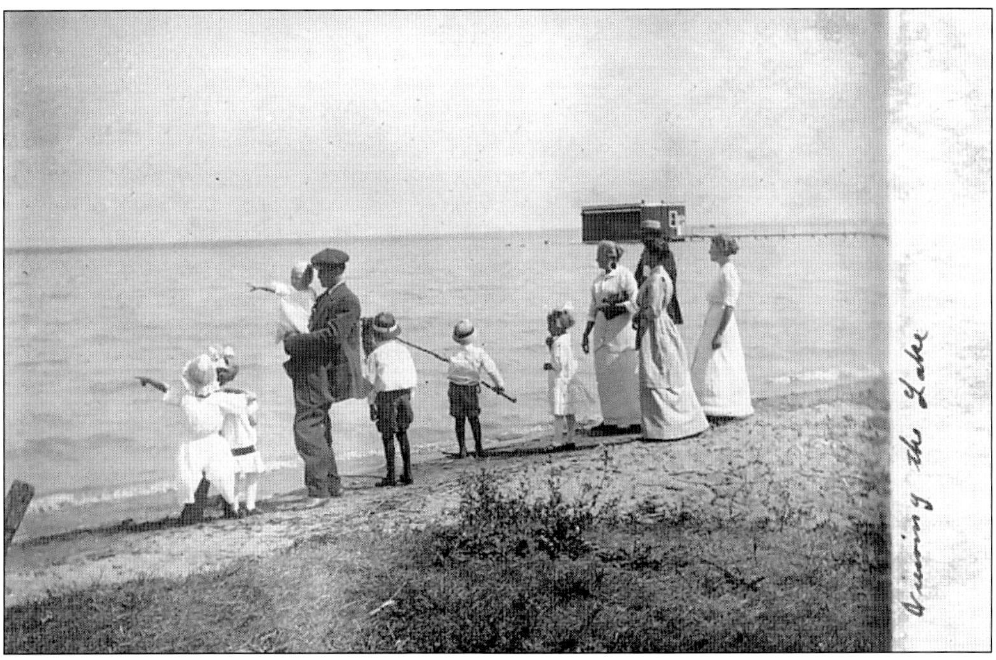

This postcard features a Victorian family "Viewing the Lake," as the handwritten caption reads. Apparently made especially for the family, the card lists the family members' names on the back, with the notation "at Lake Erie."

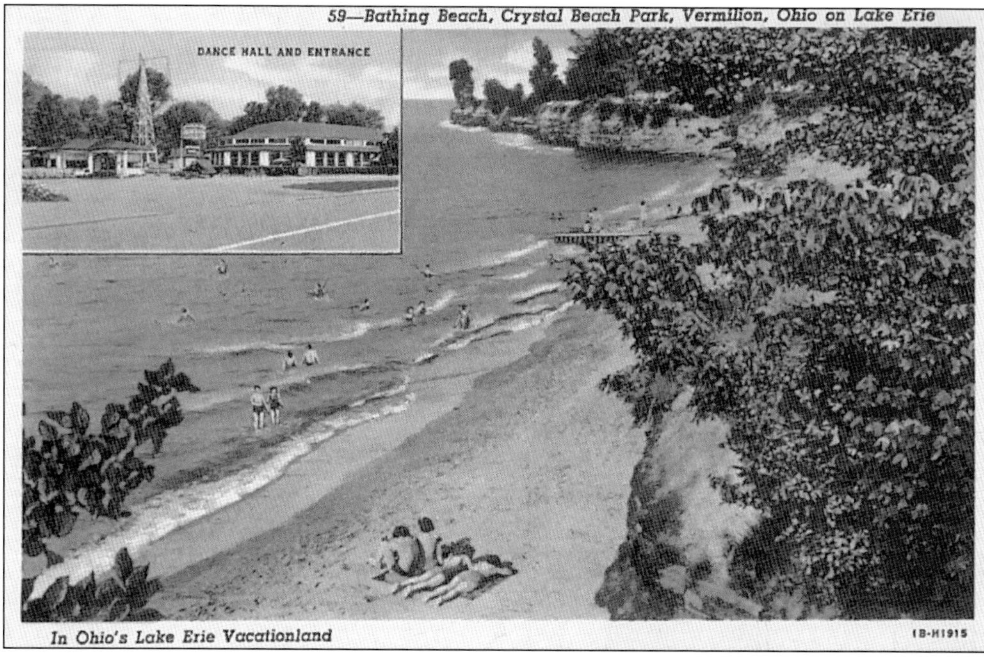

Crystal Beach Park originated in 1906 when George Blanchart purchased the former Shadduck Lake Park and renamed it after the "crystal-like" sand on the beach. The park featured a dancing pavilion, beer garden, merry-go-round, shooting gallery, bowling alleys, a toboggan slide into Lake Erie, and (of course) a wide sandy beach. The park closed in 1962.

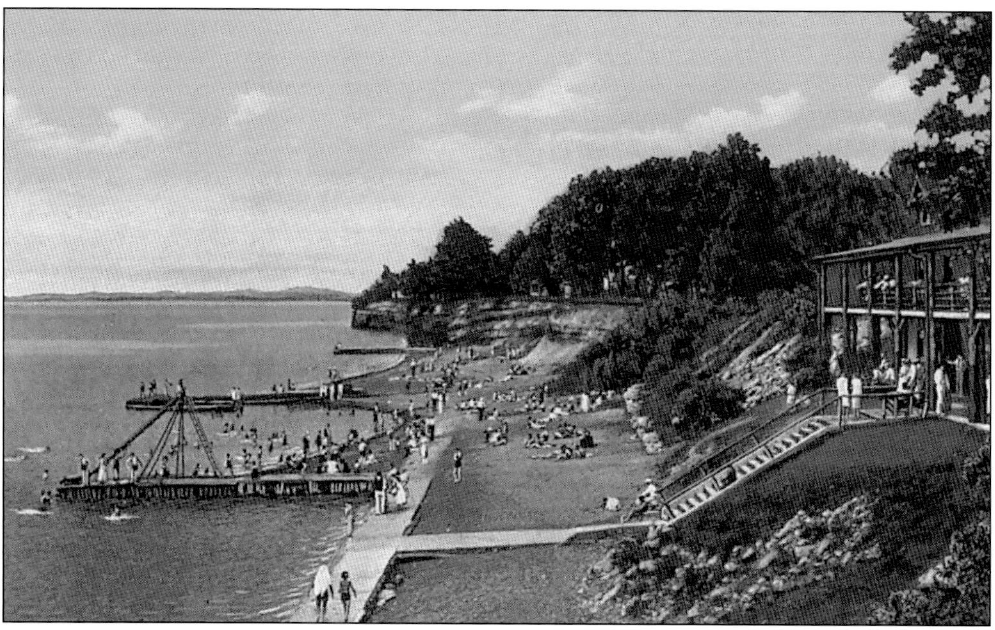

Vermilion-on-the-Lake, another popular beachfront attraction in the early 1900s, even featured a boardwalk and waterslide.

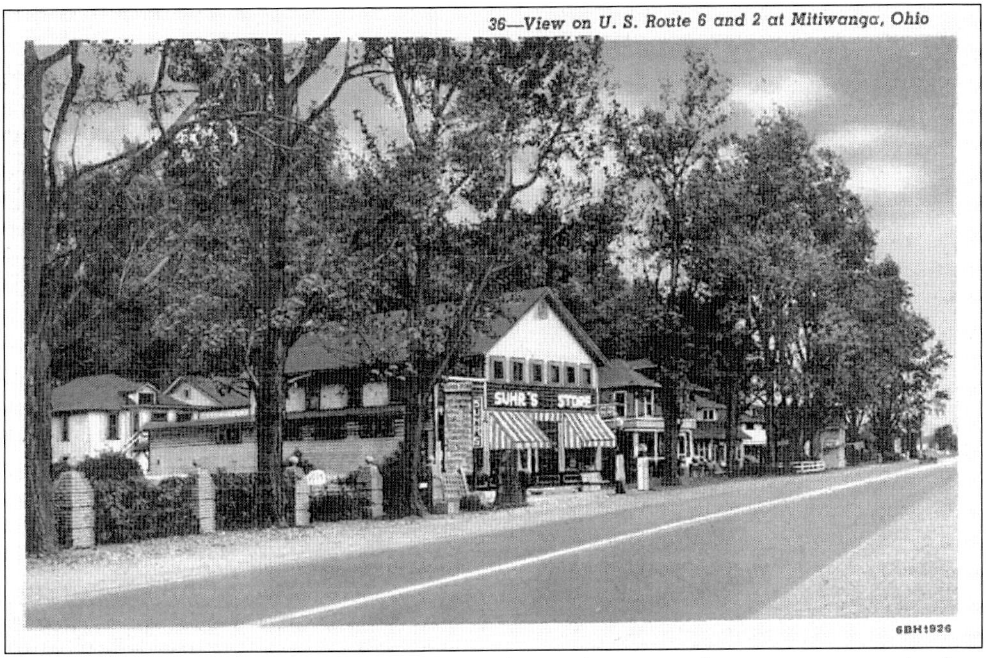

Mitiwanga, along the Lake Erie shore west of Vermilion, is no longer a town entity, but most of the pictured structures still exist.

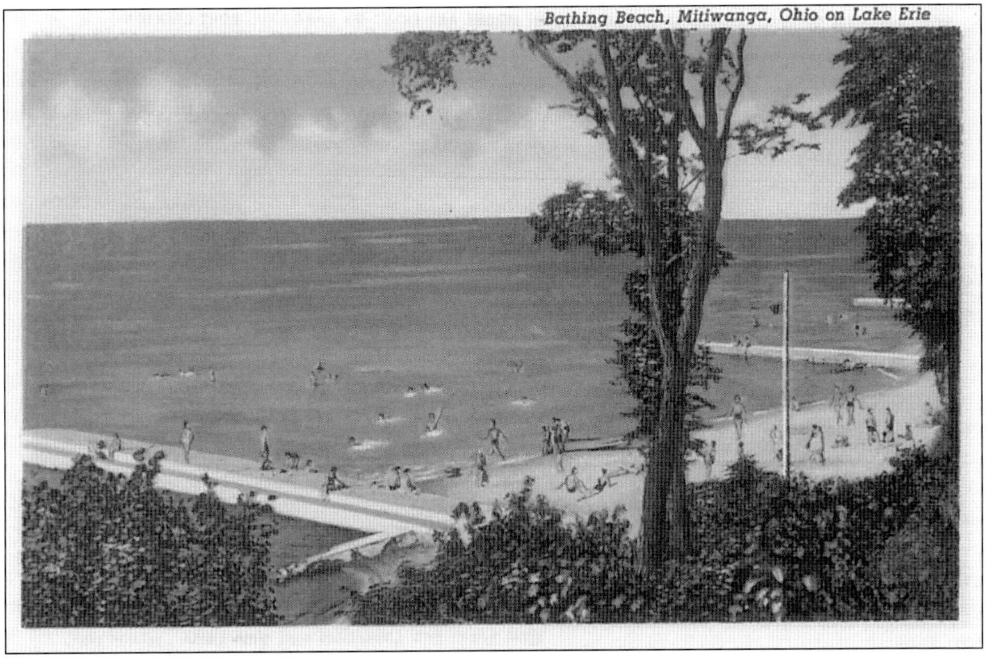

Bathers crowd the beach at Mitiwanga in the 1940s.

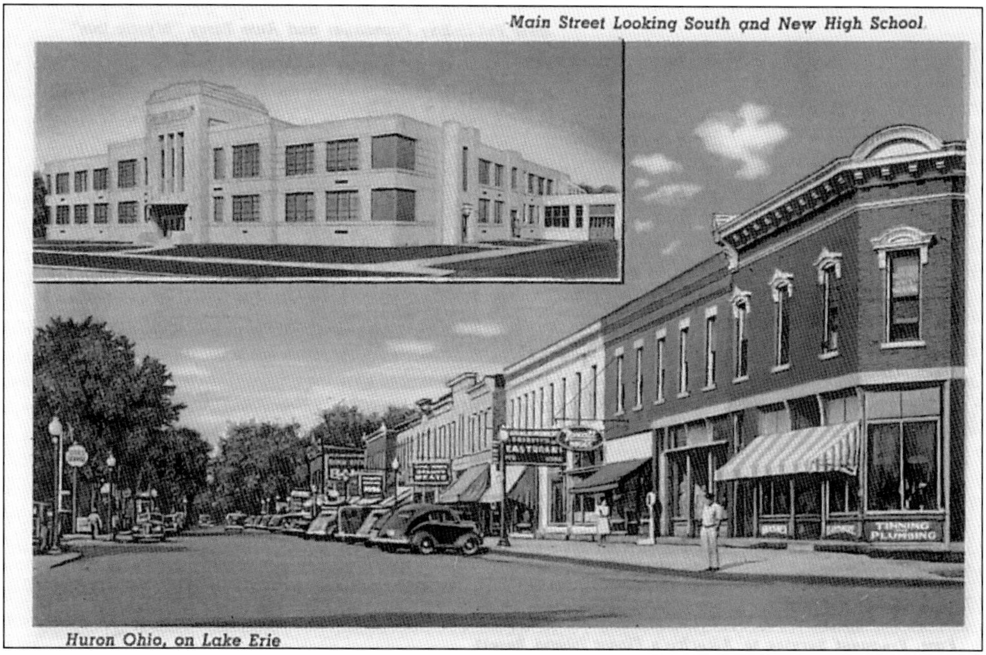

Downtown Huron, Ohio was a thriving place in this 1940s view. The entire downtown area was razed in the early 1960s, a victim of urban "renewal."

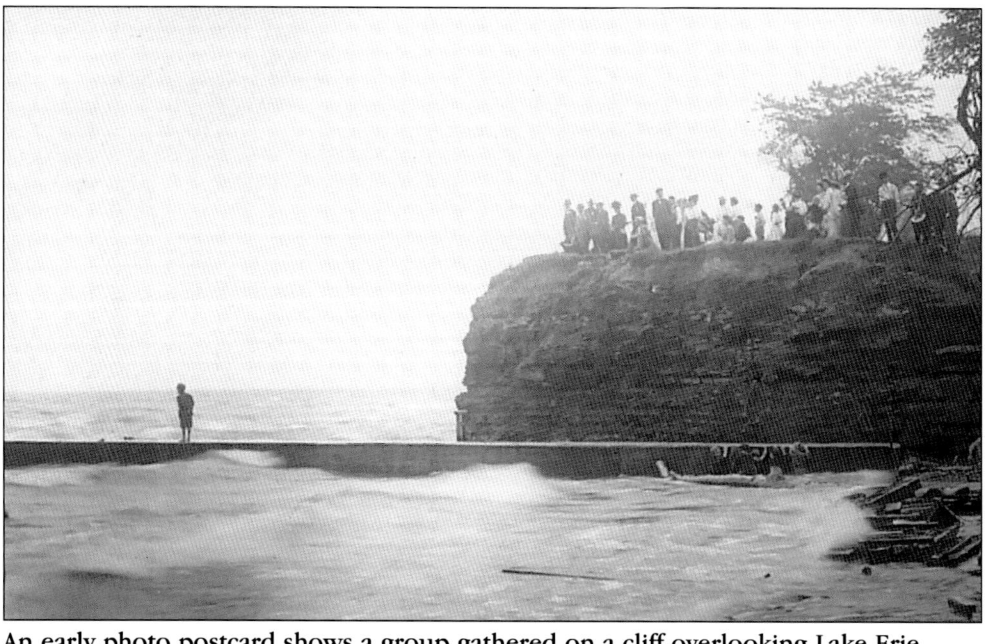

An early photo postcard shows a group gathered on a cliff overlooking Lake Erie.

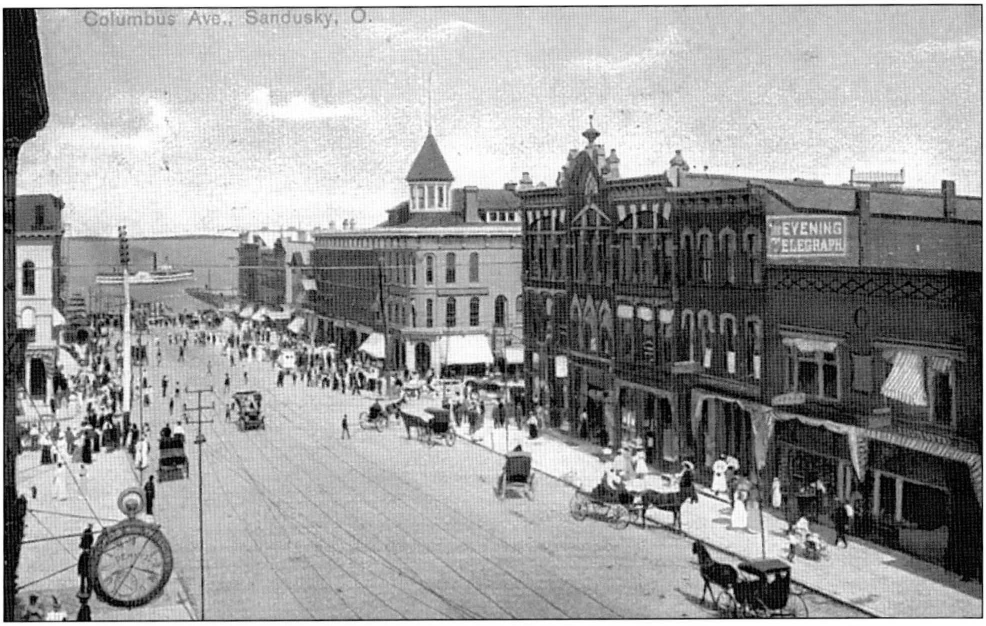

Horse-drawn carriages and lake steamers were the primary means of passenger transport in this 1915 look down Columbus Avenue in Sandusky. The clock shown at the lower left was hung outside the Henry Dehnel Jewelry Store, and was set in perpetuity at 8:20, as were all non-running clocks of that era.

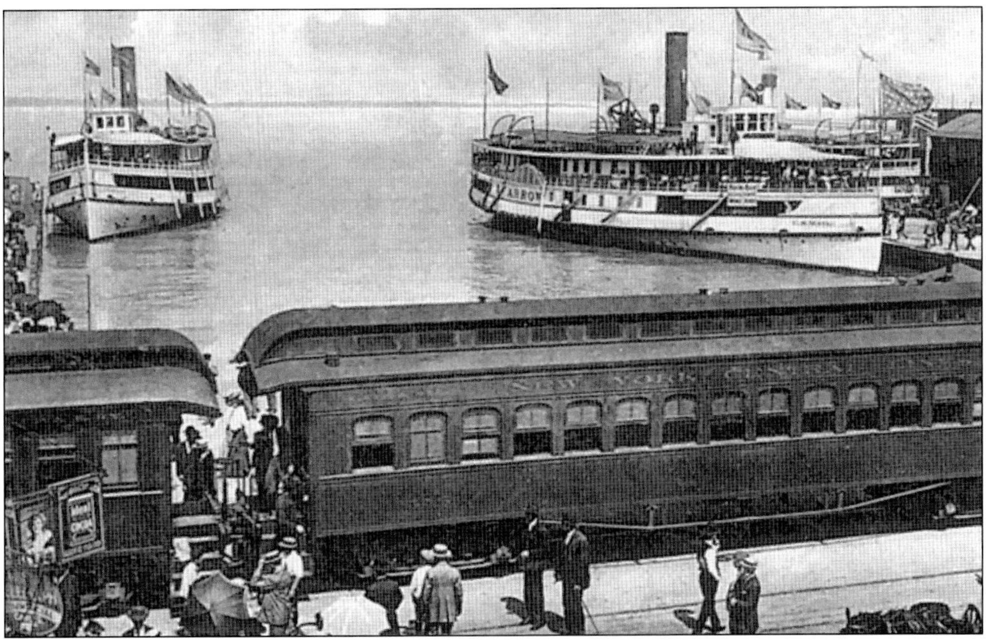
In this view, passengers are shown disembarking from a New York Central train at Sandusky landing to board the *Arrow* steamer to Put-in-Bay. The rail and steamboat lines teamed to provide dependable transportation for excursionists to the islands and Cedar Point. The *G. A. Boeckling*, which ran to Cedar Point, is visible on the left.

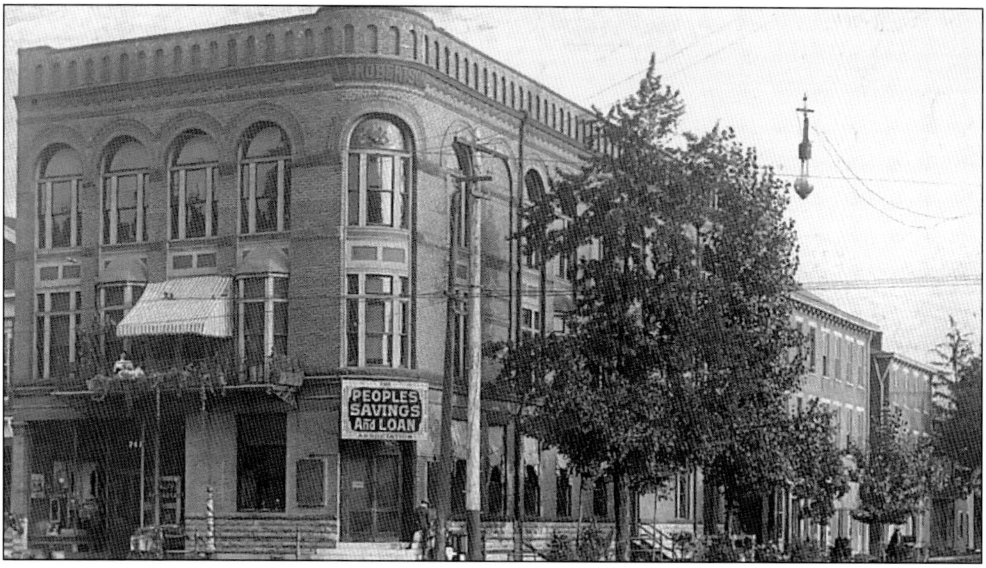

Banking institutions, such as the Savings and Loan in downtown Sandusky shown here, were pillars of the town economic structure in the early 1900s. Note the early street lamp at the top right.

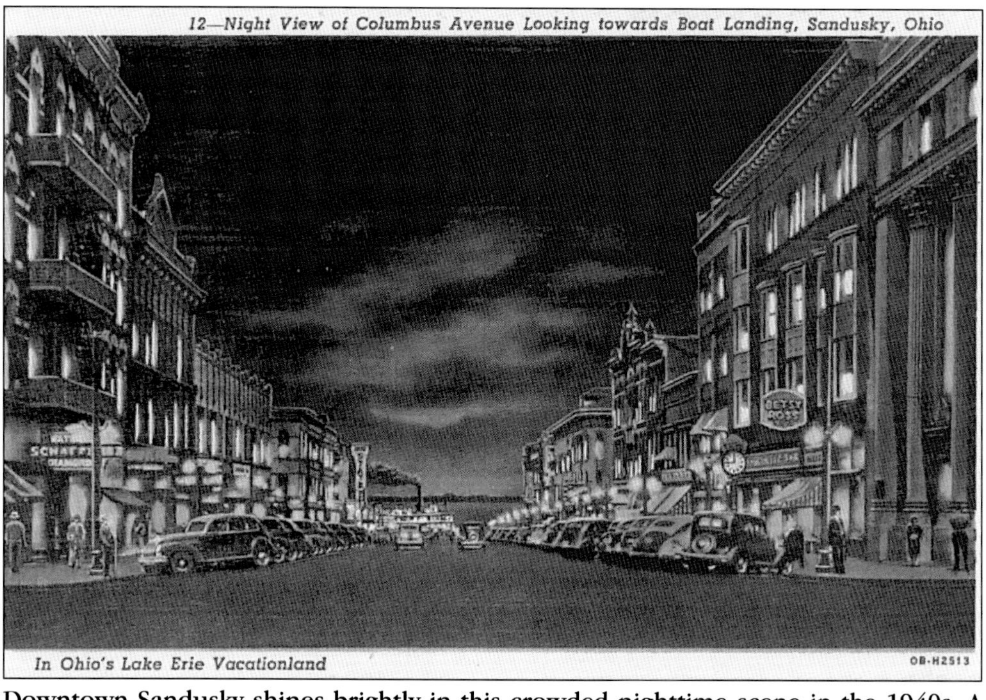

Downtown Sandusky shines brightly in this crowded nighttime scene in the 1940s. A steamship can be seen at the dock in the distance. Sandusky today has preserved most of its original downtown, and a walking tour identifying historic buildings is available.

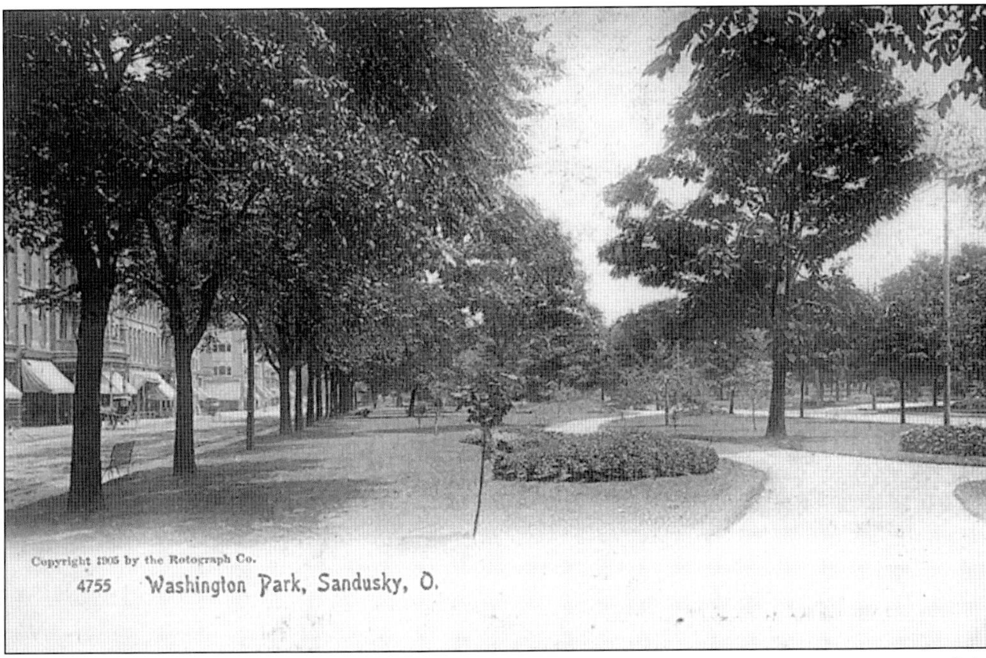

Washington Park, Sandusky's beautiful downtown oasis, is an extensive green area laid out with walkways, formal gardens, exotic plantings, and shade trees. Only the horse carriage on the left disrupts its peaceful visage in this 1905 view.

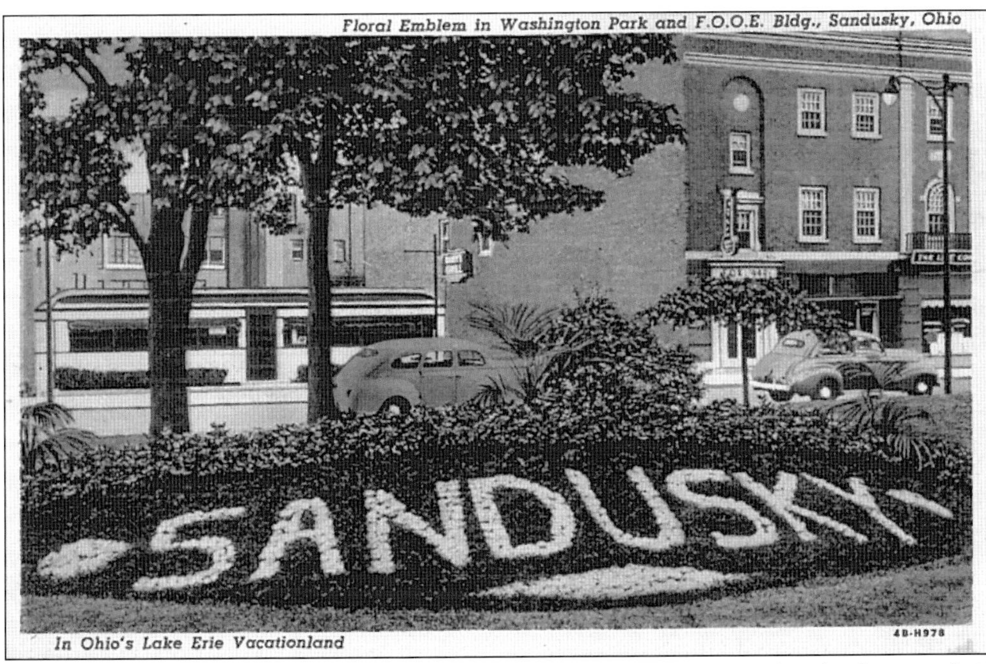

This plant sculpture spells out the name of the city. In the background is the F.O.O.E. Building.

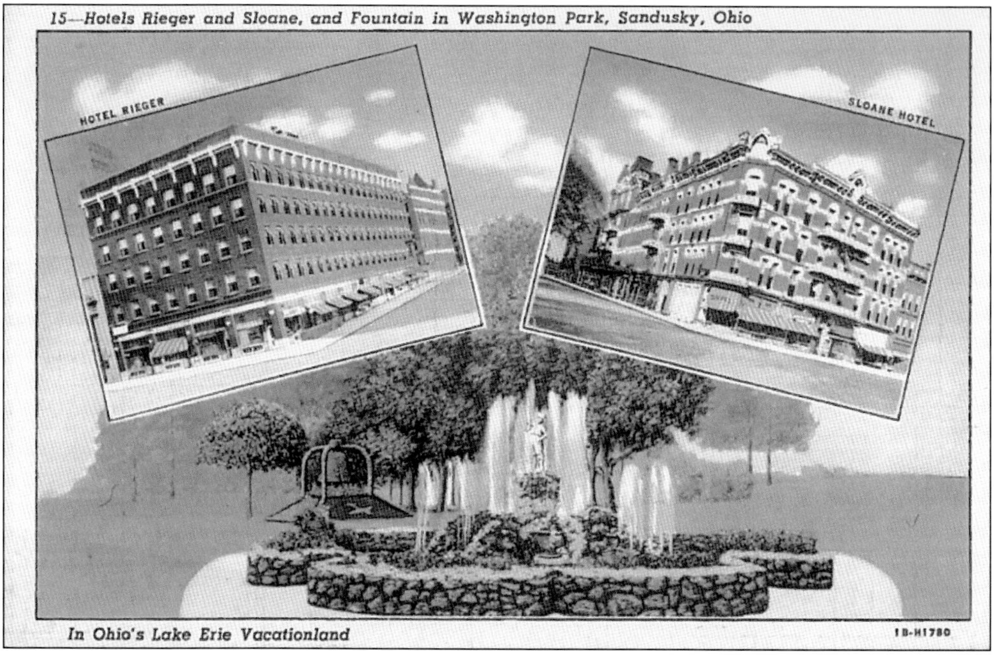

Sandusky's proximity to area attractions, it excellent harbor with steamship and rail connections, and its status as the metropolis of the region made it a popular overnight stop for tourists. Sizable downtown hotels, such as the ones shown, were built to accommodate the influx of visitors.

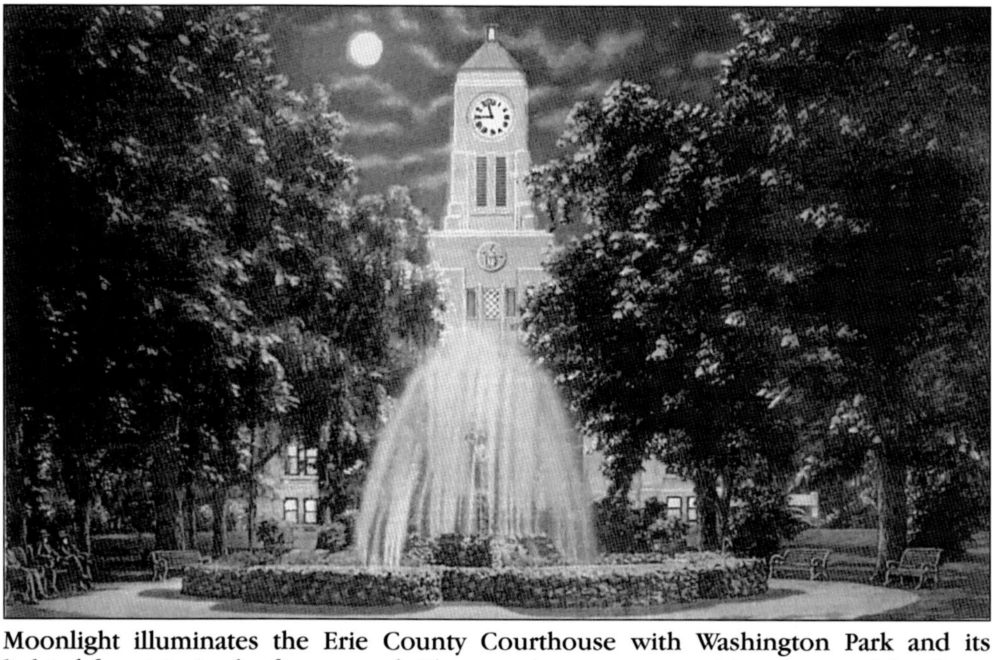

Moonlight illuminates the Erie County Courthouse with Washington Park and its lighted fountain in the foreground. The courthouse was considered one of the finest public buildings anywhere in the country when it was completed in 1874. It underwent extensive renovation in 1936 as part of a WPA project.

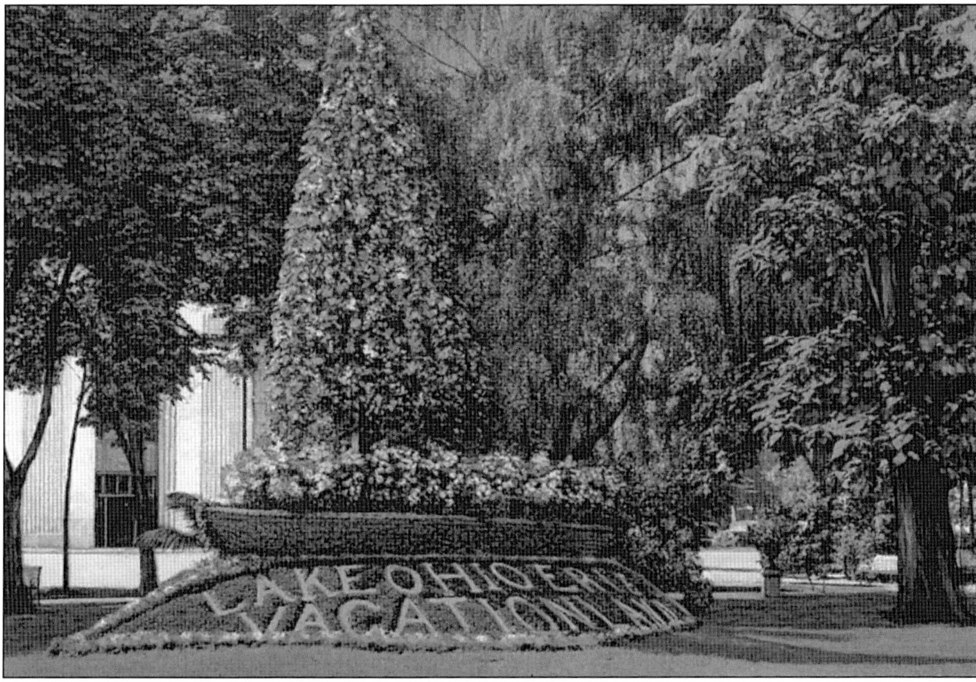

Formal plantings were popular at Washington Park in the 1940s. This elaborate sculpture celebrates Sandusky's location in the heart of Ohio's Lake Erie Vacationland.

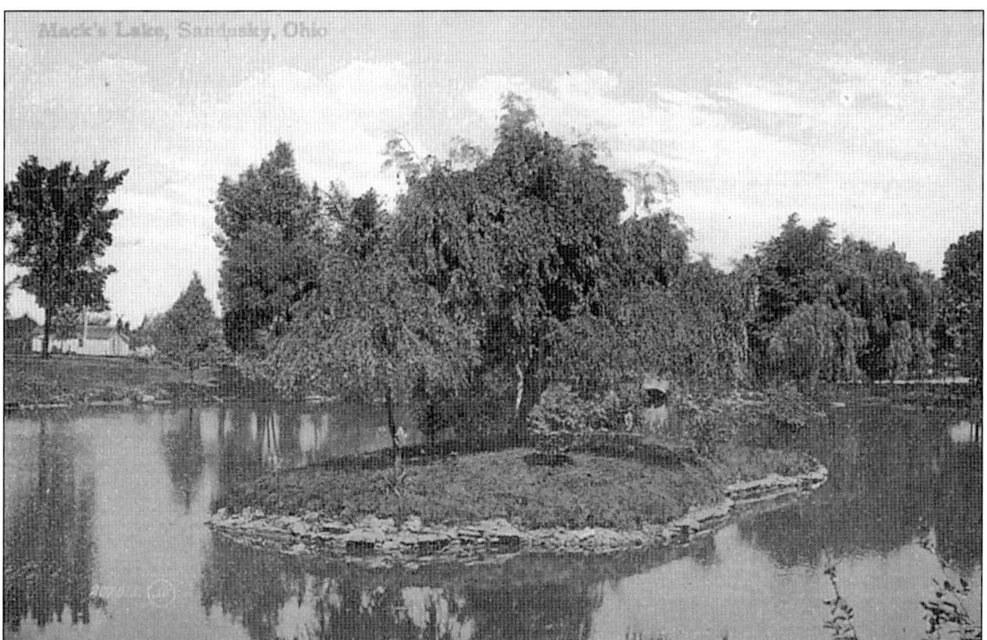

Mack's Lake in Sandusky is pictured in this 1910 scene.

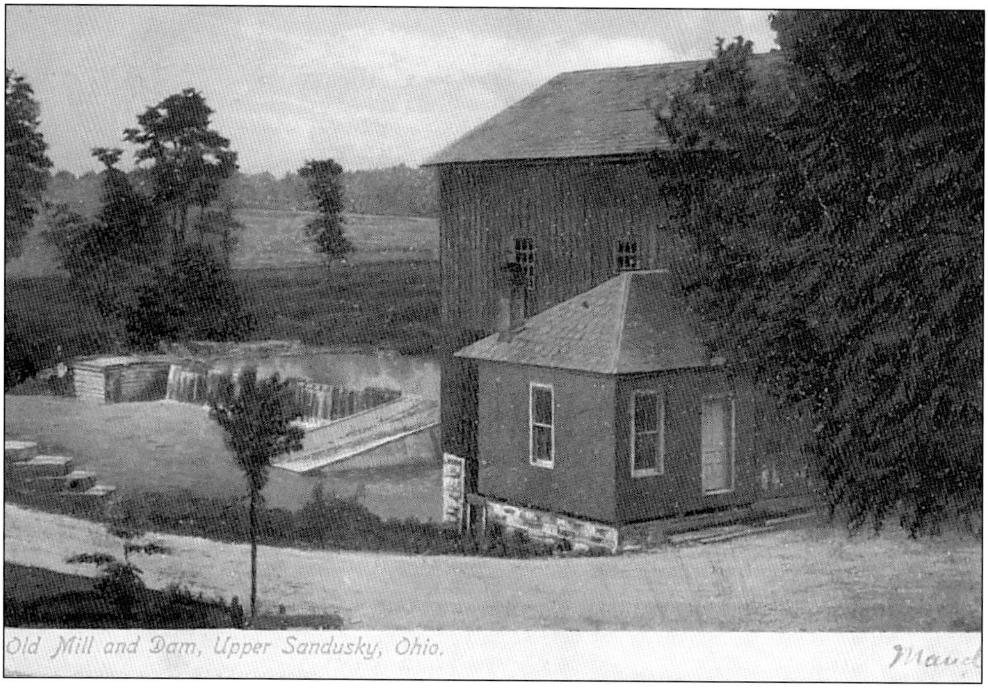

The Sandusky River, which flows from the west end of Sandusky Bay south through the Firelands, offered a number of attractive mill sites. Here are two mills, one at Tiffin (below) and the other in Upper Sandusky (above). The waters of the river powered grain mills, sawmills, and other local manufacturing.

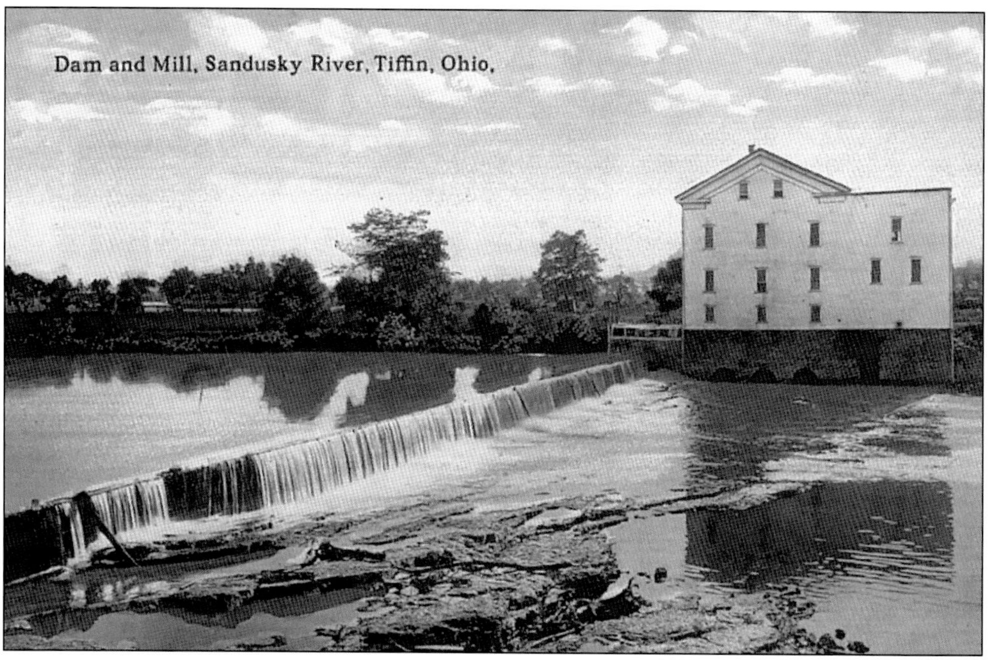

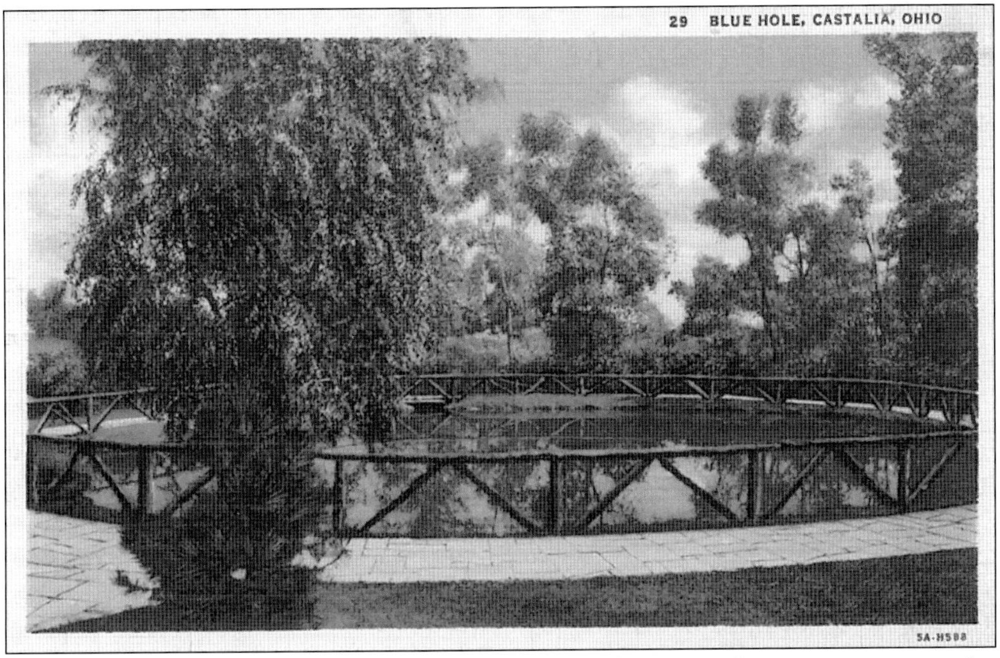

The Blue Hole, known for its "bottomless" pool and mammoth trout, was a popular area attraction until the 1990s, when it closed to become part of a trout club.

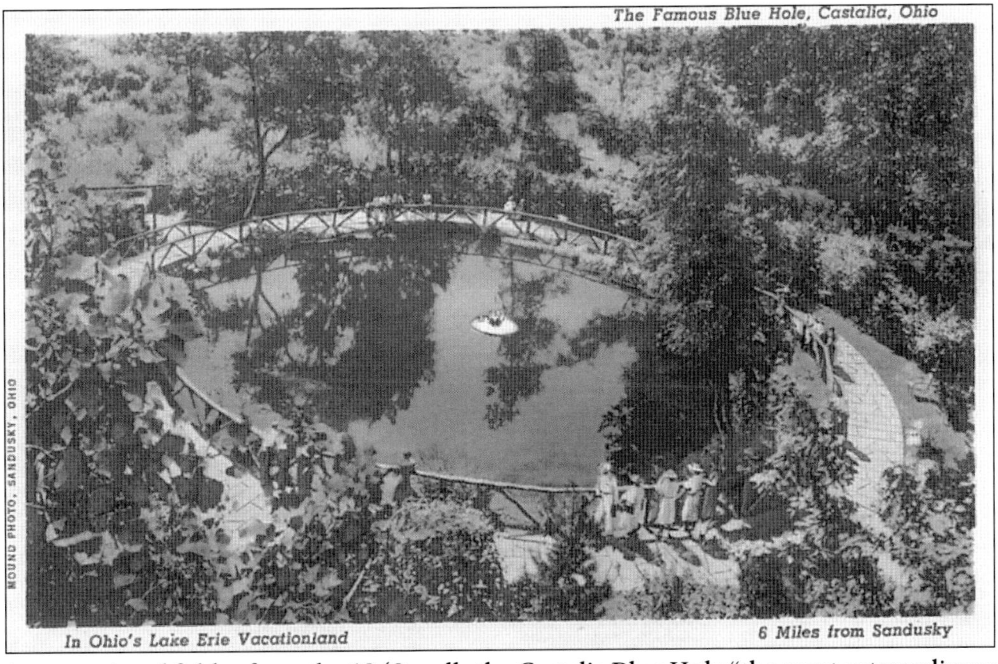

A promotional folder from the 1940s calls the Castalia Blue Hole "the most extraordinary artesian spring on the continent." It goes on to say that "visible depth is apparently 50 or 60 feet but actual depth and source are unknown. Seven million gallons of water flow daily from the spring, feeding a stream teaming with trout."

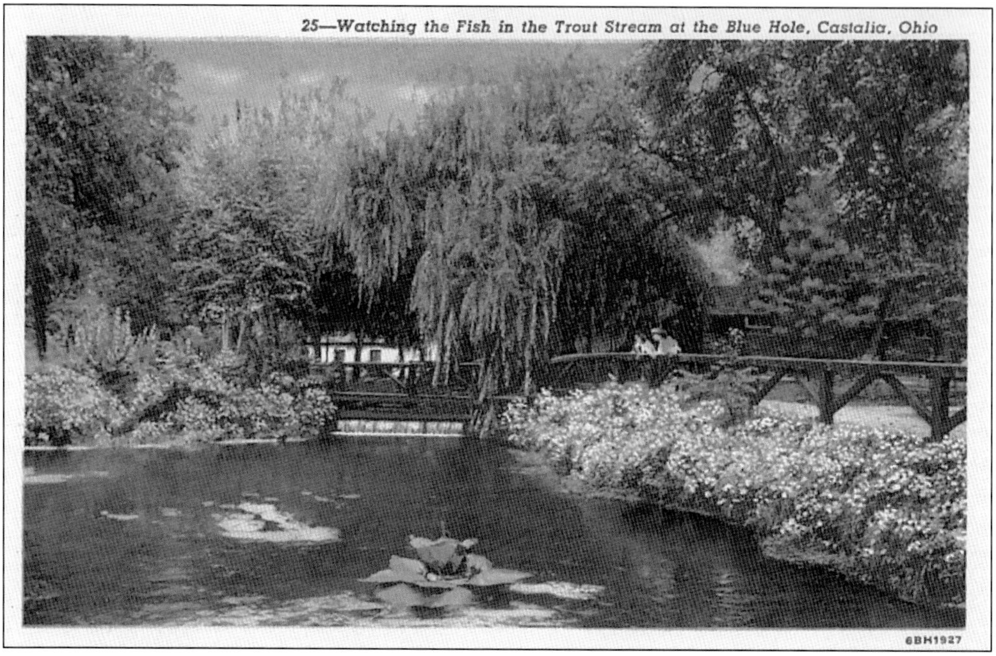

Beautiful grounds and a trout stream surround the Blue Hole, a longtime popular tourist attraction until it closed in the 1990s. According to the card, "Fish cannot live in the Blue Hole, as it is absolutely free from air or food." The water temperature was said to be 45 degrees year round.

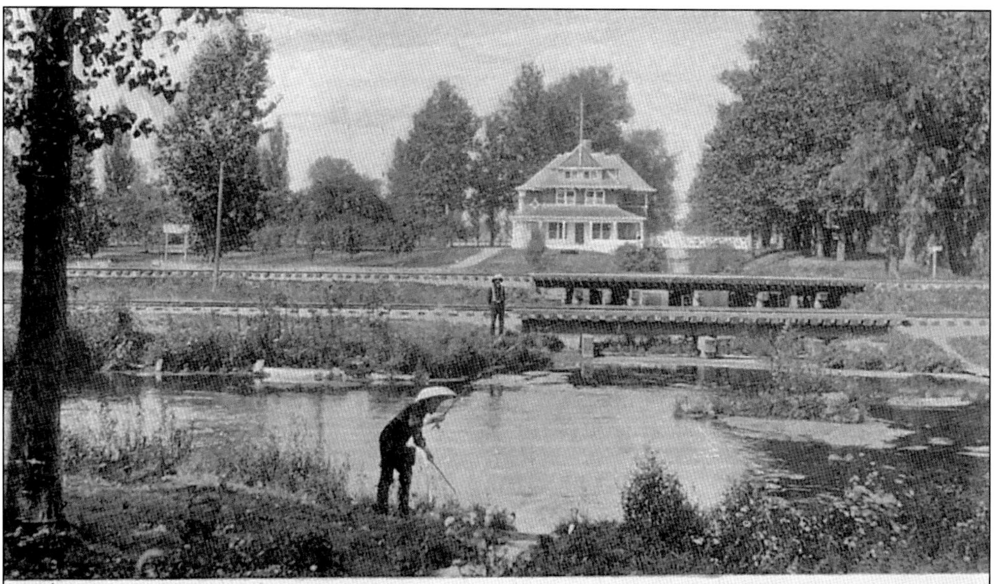

Fishing for trout at the area near the Blue Hole at Castalia in 1909.

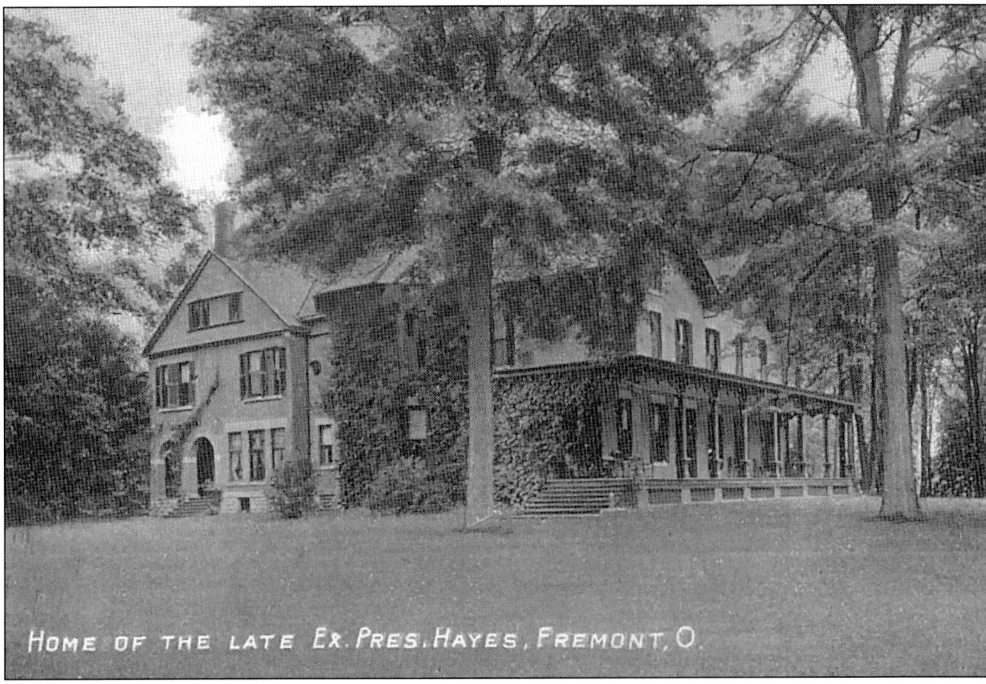

The Hayes Presidential Center in Fremont honors Rutherford B. Hayes, 19th president of the United States. The center features Spiegel Grove, the 33-room Victorian home of the president.

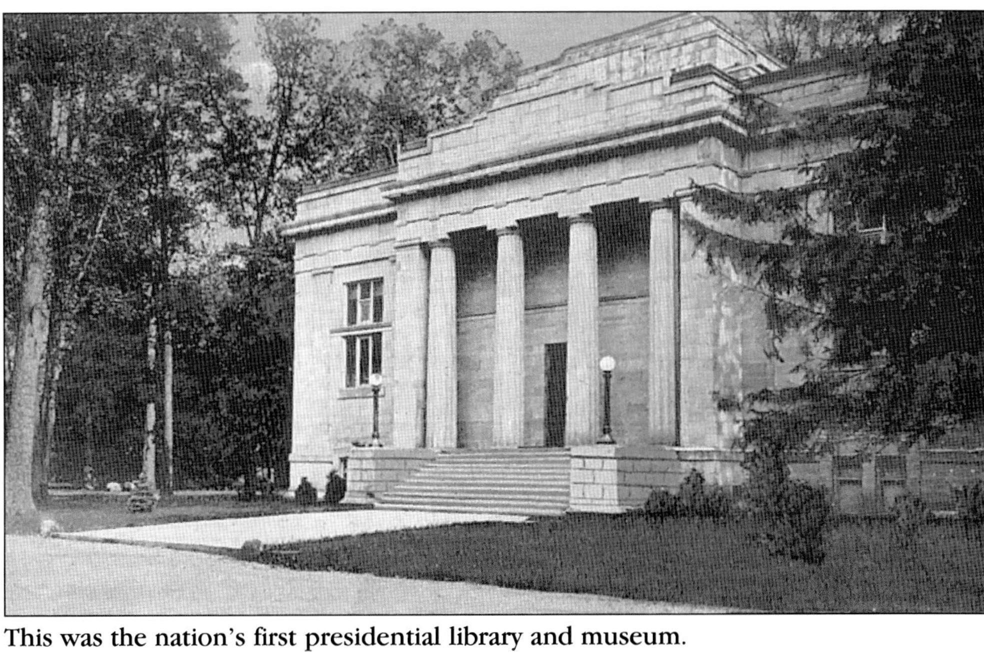

This was the nation's first presidential library and museum.

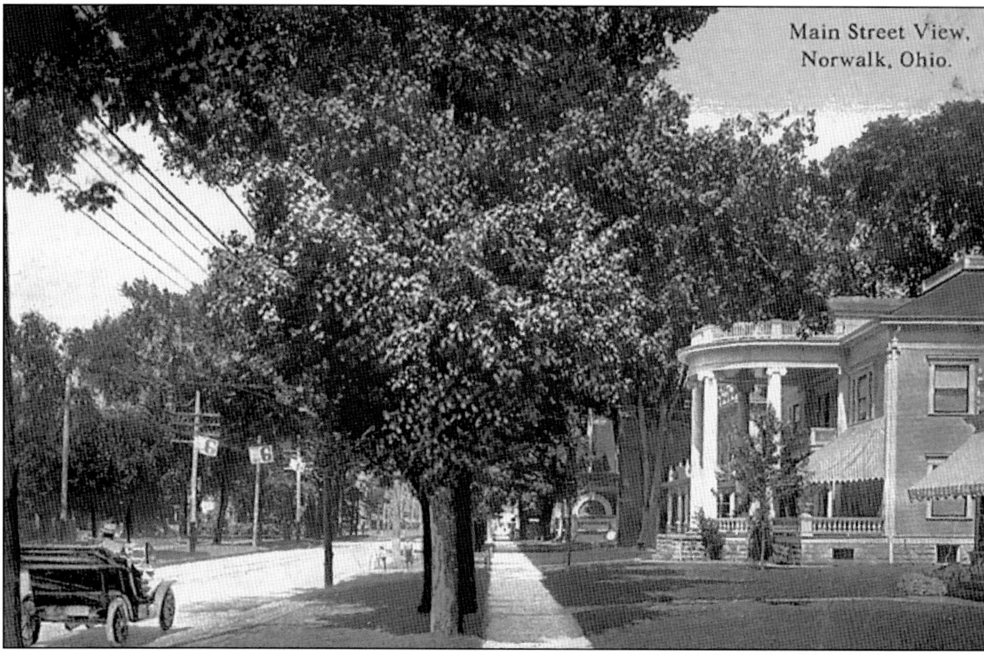

Stately homes line Main Street in Norfolk, home of the Firelands Museum. The region is known as the Firelands because land was given to New England settlers in the late 1700s as compensation for Revolutionary War fire destruction. As a result of settlement by these veterans and their families, many parts of the area have a classic New England look similar to the Western Reserve of Northeastern Ohio.

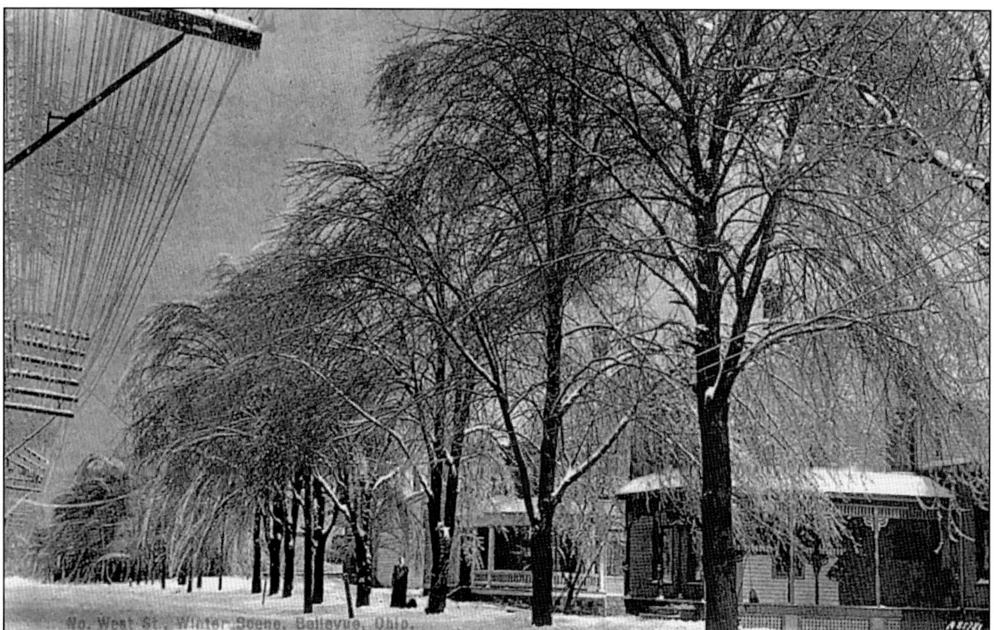

Winter often brought snow, ice, and downed power lines, as this scene at Bellevue, south of Port Clinton, shows.

Six

LAKE ERIE STEAMERS

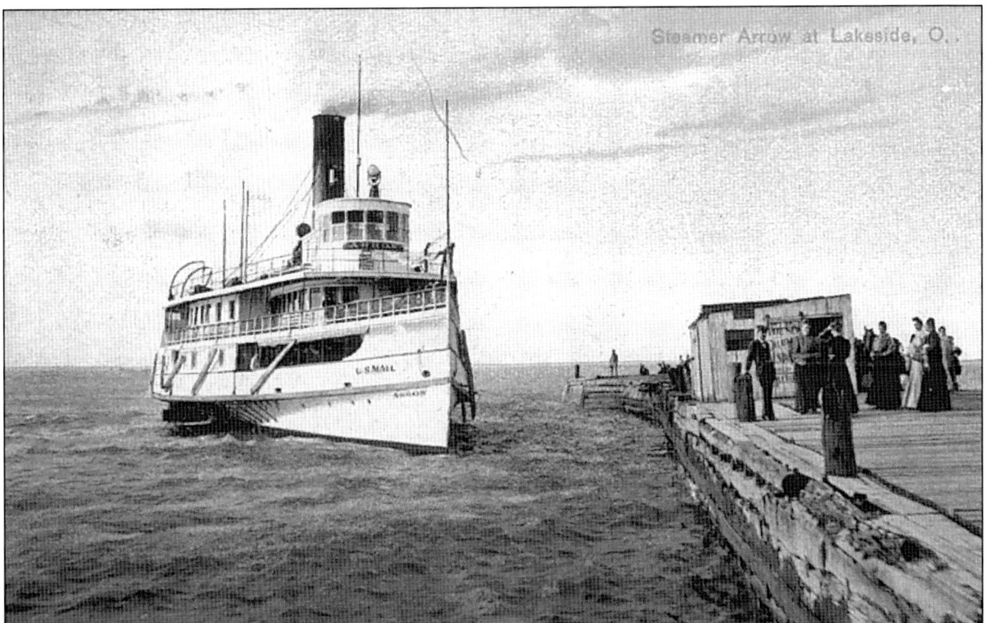

The steamboat *Arrow*, that offered service from Sandusky to Lakeside and Put-in-Bay between 1895 to 1922, is shown heading to the Lakeside pier. The *Arrow* burned at the dock in Put-in-Bay on October 14, 1922.

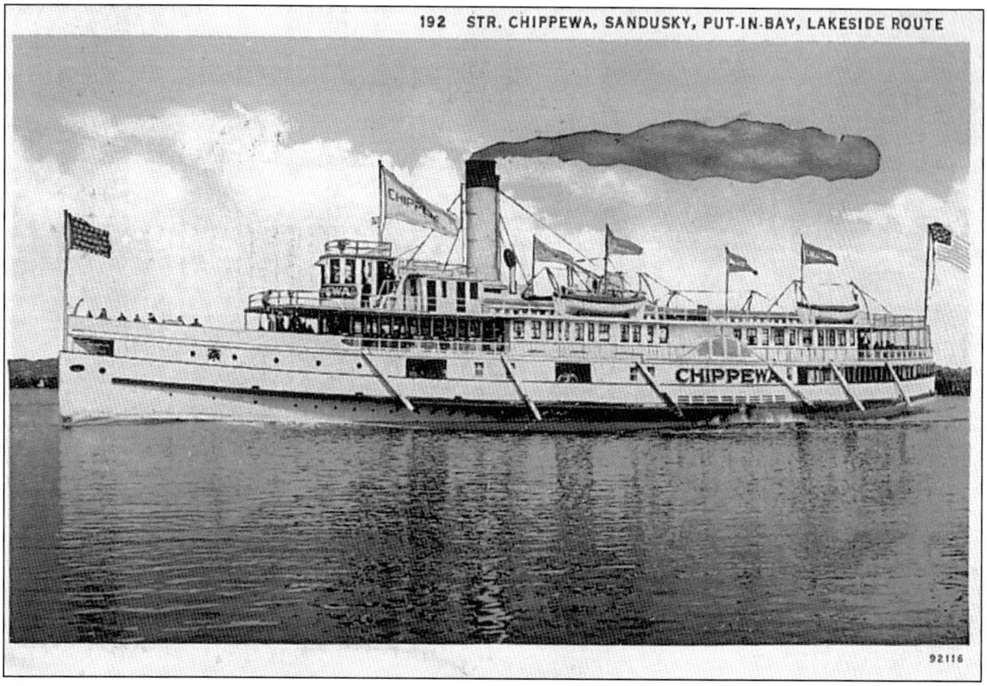

After fire destroyed the *Arrow* in 1922, she was replaced by the *Chippewa*, built in 1884 as a U.S. revenue cutter. The boat was converted to a passenger steamer in 1908 and began the Sandusky–Put-in-Bay–Lakeside route in 1923. The *Chippewa* provided passenger service until 1938.

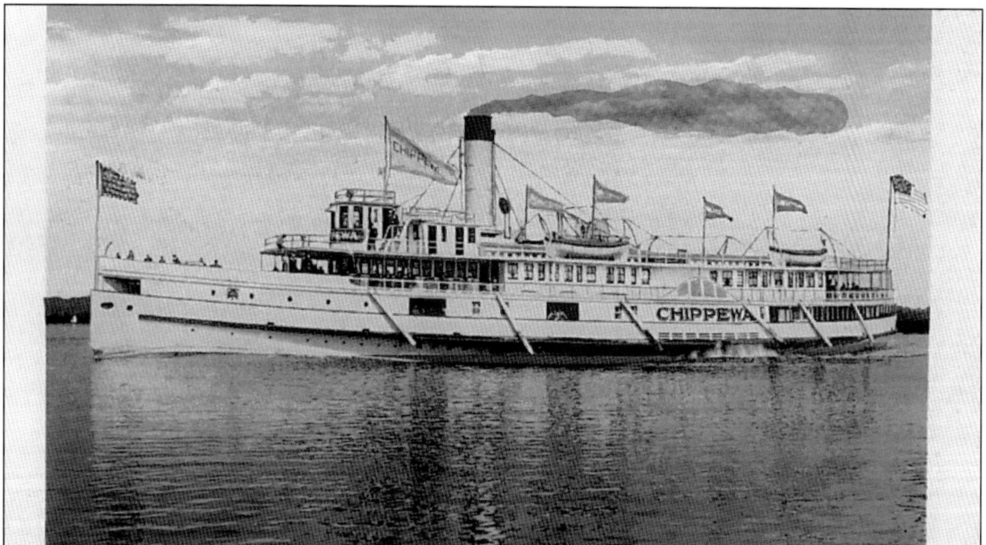

The *Chippewa* plied a Sandusky–Put-in-Bay–Lakeside route during the period 1923 to 1938. The boat was built in 1884 as the U.S. revenue cutter *Fessenden* then converted to a passenger steamer in 1908 and given the name *Chippewa*. The boat was purchased from owners on Mackinaw Island before being put into service here in 1923.

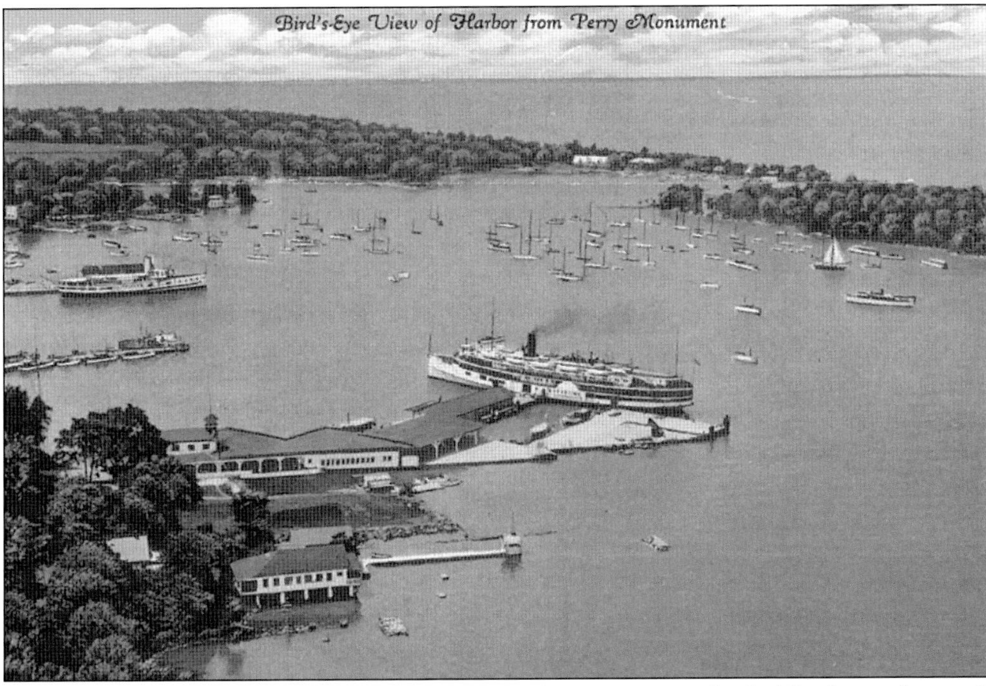

The steamer *Goodtime* can be seen here at the Put-in-Bay dock. The boat, formerly *City of Detroit II*, was acquired by the C & B (Cleveland and Buffalo) steamship line in the 1920s and renamed the *Goodtime*. It ran the Cleveland–Cedar Point–Put-in-Bay route until it was sold for scrap in 1939. The *Goodtime II*, formerly a Cleveland harbor tour boat, is now a ferry running from Sandusky to the islands, while the new, larger *Goodtime III* is Cleveland's premier sightseeing boat.

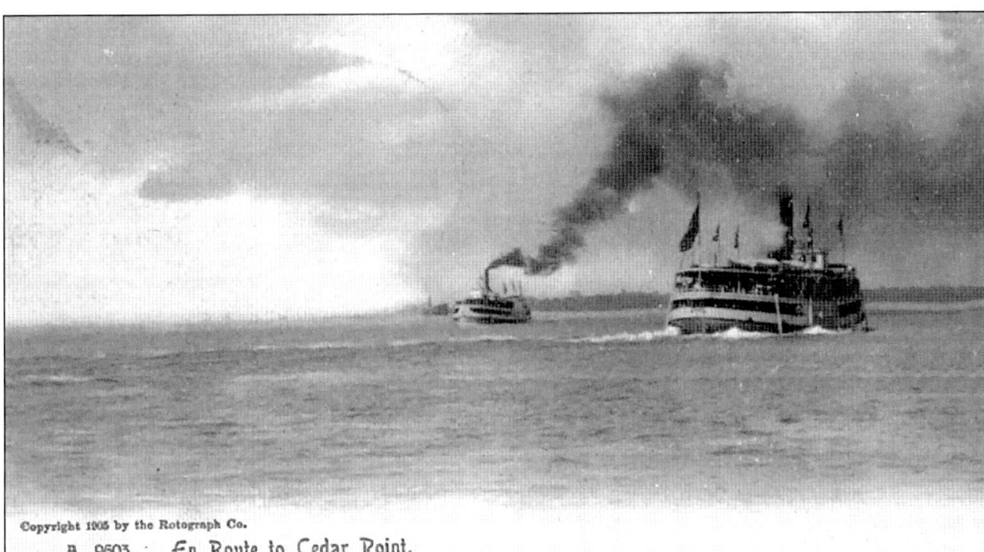

Here, steamboats bring excursionists to Cedar Point in 1905.

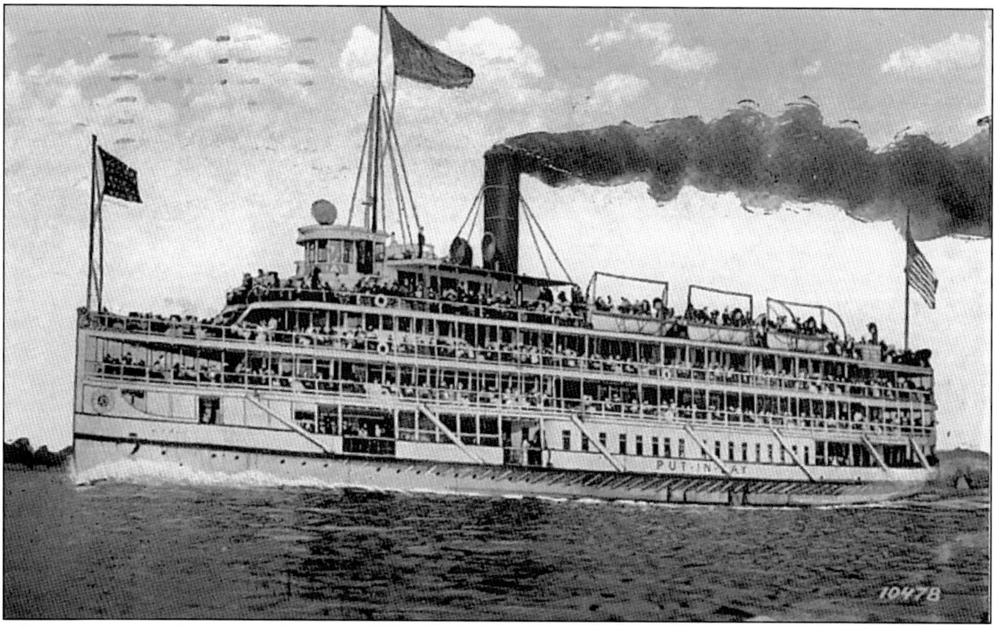

The *Put-in-Bay*, one of the finest excursion ships on the Great Lakes, was built to take advantage of the twin pleasures of the day—cruising and dancing. An elegant ballroom offered passengers the opportunity to participate in the latest rage of the early 1900s —ballroom dancing. The observation deck and elegantly appointed lobbies and staterooms provided luxurious passage in the steamer's appointed route from Detroit to Put-in-Bay and Sandusky.

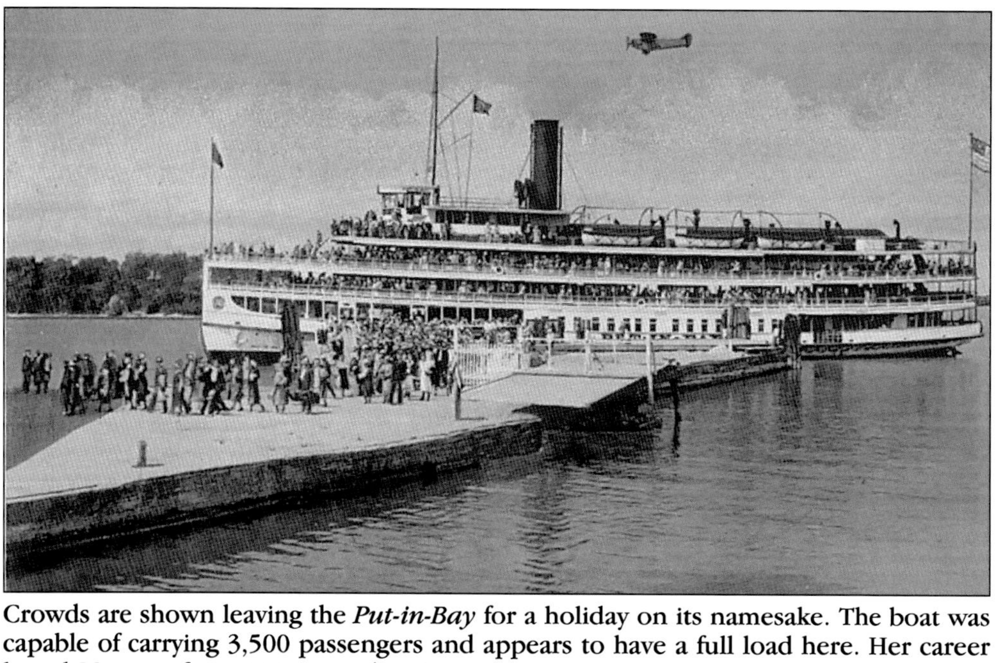

Crowds are shown leaving the *Put-in-Bay* for a holiday on its namesake. The boat was capable of carrying 3,500 passengers and appears to have a full load here. Her career lasted 38 years, from 1911 to 1949. The great ship was sold for scrap in the early 1950s and set afire in Lake St. Clair on October 3, 1953.

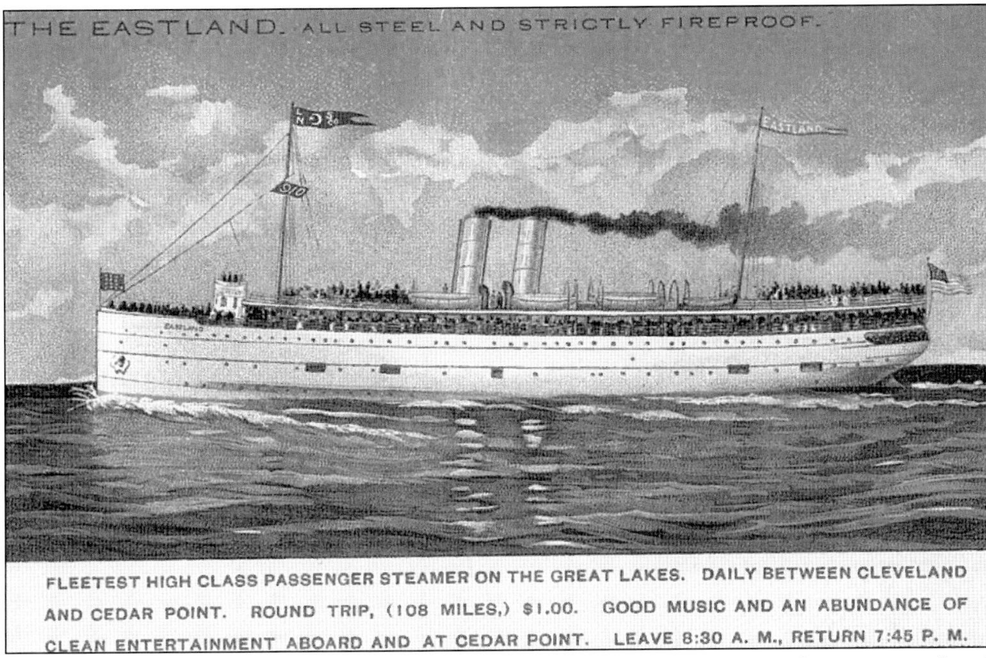

The *Eastland* billed itself as the "fleetest high class steamer on the Great Lakes." The steamer, which belonged to the Lake Shore Navigation Company, initiated the Cleveland to Cedar Point route in 1907. By 1913, she had taken over two hundred thousand people to Cedar Point. That same year, the *Eastland* was moved to Chicago where, in 1915, she capsized, drowning more than eight hundred people.

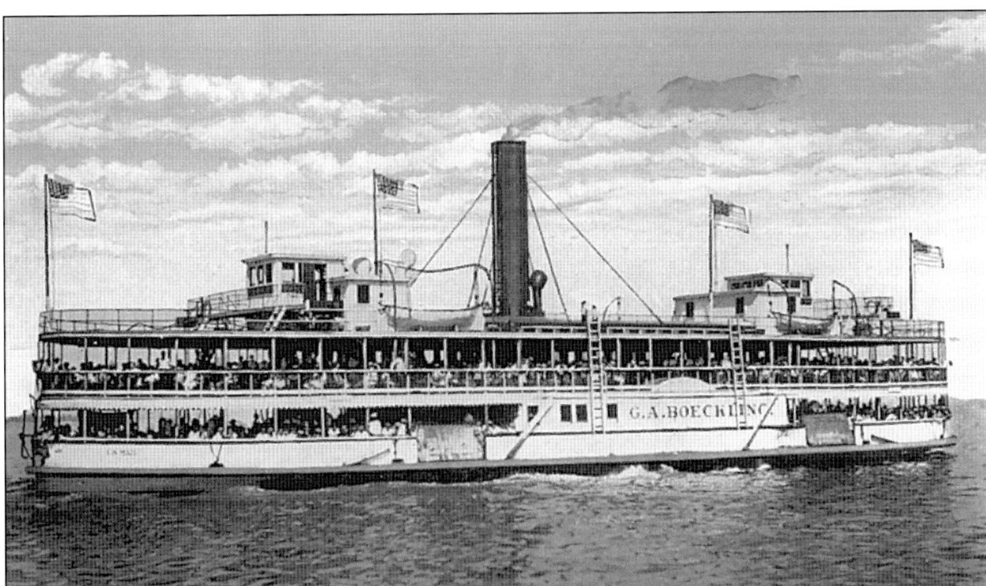

The old steamer *New York* was refurbished in Detroit and sent to Sandusky, where it was christened the *G.A. Boeckling* on June 26, 1909 in honor of the legendary General Manager of Cedar Point. The ferry ran the Sandusky–Cedar Point route for more than 40 years.

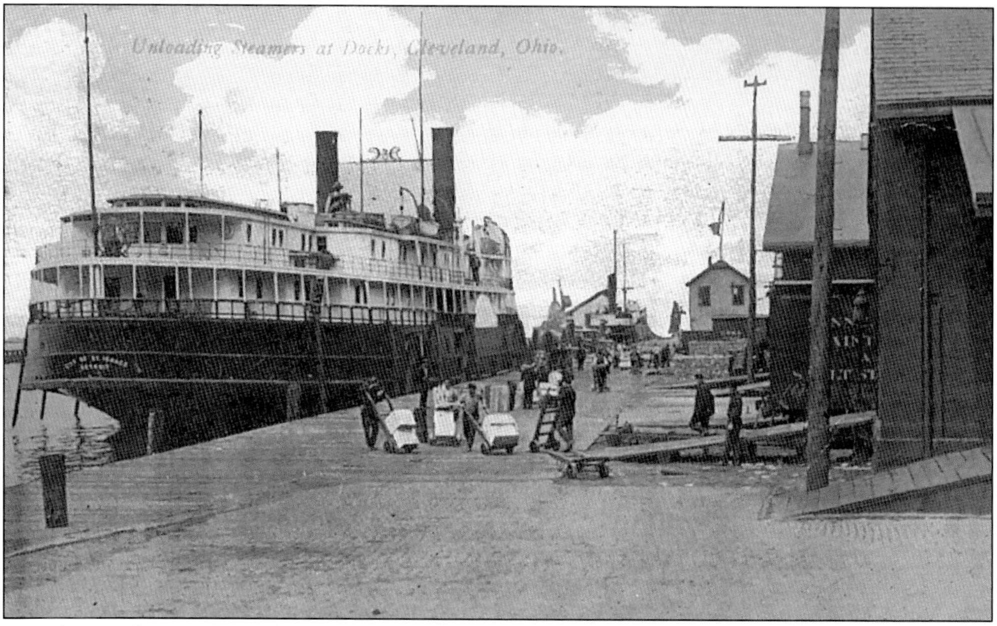

Freight is shown here being unloaded from the *City of St. Ignace* at the docks on the Cuyahoga River in Cleveland (1911). The steamer was a sister ship of the *City of Detroit II* and was part of the Lake Erie Division of the D & C line. It ran from Detroit to Cleveland.

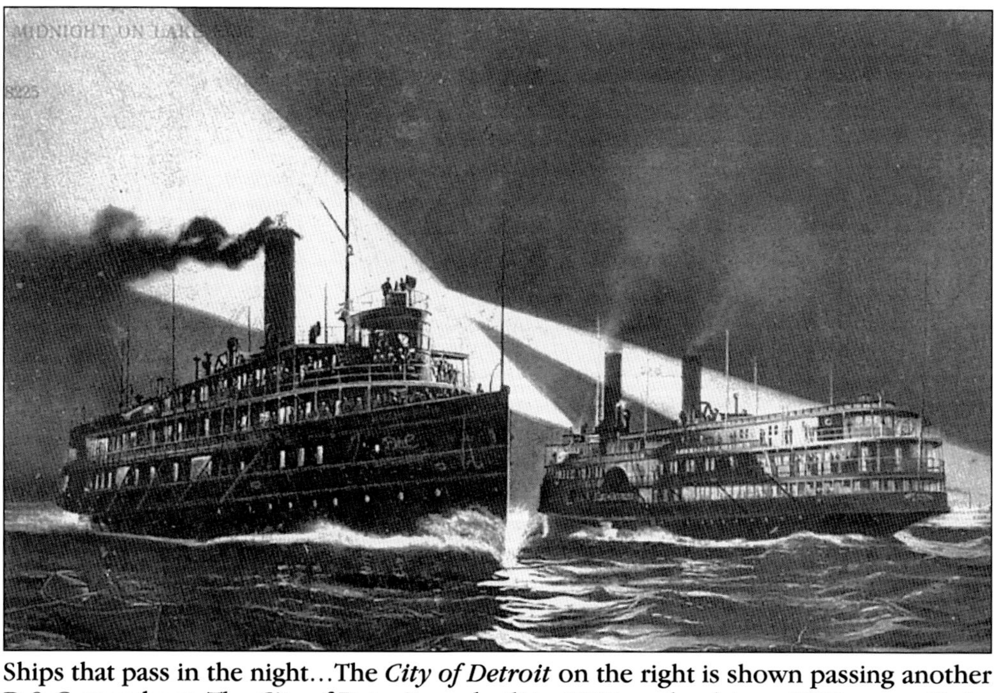

Ships that pass in the night...The *City of Detroit* on the right is shown passing another D & C steamboat. The *City of Detroit* was built in 1889, and as late as 1910, was still the second largest ship in the company's fleet. It also ran from Detroit to Cleveland.

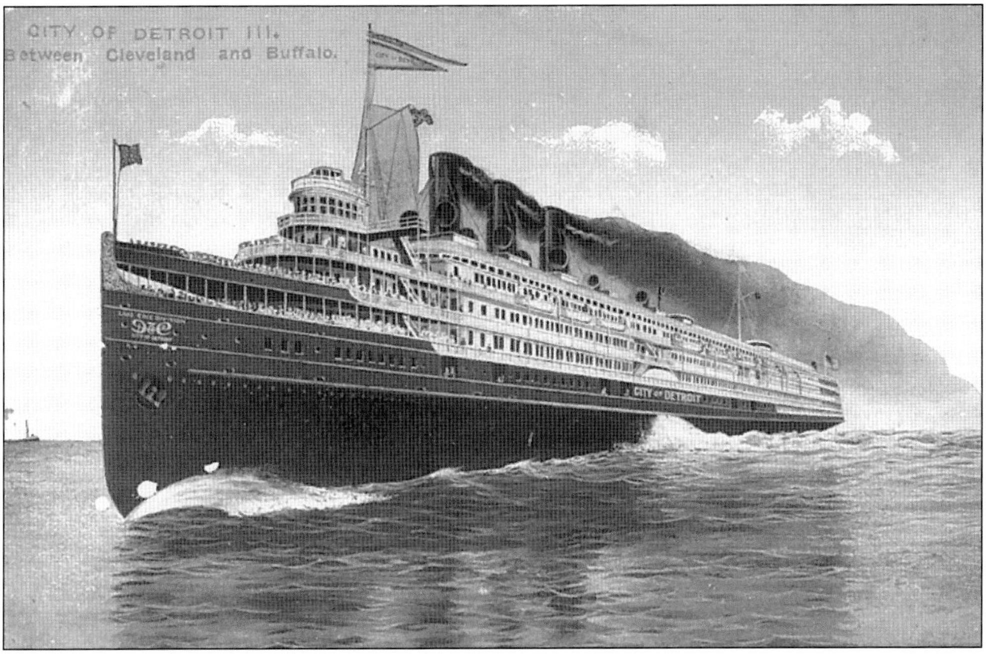

When it was launched in 1912, the *City of Detroit III*, pride of the D & C (Detroit and Cleveland) Line, was "the largest and finest side wheel steamer afloat", according to a promotional brochure published by the company. The huge ship was five hundred feet long by one hundred feet wide, with six decks, six hundred staterooms, and a passenger capacity of five thousand.

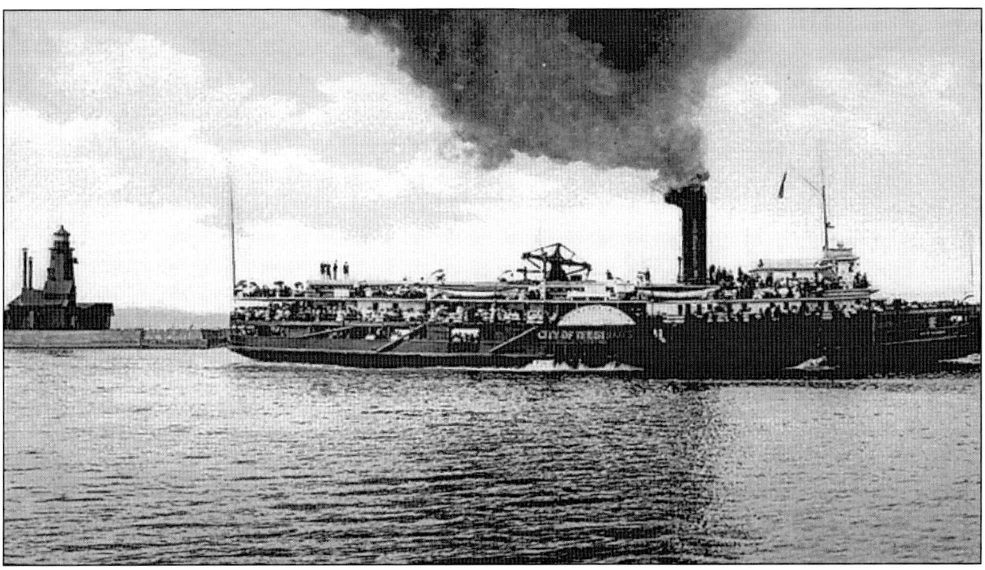

The *City of the Straits* is shown approaching the old Cleveland lighthouse. The boat, formerly *City of Detroit*, was another popular steamer of the D & C (Detroit and Cleveland) line, and ran the Toledo–Put-in-Bay–Cleveland route from 1896 to 1913.

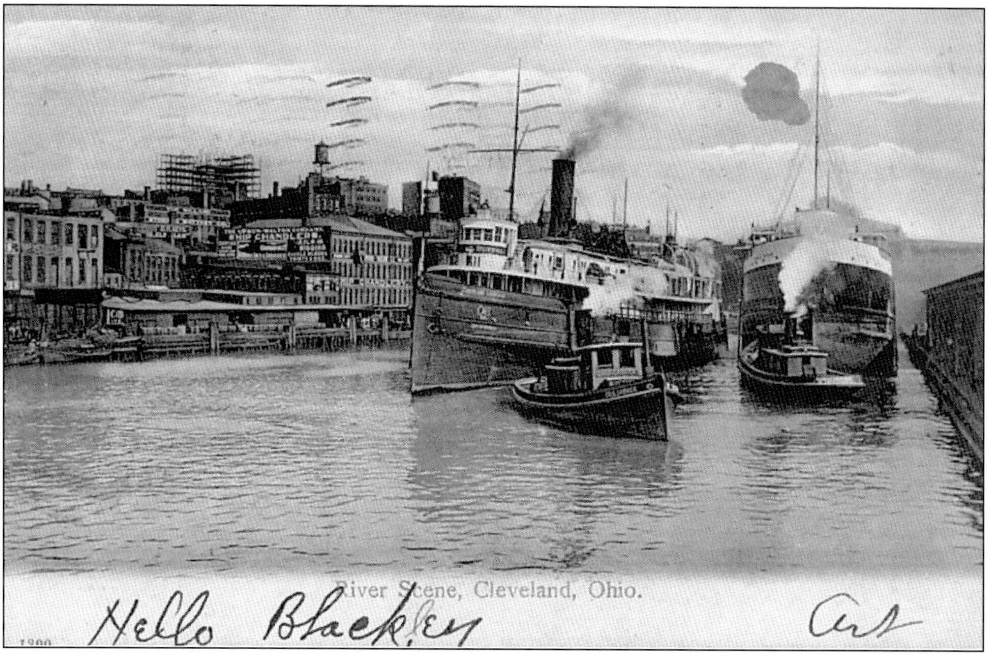

The *City of Buffalo* (at left) is being pulled by a tug in Cleveland's Flats district in 1906. The boat was part of the popular Cleveland and Buffalo (C & B) transit line, founded in 1885. Destruction of the boat by fire in 1938 helped cause the bankruptcy and liquidation of the C & B line in 1939.

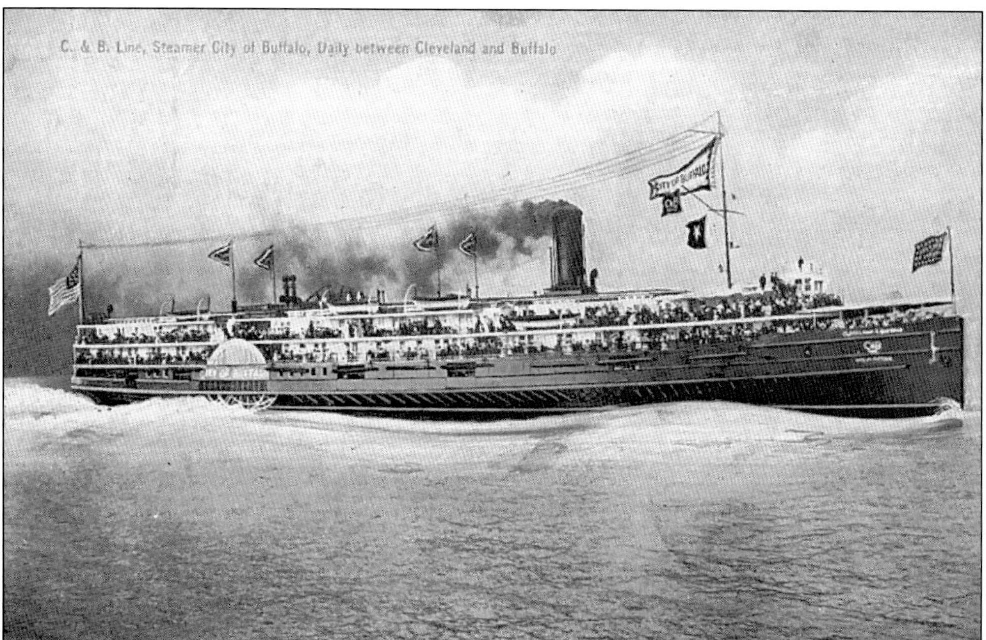

This view shows the *City of Buffalo* speeding along the high seas of Lake Erie.

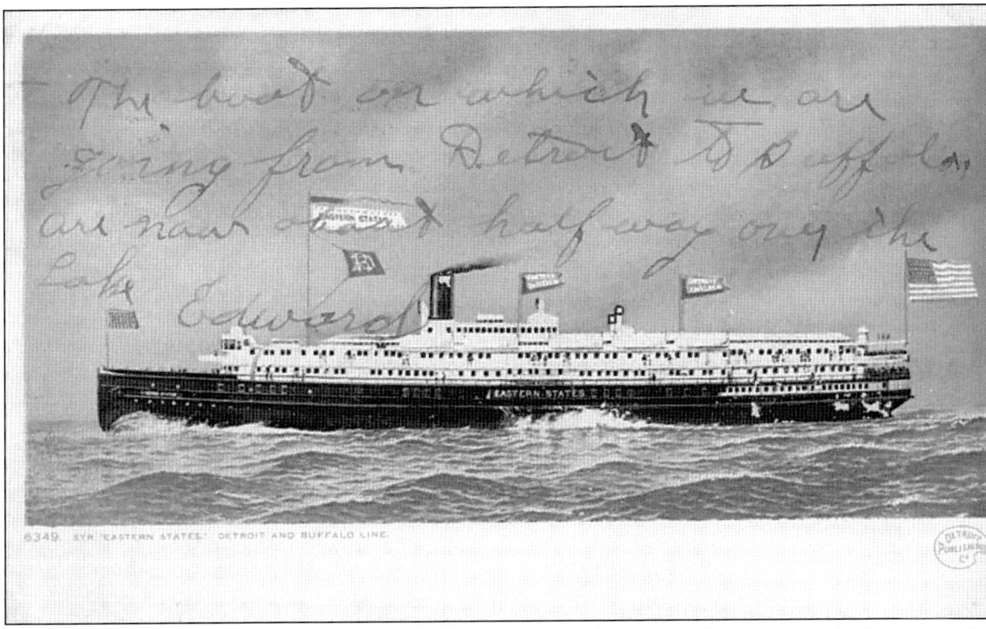

The *Eastern States*, D & C line's third largest boat in the early 1900s, ran the Detroit–Cleveland and Detroit–Buffalo routes. In later years, service was expanded to include Sandusky, Put-in-Bay, and Cedar Point. The boat ran until the early 1950s, at one time alternating service to Cedar Point with its sister ship *Western States*. The postcard inscription, from July 1908, reads "The boat on which we are going from Detroit to Buffalo. Are now about halfway over the Lake. Edward."

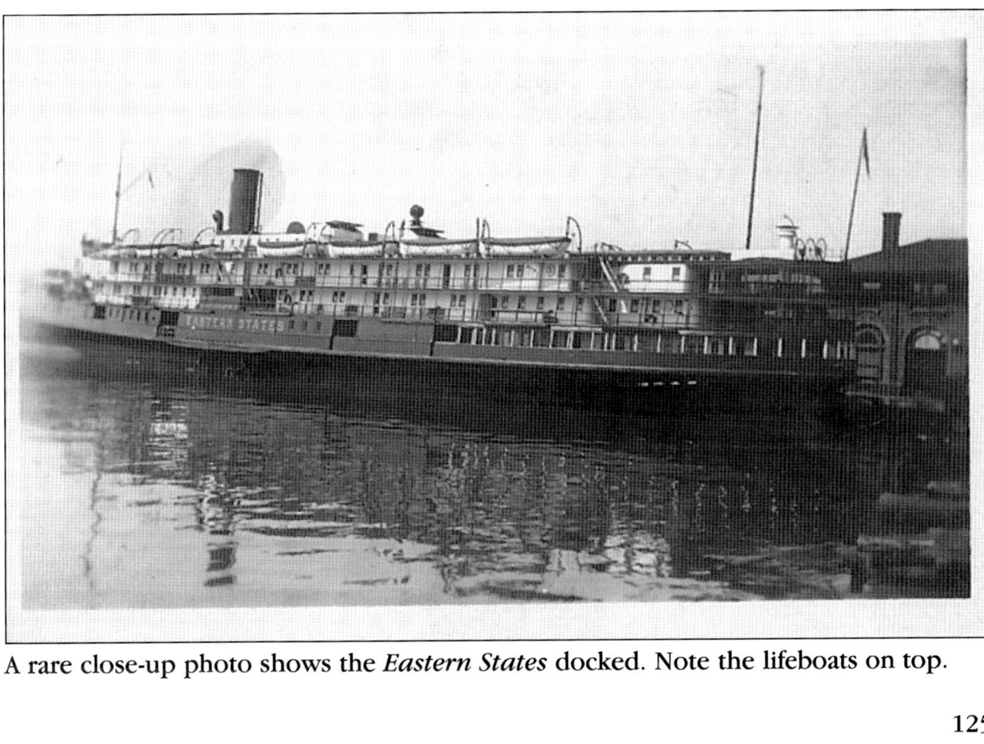

A rare close-up photo shows the *Eastern States* docked. Note the lifeboats on top.

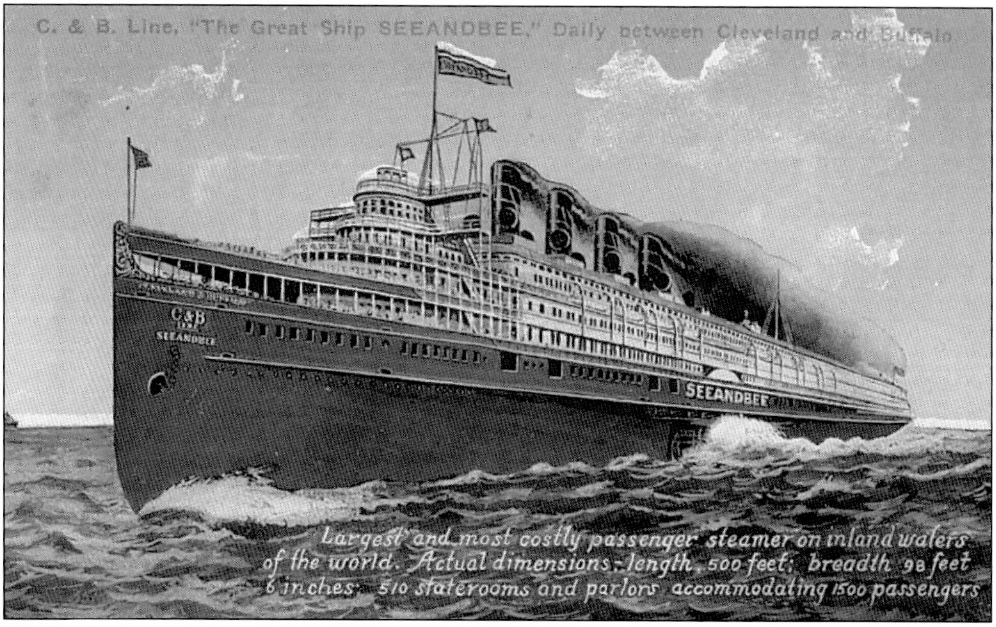

The *SEEANDBEE* was the flagship of the Cleveland and Buffalo (C & B) line and claimed in the early 1900s to be the largest and most costly passenger steamer on inland waters. The ship featured an elegant ballroom and boasted 510 staterooms and a capacity of 1,500 passengers. It began operation on November 6, 1912, and ran directly between Cleveland and Buffalo until 1942, when it was acquired by the U.S. Navy and became the *USS Wolverine*. It was scrapped after World War II.

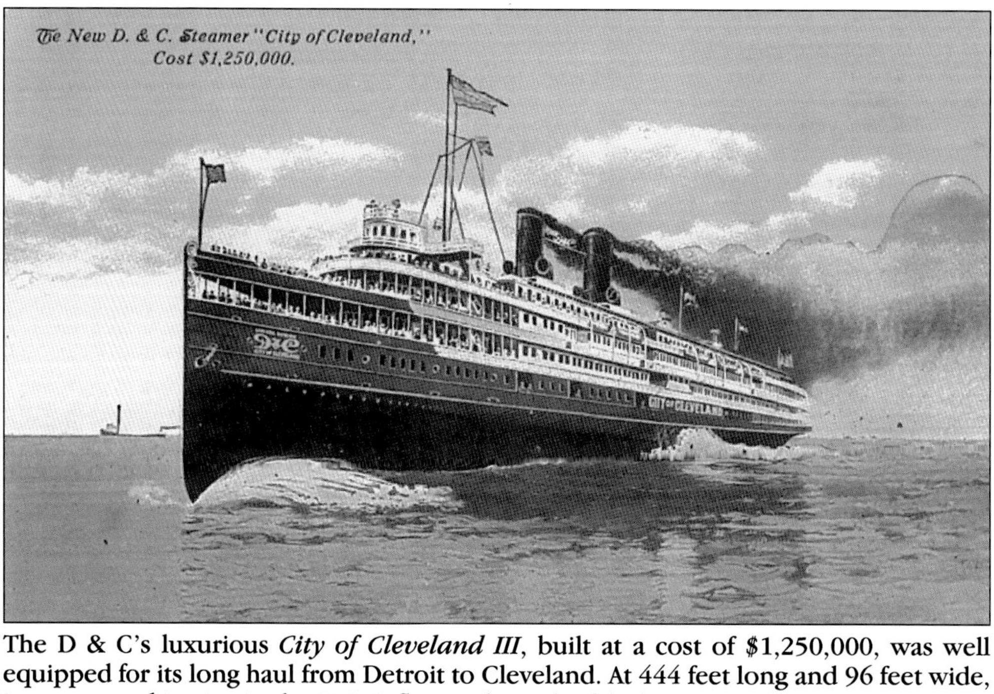

The D & C's luxurious *City of Cleveland III*, built at a cost of $1,250,000, was well equipped for its long haul from Detroit to Cleveland. At 444 feet long and 96 feet wide, it was second in size in the D & C fleet only to the fabulous *City of Detroit III*.

The Grand Salon of the D & C Line's luxury steamboat *City of Cleveland* was indeed grand as this view attests. Palatial surroundings greeted guests on the large passenger ships as the steamer lines sought to outdo themselves in constructing even larger, faster, and more luxurious boats.

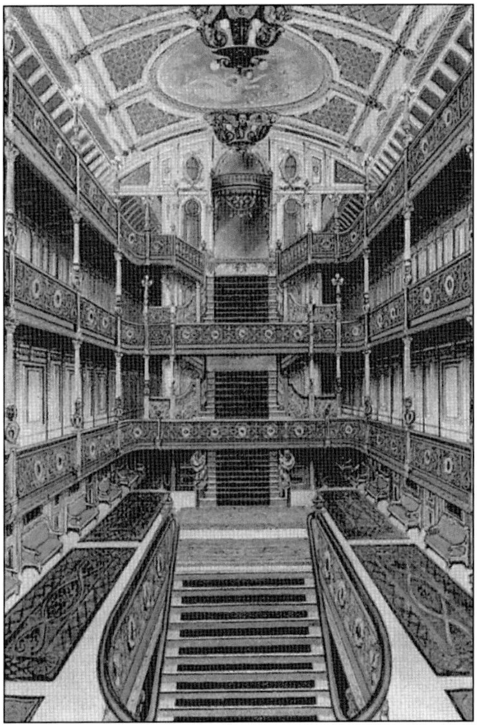

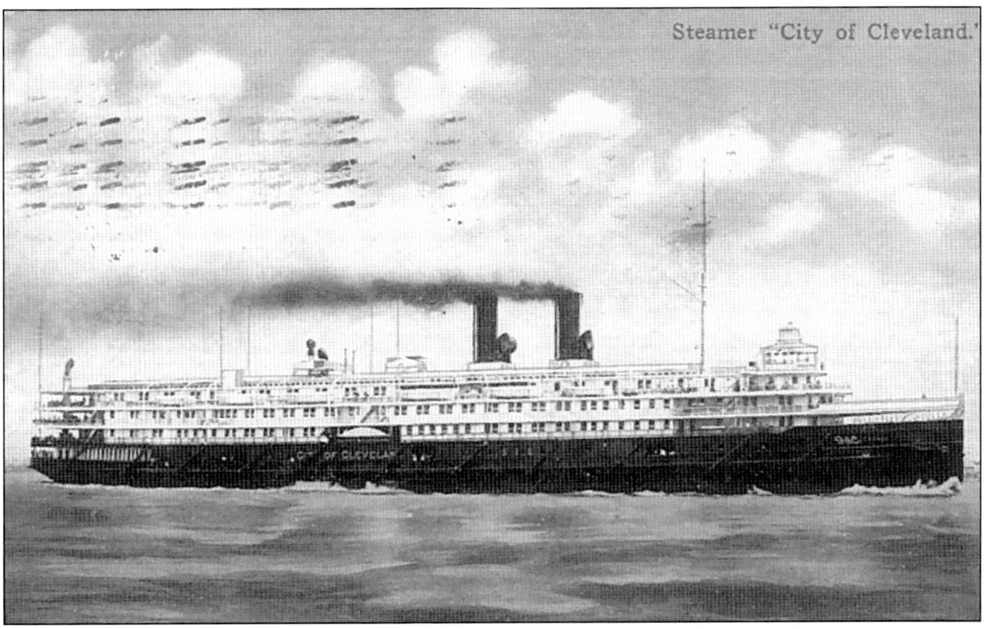

The original *City of Cleveland* was a smaller boat, shown here in 1910.

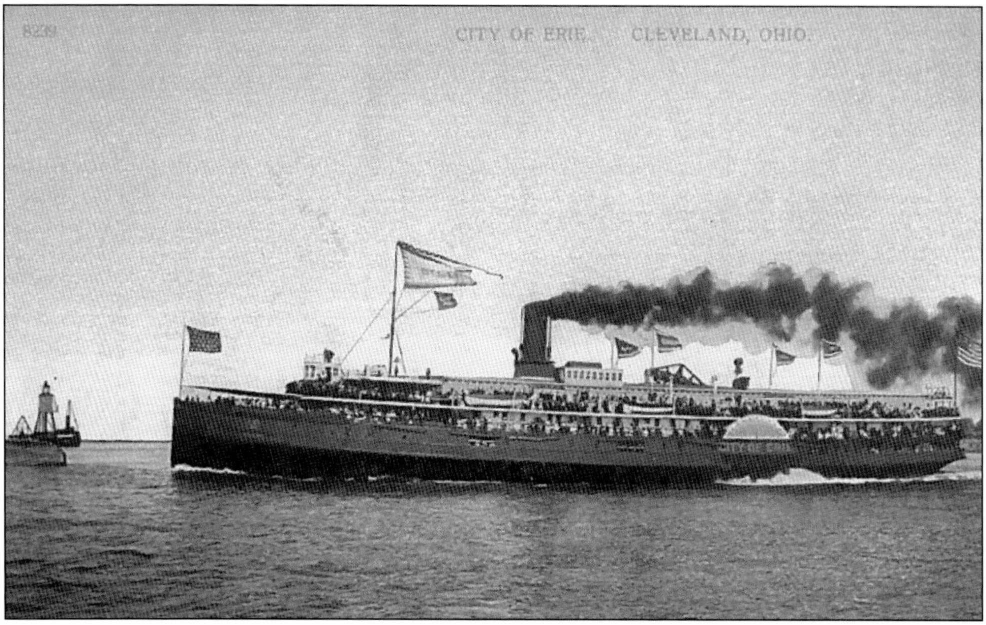

The *City of Erie* and the *City of Buffalo* were billed in a 1912 advertisement as "twin flyers of the lakes," and "the fastest, finest, and staunchest steamers on the Great Lakes, unsurpassed for comfort and convenience." The boats offered daily service between Cleveland and Buffalo.

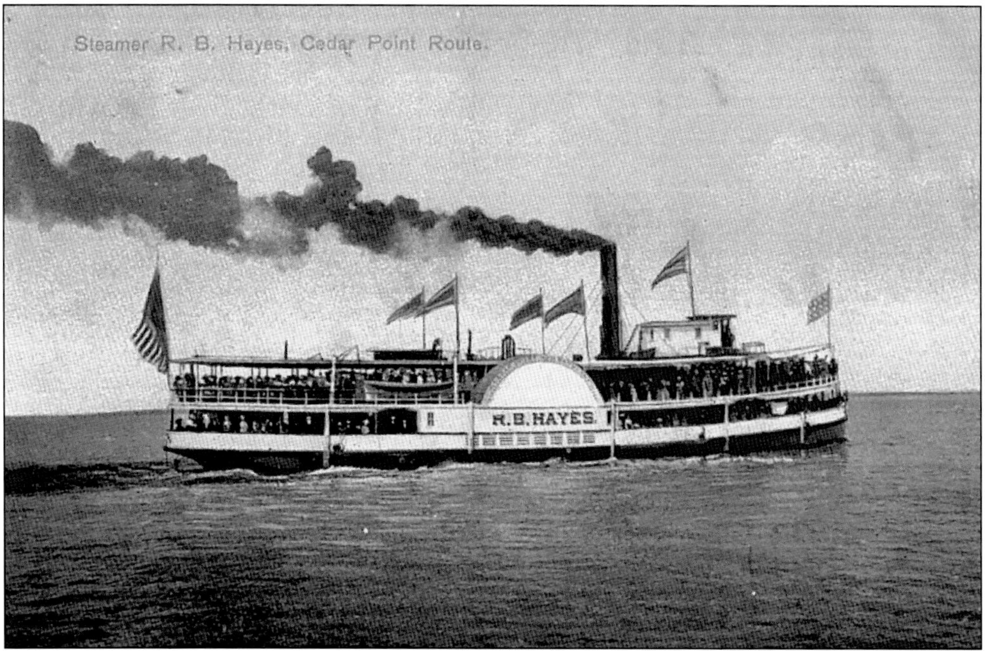

The *R. B. Hayes*, named after U.S. President Rutherford B. Hayes, was the workhorse of the Sandusky to Cedar Point ferries, from the time of her construction in Sandusky in 1876 through World War I. She was withdrawn from passenger service after the July 4, 1917 holiday, and dismantled in 1921. The boat is shown here in 1908.